MILITARY MONOGRAPH 221

Not Me!

The World War II Memoir of a Reluctant Rifleman

Alexander H. Hadden

Merriam Press
Bennington, Vermont
2007

— Not Me! —

First published in 2007 by the Merriam Press

Fourth Edition

Copyright © 2007 by Alexander H. Hadden (text and photographs except where noted)
Maps copyright © 2007 by John Hadden
Book design copyright © 2007 by the Merriam Press
Additional material copyright of named contributors.

All rights reserved. No part of this book may be used or reproduced in any manner whatsoever without written permission, except in the case of brief quotations embodied in critical articles or reviews.

The views expressed are solely those of the author.

ISBN 978-1-57638-350-6 (paperback)
ISBN 978-1-57638-094-9 (hardcover)

Printed in the United States of America.

This work was designed, produced, and published in the United States of America by the

Merriam Press
218 Beech Street
Bennington VT 05201

E-mail: ray@merriam-press.com
Web site: merriam-press.com

Both the author and the Publisher welcome and encourage comments and corrections to the material appearing in this work. Please send them to the Publisher at the above address.

The Merriam Press is always interested in publishing new manuscripts on military history, as well as reprinting previous works, such as reports, documents, manuals, articles and other material on military history topics.

For a copy of the current edition of the Merriam Press catalog describing dozens more Monographs, Memoirs, and Journals send $2.00 (U.S. first class or foreign airmail delivery).

To order additional copies of this book
visit the Merriam Press web site or write to the address above.

Contents

Introduction 5

Distant Drumming — 1941-43 13

The Army Air Corps — March-June 1943 19

My "Phony War" — June 1943-April 1944 23

The Infantry and Camp Rucker — April-September 1943 33

En Route to Europe — September-October 1944 45

England and an Introduction to German Weapons — October 1944 51

The War is Being Won Without Me; I Land in Europe — October 1944 55

Carentan, France; I Meet René Bucaille and Family — October 1944 61

Through the Repple-Depples; Verviers; Christine — October-November 1944 65

I Join the 28th Division in the Hürtgen Forest — November 11, 1944 77

The 28th Division Through Hürtgen 83

More on Hürtgen — November 1944 91

My Second Phony War — November 16-December 16, 1944 95

The Ardennes Offensive: The Strategic Background — July-December 1944 111

The Ardennes Breakthrough — December 16, 1944-January 16, 1945 117

Alsace; The Colmar Pocket — January 17-February 19, 1945 165

Back Into Germany and to the Rhine; My Shooting War Ends and I Am Alive —15 February-6 April 1945 183

Combat: A Summing Up 197

Officer Candidate School, Fontainebleau, France — April 6-June 11, 1945 213

Back Into Germany; The Potsdam Conference — June 12-August 2, 1945 221

Berlin; Paris; The Trip Home — August 1945-July 1946 249

Afterthoughts 287

Appendices

    Journal of European Trip: August 18-September 6, 1990 291

    "Unconditional Surrender": The Wrong Policy 341

    Baker Company's Reunions — June 1992 and August 1994 347

Introduction

WHEN I was a schoolboy in the 1930's, a fixture on the coffee table in the library of our home in Cleveland, Ohio was a two volume photographic history of the experiences of the American Expeditionary Force in France in what was then known as "The Great War." On the books' soft brown leather covers was an embossed likeness of a steel-helmeted doughboy thrusting his bayonet at an unseen enemy.

The pictures were unsparing in their depiction of the front lines. Here in sepia rotogravure were exhausted horses toiling to move artillery caissons and limbers through deep mud. On the next page their disemboweled carcasses were being manhandled to the side of the road by handlers who had been wounded by the same shells that had killed them. Quickly passing images of generals at parades, I would flip to a sequence of the 42nd Division's blood-bath in the Argonne Forest: men with gas masks and fixed bayonets scaling the trench parapet; others cowering in a water-filled shell hole ringed with barbed wire; wounded men being carried from the front by litter bearers past sullen German prisoners; and finally an overhead view from inside a vast French cathedral whose floor was crammed with stretchers of soldiers with bandaged heads and limbs.

There was one startling photo in particular which I have never forgotten: it showed an infantry soldier prone at the lip of a shell hole with his rifle, bayonet and helmeted profile limned against a flare-lit night sky. The photo had obviously been included as an example of courage and grit, but I knew better: that wasn't bravery in his face, he was just plain scared!

The books belonged to my father. He had served in the Ohio National Guard in the abortive campaign on the Mexican Border in 1916 in pursuit of the elusive Pancho Villa, and later was Captain of an artillery battery which saw action in France in 1918. He never spoke much of his military experiences. Oh, he would tell about his horse "White Sox" on the border and would relate humorous anecdotes about the men in his battery, but I never could get him to convey any sense of what it was really like.

On the other hand it was crystal clear that his military experiences meant a great deal to him. He attended reunions of his battery on every possible occasion, and the presence of the books told its own story: they certainly were not in the library because my mother wanted them there. But I never did see him looking at them, and it has belatedly occurred to me that it is just possible that they were meant to be a message to his two sons. If so, it is one that really "took" in my case.

I had been as captivated as any kid with the sweep and excitement of the Odyssey and the romance and daring of Robin Hood and the knights of Camelot, but after exposure to my father's books, I was never in any doubt as to the difference between such adventure stories and the harsh reality of modern warfare. The notion that there could ever be romance on the killing fields had been forever destroyed. They held nothing but fear, pain, discomfort and death, and the lesson I took from them was that if I should ever have the bad luck to be involved in a war, I should do all in my power to avoid them.

Viewed in long retrospect there now seems more than a little irony—one might almost say an inevitability—between my early and total recognition of the horrors of war and my eventual and total immersion in them. I would say "Not me" again and again, but as it turned out, I had as much chance of escaping as a cobra does from a mongoose or a moth from a flame.

This book attempts to depict how and why this chain of circumstance came about. I am hopeful that it may also shed some light on how a youth as emotionally ill-prepared as I was was able in spite of himself to confront and eventually, with generous assistance from providence, even benefit from the very terrors that again and again came close to undoing him.

There has been a considerable evolution in the purpose and scope of my effort. At the outset, what I had in mind was simply to put on paper a chronological account of my military service, starting with my earliest recollections of its looming approach and setting down the events that are lodged in my memory as the significant milestones, including times in training, combat experiences and the wildly unpredictable events which followed after the European armistice. My purpose was to record for my own satisfaction what seemed to be important and to try for my own two sons, who were mercifully too young to be caught up in the vile meat grinder that was Vietnam, to fill the void about *my* military career that I had felt about my father's. In other words, what I set out to do was to record to the best of my ability what *I* remembered to be accurate and not to worry much about any broader context.

But this initial effort developed in an odd and unexpected way: I found that the things that I remembered were in many instances not at all the same as those which I contemporaneously recorded in my letters home (a fairly complete file of which had been kept by my father), and that they were often quite different from the events and experiences which would be regarded in any objective sense as "important" or "historical." In other words, they tended to be random, unpredictable and sometimes even trivial. They were also full of contextual gaps that would need to be filled in to produce a balanced and readable narrative. Yet they *were* the things that had survived *my* subconscious test as "historical" (read "memorable"), and I resolved therefore to retain them as the primary framework of my account, while at the same time filling in gaps in appropriate ways as I went forward.

In the process of "gap filling" a realization gradually developed that what I was writing might just possibly be of interest to a wider audience than first envisaged. Whether that will be so remains to be seen, but once I recognized the possibility, I found that a somewhat different voice— less personal, more descriptive and general—was speaking. I hope that the variations in tone which have resulted do not prove disorienting to readers.

There were also a number of exterior events as I wrote which dramatically altered its scope and content. The first was a telephone call which I received one winter Sunday in Vermont from an old wartime buddy in my infantry company in Europe. The caller was Cliff Hackett from Greenville, South Carolina. He had seen my name in an article in *Time* magazine and somehow found out how to reach me. The call seemed providential from the point of view of my writing effort, because at the war's end Cliff had been named official "historian" of our Company and he had decided to rewrite the chronology of its engagements which he promised to send me. This document, complete with maps, provided invaluable assistance in lending temporal and geographical precision to the very rough accounts I had started to prepare. Our letters and phone calls also served to highlight a number of instances in which both recollection and record were in doubt (was it at Utah or Omaha Beach that our detachment of infantry replacements had landed in Normandy in October 1944?). They also led me to wonder what had happened to some of the people I met, and how the last half of the Twentieth Century had dealt with them and with some of the places that were burned into my memory like Normandy, the Ardennes, Alsace and Berlin.

The second transforming event was precipitated by my awakening one night in the Spring of 1990 knowing all of a sudden that I should go back and see. Eventually, in August and September of 1990 with wife Susan, daughter Kate and two small poodles, I did so. The results and insights were in many respects moving and astonishing, and I have folded some of them into my account to give an extended dimension to it. For those interested in a more detailed account of that trip, I have attached a diary of it as Appendix 1.

In March of 1992 another unforeseen development occurred. Out of the blue I got a phone call from a man who identified himself as George Knaphus of McCallsburg, Iowa. He said that he, too, was one of the few survivors of Company B ("Baker") of the 112th Infantry Regiment and never could forget my having been struck in the head, back and arm by German machine gun bullets in Belgium in January 1945, because they had miraculously torn up only my steel helmet, helmet liner, sleeve and shirt and not me, at least not badly. George had seen my name in a newspaper account some years earlier concerning a litigation in which I had been involved as attorney for major league baseball and had succeeded in tracing me to my home in Vermont. He had called to renew acquaintances and to be sure that I was aware of plans for a reunion of Baker Company to be held in Minnesota in June 1992.

I was almost as stunned by George's call as I had been by the German machine gun. Although I could not have failed to know him well at the time (he was our company communications sergeant), it took a face-to-face encounter to revive my memory of him. It turned out that Knaphus and another member of Baker's handful of survivors, Charlie Haug, had been quietly collecting names for several years and that when a total of fourteen of us had been identified, it was as though—almost fifty years after the event and well into the seventh decade of our lives— a critical mass was finally at hand and it was time to schedule a first reunion.

It would be an understatement to say that the event was a revelation.

It was that and much more besides, and many of the memories which it revived have found their way into later pages of this effort.[1] It also had the not so incidental benefit of permitting me to draw a more complete picture of some of the events which befell my Company B both in the Ardennes and later in Alsace. (For example, Charlie Haug was able to solve a mystery surrounding the destruction of a column of German tanks which had attacked Baker at Lutzkampen, Germany, on the first day of their "Bulge" offensive.) My own knowledge of these happenings was fragmentary at best, and while some of the facts learned from my fellow soldiers, it's true, don't lie within my own knowledge I am one hundred per cent certain of their accuracy. In the instances where my account relies on such information, I have clearly said so.

What started out simply has thus greatly mushroomed. I have in the main, however, tried to remain faithful to my original purpose: to try to explain to what I had supposed would be a very narrow audience what "it was really like." Especially have I tried to convey some sense of what combat was really like and to describe some of the thoughts, emotions and changes that affect a raw 19-year-old replacement as he is exposed to it. While the final result inevitably falls short of making the experience come alive even for me, I am hopeful that it will perhaps give those who have been lucky enough not to have been exposed to the first hand experience a little better idea of its essential nature.

I should warn readers about the tone of my text. There have been many accounts of infantry combat as seen through the eyes of authors— they are usually but not always higher ranking officers—who express eagerness and even delight at its excitement and adventure. Their soldiers can't wait for the order to attack, and are bitterly disappointed when directed to retreat. If they feel fear it is a momentary inconvenience, like hunger or wet socks. That is *not* this book, nor is it in my opinion an accurate depiction of how combat infantry soldiers really think and act. If the reader seeks such inspirational or fictional accounts he should look elsewhere.

---

[1] The 1992 reunion was such a success that Charlie and George organized a second one in August 1994 which was enthusiastically attended by most of us who were at the first plus two others who were later identified as Baker vets. Some of the information which surfaced at the later reunion is also included. Those attending are briefly profiled in Appendix III.

I cannot move to my narrative without expressing heartfelt thanks to my wife Sue and daughter Kate for their unfailing support and enthusiasm for this project, which included accompanying me on our 1990 trip to Europe to revisit my venues of 1944-45, details of which are recorded in Appendix 1. It included much that was enjoyable and fascinating, but it also entailed a trip of over 5,000 kilometers in a space of two weeks in a compact Opel sedan, the back seat of which held two dogs and lots of baggage in addition to Kate. She and her mother both bore up splendidly. Their editorial suggestions have likewise been penetrating and extremely useful. Thanks also go to my son David whose interest has been keen from the start and who has read various drafts with suggestions which have been very much on the money. His younger brother John has also made an enormous contribution in first persuading and then patiently guiding his father out of paraplegic dependency on stenographers and into the brave new world of computers where John often had to man a computer hotline at odd hours of the day and night. It would be a large overstatement to suggest that computer literacy has resulted, but I now wonder how it could have been that I ever got along without my Mac laptop. John's help and expertise have also been invaluable in the preparation and production of the dust jacket and the creation and processing of both maps and photographs. I am confident that these have immeasurably enhanced the attractiveness of the book.

    I wish also to offer thanks and expressions of warmest friendship to Cliff Hackett, without whose providential phone call in the winter of 1990 and subsequent prompting I might easily have given up my effort, to Charlie Haug of Sleepy Eye, Minnesota, who has been the spark, the inspiration and the host for the 1990's reunions of Baker Company's scant remnants, to Bill Kleeman, with whom I rekindled such a strong and instantaneous bond at those reunions, magically bridging the fifty years of our civilian lives, and to George Knaphus, who through the force of his warm personality and intense interest has become the keeper of the flame for Baker Company, for its members and survivors, and for its sadly obscure but permanent legend.

    I am likewise grateful to Robert Elliott, a good friend and former Vermont neighbor who argued early on that my book was publishable, analyzed it with care and offered sage advice as to how it might be made more so, to Kenneth Koyen of New York who also encouraged me to seek a broad audience for it and counseled as to how to navigate through the publishing shoals, and to Roger Spiller, George C. Marshall Professor of History at the Army's Command and General Staff College who has found my accounts of combat and of Captain Farrar worthy of the attention of his students.

Finally, thanks are also due to the many other relatives and friends who have read and commented enthusiastically but who are too numerous to be listed. I have no doubt that they know who they are.

Distant Drumming

1941-43

THE first war-related memory I have goes back to 1941-42, my senior year as a student at Milton Academy outside of Boston. Milton was an austere Spartan prep school on the English model with a passion for scholastic accomplishment (excellence is not quite the right word), but with little apparent concern—or certainly none that I was able to detect—for the emotional well-being of those students like myself who lacked social graces or who failed to exhibit a conspicuous ability or accomplishment, especially in sports. I did play intramural basketball, baseball and tennis and was a good student, but I was excruciatingly shy, partly no doubt due to natural temperament, but more so in my eyes because of a galloping case of zits which afflicted me early in adolescence.

My academic interests tended to focus on mathematics, French and English, and I spent many hours in the Camera Club's darkroom. I could probably be accurately described as something of a loner, having few friends and only one or two close ones.

Few if any of us in those days were serious students of current events, but we were all certainly aware of some of the headline occurrences taking place in Europe, such as the dismaying success of Hitler's Blitzkrieg into Holland, Belgium and France in the summer of 1940 (there was not the slightest trace of sympathy among us for the Germans), and of the magnificent performance of the Royal Air Force in the "Battle of Britain" in the fall of that year when Göring's Luftwaffe was driven out of the English skies by Spitfires and Hurricanes. I also vividly remember the electrifying presidential race in the fall of 1940 when Wendell Willkie, the Republican candidate, opposed the third term bid of Franklin Roosevelt, who did not occupy hero status in the eyes of most Miltonians or their families. A Willkie motorcade drove past the Milton campus one fall afternoon to the accompaniment of tumultuous cheering from the sons of the comfortably conservative.

I can't say today whether our awareness extended beyond these headline events to others of more ominous significance, such as the September 1940 transfer of fifty old destroyers from the U.S. to the Royal Navy in exchange for naval bases in British Atlantic possessions, or "Lend-Lease," the pre-Pearl Harbor program worked out in March 1941 between Roosevelt and Churchill for the furnishing of U.S. munitions and financial credits to Britain. While we were to a man four-square behind England in its plucky underdog resistance to the Germans, I very much doubt that we understood the trend toward American involvement which was hotly contested by the conservative "America First" movement but which would soon be seen to have been inexorable.

However that may be, our insouciance vanished on Sunday, December 7, 1941, the date of the Japanese attack on Pearl Harbor. I vividly recall being in study hall when the word was flashed that Pearl Harbor had been bombed. We were stunned. There had been news reports for months of desultory negotiations in Washington between Japanese diplomats and the State Department. None of us had paid any attention. But now the bastards had attacked U. S. territory (and though it was not revealed at the time sunk a large part of the U.S. Pacific Fleet)! We were outraged!

Some of my classmates reacted like George Bush who was also in his senior year at nearby Andover. According to a December 1991 interview in *Life* magazine, his immediate reaction was to scrub any and all plans of going to college and to head straight for enlistment as a naval aviator. Not me! After the immediate sense of outrage had somewhat cooled, the predominant emotion resonating in me was one of the ominousness which now overhung the future. I knew that the war could not fail to have a drastic effect on my life; perhaps even a dangerous one. What it would be I could not then know, but I had no instinct to accelerate it!

In any case, Milton Academy moved rapidly to a wartime footing. With hindsight, it's clear that what happened was based in good measure on wartime hysteria, but the school was very much in step with the rest of the country, particularly coastal areas, in its reaction. Use of lights at night was curtailed. More dramatically so far as the individual student was concerned, a regimen of nocturnal sky-watching was inaugurated. All boarding students were required in pairs to man a lookout post atop the school chapel, a stone Tudor edifice with a 70-foot high square tower, topped by a crenelated battlement on which a temporary roof had been installed for partial shelter. It was, however, open to the winter winds and it was often very cold. Hot coffee or cocoa was provided as was a telephone for communication to some central headquarters to which all aircraft sightings had to be reported. For me and my partners these occasions were entirely frivolous: We knew the likelihood of an attacking plane was just about zero and that the approach of faculty snoops could be discovered well in advance; hence we were able single-mindedly to savor the forbidden rituals of tobacco, even though in the tower's darkness we could not fully relish the plumed elegance of the smoke leaving our nostrils.

Intimations of reality were gradually borne in upon us. The Selective Service Act, in effect since September 1940, was tightened and college deferments were largely eliminated. Most colleges went to a twelve-month curriculum—no more summer vacations. Military service was clearly in the future of every single one of us who was found to be physically capable.

I graduated from Milton in June 1942. A somber commencement address was given by a man named Jan Masaryk who at the time was Foreign Minister of the Czechoslovakian Government-in-Exile in London. He had held the same post in his country in 1938 at the time of the Munich crisis. At Munich, his country had been partially dismembered by the shameful agreement between Hitler on the one hand and Neville Chamberlain and Edouard Daladier, Prime Ministers of England and France on the other. The "peace in our time" epigram, which was the returning Chamberlain's distillation of the meaning of this craven appeasement, was shown for its true value some months later when Hitler's legions stormed into Prague, making the country a puppet state and sending Masaryk into exile.

Mr. Masaryk's lasting impact on me arose less from any remembered words—there were none—than from who he was and what he had been through: as a symbol of the suffering of his country, he brought home to us that Hitler's hunger for conquest with his panzer divisions was real and devastating and not a mere headline abstraction. His presence made our own small wartime deprivations seem trivial.

I recently obtained and reread the text of his short speech. Four days before he spoke, the small Czech town of Lidice had been leveled and all its inhabitants slaughtered by the Nazis in reprisal for a Czech patriot's assassination of Reinhard Heydrich, a sadistic Nazi gauleiter. Masaryk referred to this ghastly event to illustrate the point that both his country and the rest of the world, including America, would undergo enormous hardship and privation, but in the end the Allies were certain to prevail; the most difficult task would be the post-war rebuilding of Europe. How accurately, and even clairvoyantly, he spoke.[2]

In July 1941, Hitler had unleashed "Operation Barbarossa" against the USSR, and his armored units made lightening progress deep into Russia where it appeared that the Soviet Union would soon be eclipsed just as France had been. The Russian lines solidified just short of Leningrad and Moscow, however, in December of 1941, and a ray of hope was seen. But then, in May of 1942, the Nazis resumed their Russian campaign and new German successes were achieved in July. Finally, the battle initiative appeared to swing over from the Germans to the Russians, and a "high-water mark" was reached by the Germans at Stalingrad, when they were repulsed there with the capture of hundreds of thousands of troops in October of 1942.

Something of the same pattern was discernible (though I doubt I discerned it) in the other theaters of war, such as North Africa and the Pacific, where Allied and U.S. efforts were being greeted with some success. While optimistic remarks were sometimes heard ("The worst is over!" — "It's only a matter of time!"), by any realistic view, there was still a long uphill campaign to wage.

By the spring of 1942, the U.S. Selective Service System had moved into high gear. But while 17-year-olds like me could volunteer, they were subject to being drafted only at age 18, which I would not reach until December. As noted, I was not tempted to rush towards warfare. On the contrary, from late June 1942 until February 1943 I pursued my freshman year at Yale. The campus was alive with both civilian and uniformed students, the latter in a variety of ROTC and Naval Officer Train-

---

[2] After the war was over, Masaryk returned to Czechoslovakia and resumed his position as Foreign Minister in its reconstituted government. Though he saw the need to attempt to coexist with the Soviet Union, he nonetheless attempted to maintain ties with the West and was bitterly disappointed by the Communist takeover of his country in 1948. A few months later he fell to his death from a building in Prague; it has never been clear whether it was murder or suicide.

ing programs. They marched from class to class in formation, while we straggled here and there as though on a different planet, which we almost were. But we were trying to get as much education under our belts as possible before scattering to the four winds.

I recall this time as one of suspended animation. French literature and introductory philosophy and economics courses, all totally civilian educational pursuits, seemed relevant to nothing at all. I doubt that at this point anything would have.

When I completed my freshman year in January 1943, it was apparent that I would be drafted in the next two or three months and it therefore made no sense to start my sophomore year. Accordingly, I went back to Cleveland and "volunteered for the draft." This phrase, which was one of many oxymorons with which I would become familiar in the military, meant that you would become a soldier several weeks more quickly than if you waited for the form letter of "Greetings" from the President. But even at that it took about two months before I could be "processed," to use the then-current military phrase. In the interval, I took a two-hour-a-day one-on-one Berlitz course in conversational French from which I emerged if not fluent, at least comfortable. As matters turned out, this was a very good move indeed.

My pre-induction physical took place in one of the nineteenth century loft buildings in downtown Cleveland: high embossed-steel ceilings, splintery wood floors and wintry drafts. We paraded around naked or half-naked, stood in line, and were barked at by non-coms, a foretaste of what was to follow for the next two years of my life.

There was very little to distinguish me in this motley parade from the scores of other young draftees. I was about six feet two inches tall, weighed all of 175 pounds and had curly red-brown hair. My father's favorite nickname for me was "Skinny McGeedle," from a comic strip character of his youth, I think.

The climax came at the swearing-in ceremony. Our group of about a hundred sullen "inductees" stood at attention (now with clothes on) with right hands raised. An officer ascended the podium to lead us in the oath of allegiance, whereupon a non-com reached up to a window shade pull to the officer's side and pulled down from a roller a large American Flag for us to contemplate during the ceremony. Thirty seconds later, now formally inducted, the non-com reached up, tweaked the pull string and the flag snapped back up on the roll. If I felt any patriotism during this ceremony, it retracted just about as fast as the flag.

As I marched off to war, much had changed on the American home front. Women by the thousands were at work in munitions factories. Rationing of some foods (meat, sugar) had become effective, and those not obliged to travel on wartime business were issued an "A" decal for their windshields and could buy only six gallons of gas a week. In January 1943, at Casablanca, Morocco, Roosevelt and Churchill had conducted the third of their wartime meetings which became known as the "unconditional surrender" conference because of its adoption and promulgation of that policy as the sole basis on which the Allies would end the war. No doubt I nodded sagely at the headlines proclaiming this development, but I could not have had even the dimmest appreciation of its future meaning for me.

The Army Air Corps

March-June 1943

MY first stop was Camp Perry, Ohio, just east of Toledo. After a few days it became known that a train load of us had been assigned to the Army Air Corps for basic training and we were sent on our way to Florida.

The Air Corps! "Terrific!" was the reaction of most of us, myself included. There was the prospect of flight training, gunning the engine on the flight-line, silk scarf in the slip stream, etc., etc. Moreover, the destination of our train was St. Petersburg, Florida. Surely that could not be bad in the month of March!

Illusion abruptly gave way to reality. Basic training had nothing to do with aviation. It was eight weeks of 5 a.m. arisings (sometimes seeming bitter cold because we had no warm clothing), infantry and weapons drills, calisthenics, close order drill, parades, classes on military courtesy (another oxymoron), discipline, and venereal disease and how to prevent it, until 9:30 lights out. I was an innocent 18-year-old and couldn't believe what were called "short-arm" inspections—unzipping flies for visual inspection while in military formation—or the hideously graphic movies they showed us. (There was a memorable "Sad Sack" comic strip which showed the hapless recruit emerging from one of these training films and being introduced to a young lady; he would not shake hands with her until he had donned a pair of rubber gloves.)

The trouble was they weren't ready for us in "St. Pete." We were taken to a newly opened camp called "Tent City" on the shores of Tampa Bay where each train load of recruits was installed on a new street of pyramidal tents just opened up in the palmetto scrub, supposedly with all necessary appurtenances for feeding, housing and sanitation. Before long there were thousands of us marching, toiling and sweating under the fierce southern sun. If it was cold at night, it was searing during the day.

We ate from mess kits which had to be "washed" in galvanized garbage cans filled with water. The water was supposedly heated to bacteria-killing temperatures by gasoline-fired burners which belched smoke and flame when operating properly, which they didn't most of the time. You'd immerse your dirty mess kit in the first can, said to contain soapy water. Rings of grease and gobbets of food would float atop the water. Then you'd rinse it in "clean" water, not noticeably dissimilar from the water in the first can, and now you were ready for your next meal.

Soon the whole camp was down with "G.I. shits" (G.I. = Government Issue) only in my case it turned out to be dysentery, with a high fever. Mercifully, it was the last time I was to see Tent City because while I went to an army hospital which had taken over a pink wedding-cake hotel out on St. Pete Beach called the "Don Cesar," Tent City was condemned and all troops previously assigned there were instead billeted in various St. Petersburg hotels that had been taken over by the military.

It took me many days to shake the aches and fever because the drugs that are now available were not then on hand. Returned to my unit, I found myself in an ancient three-story wooden hotel on the main downtown street, called with florid irrelevance the "Poinsettia." Here twelve guys were lodged in an ordinary smallish hotel room sleeping on wooden two decker bunks and straw mattresses. Never mind; it was dry, warm and comparatively insect-free. The training regime, including classes in close-order drill, calisthenics and the like were conducted at the minor league baseball park down the street where thirty years later and in unforeseeably different circumstances, I would watch spring training baseball games when I worked in the office of the Commissioner of Baseball.

As my company of recruits made its way through the basic training curriculum, we were gradually made aware of a veritable smorgasbord of further training options which were available to those of us who were qualified. I was eligible for just about anything I wanted, having scored well on the Army General Classification Test (AGCT) which was the rough equivalent of a scholastic aptitude or IQ test.

The range of choice was really dazzling. On the one hand was flight training, which offered a whole spectrum of opportunities including being commissioned as an officer and serving as a fighter pilot or as a member of a bomber crew, in which pilots, co-pilots, navigators, bombardiers and engineers were all commissioned officers. Alternatively, if you didn't want to be "bothered" to become an officer, you could still go flying as a machine gunner or a radio operator. We attended lectures outlining these "military occupation specialties" ("MOS"). One MOS number that I noted was 745, "Infantry Rifleman," and I shuddered with mixed gratitude and angst that I had escaped that fate.

To be an officer and a pilot held enough attraction for me to get me into the lecture hall but no further. The news was now full of U.S. and RAF bombing raids over Germany, virtually all of which were depicted as smashing successes, but each with its quota of bombers and fighters which "did not return." This information seemed only to enhance the enthusiasm of many of my cohorts who quickly signed up and were shipped off to various flight training bases around the country. Not me! The casualty figures might not appear in the headlines, but they did not have to be in Technicolor to teach me their lesson.

I was thus remitted to pondering the remaining alternatives, which included such specialties as weather forecasting, radio operation, aircraft repair and maintenance, personnel administration and the like. If I had been forced to the choice, I think I might have plumped for meteorology, but suddenly, another option became available. This was known as the Army Specialized Training Program (ASTP).

The ASTP was an odd concept indeed. I learned much later that it was a pet project of Eleanor Roosevelt, who had become concerned over the economic plight of the nation's universities whose undergraduate male populations had been decimated by the draft. The program was designed in part to alleviate the problem by assigning large numbers of recent recruits—there were well over 100,000 soldiers in the program at its peak—to college campuses for intensive training in two general areas, engineering and languages.

One would suppose that before such a large and costly program could be put in motion, some sort of at least quasi-military justification would have to be demonstrated, but never throughout the eleven months that I spent in the program did any such become remotely apparent.

There were about ten "engineers" to every "linguist." Most of those who were engineers were kids drafted out of college who took basic math and science courses with some smattering of introductory engineering. But what near- or longer-term objective could have been envisioned for this training was then and now remains a total mystery. At one point I wrote home that there would be enough engineers emerging from the program to plumb every toilet in Europe. I was a lively wit even then.

The language classes would be open only to those who were already "fluent" in French, German, Italian or Spanish. The U.S.-British invasion of Sicily would take place in early July, and it was more or less of a given that a cross-channel invasion of France and Germany would take place in due course, and I could therefore conceive that French, German and Italian fluency might be beneficial to the war effort, but *Spanish*? And there were other questions: How long would the program last? What would be our next assignment after we completed the course? No one could tell us.

In spite of these imponderables, and despite serious qualms on the question of my fluency, I wasted very little time in signing up for the French program and I was soon handed mimeographed orders to report to the University of Alabama at Tuscaloosa. It was with no regret whatever that I said goodbye to the Air Corps and St. Petersburg in May of 1943.

My "Phony War"

June 1943-April 1944

AFTER Hitler declared war on France and England on September 1, 1939, virtually no hostilities took place in Western Europe until May 1940 when the German Blitzkrieg was unleashed on the Low Countries and France. This interlude became widely known as the "phony war." Mine now started.

My sojourn at Tuscaloosa was brief but interesting. Our purpose there was to undergo preliminary testing to determine whether we qualified for the program, and if so, to what college we would be assigned. We were installed in vacant fraternity houses just in time to witness the southern belles and their sororities in the amazing rituals of the spring prom and the election of their campus queen. Never have I seen so many picture hats or as much pink and turquoise tulle! The scene was not only pre-World War II, it was almost pre-*Civil* War!

While there, I got to know a lady in the French Department of the University whose name was Talliaferro (she pronounced it "Tolliver"). She was responsible for the testing of those who would be enrolled in the French ASTP program. She saw that I was a good bit ahead in proficiency of most of the others and asked me to help her in the testing procedures, which I was glad to do. She was a charming woman who invited a few of us to her home for meals and to campus cultural events, so the time passed quickly. But orders were soon issued for another move, this time to the University of Illinois at Champaign-Urbana.

By comparison with the Air Corps and "St. Pete," the University of Illinois was Eden. Champaign-Urbana is situated in the plains about 125 miles south of Chicago. Its population at the time was about 60,000 people, but it was a primarily college town with a student body of many thousands.

In 1943, however, there were thousands of man-starved coeds and only a handful of male students. We, the French group, about ninety of us, lived together in fraternity houses. Military discipline was lax to the point of non-existence. We drifted to class much like the real undergraduates and ate in the student union.

An insight into not only the cuisine but my less-than-total adjustment to the tough life of the ASTP is provided by a letter I wrote to my grandmother on November 29, 1943: After a grudging compliment to the quality of the Thanksgiving dinner served by the Army I say: "The meal brought home to me again how much I am missing by not being able to eat off plates and not having every course brought to you when you are ready for it." This no doubt tells a lot more about me than it meant to my grandmother.

My roommate was a man named Jerry Freshman, who was a tired 35 years old. He had been assistant manager of the Ambassador Hotel in Chicago, then the "in" hostelry of that city. He was constitutionally unable to go to bed at night or arise in the morning without a cigarette smoked in bed. He would light up in the morning without opening his eyes. Jerry had maintained a close tie with the manager of the Ambassador, a semi-legendary figure in Chicago's cafe-society named Ernie Byfield. Although the demand for rooms and restaurant reservations at the Ambassador vastly outstripped the supply, Jerry and I were frequent Saturday night guests at the hotel, having taken a crowded train up from Champaign. We were lodged in a penthouse suite and dined in the hotel's and city's poshest watering spot, the Pump Room, a restaurant supposedly modeled after a similarly-named establishment famed in the nineteenth century in Bath, England. The room was ornately hung with velvet drapes of blue, green and gold, colors which were mirrored in the uniforms of the waiters and bus boys. The illusion of opulence was tarnished, I regret to say, by the sweat-stained rings radiating from the armpits of the latter. (Why in the world is *that* stuck in my memory?)

This was from the summer of 1943 through the winter of 1943-44, and there never seemed to be any shortage of steaks or scotch at the Pump Room notwithstanding that neither could be bought in any store. And it was all on house, courtesy of Ernie Byfield. Indeed, Jerry used to avail himself in his private bedroom in our suite of other less licit delights made available to him by the management. I did not succumb to the latter attractions since I found the idea of going to bed with a painted stranger in stiletto heels both frightening and repugnant. In addition, my social life also extended to Northwestern University in Evanston, a suburb of Chicago, where there was an affectionate coed by the name of Marilyn who had a claim, in her view, at least, to my affections.

Other entertainments during this surreal interlude were manifold. Two good and lasting friends whom I got to know in ASTP were Bill Markert and Herb Magee. Herb was from the Los Angeles area, in his elderly late twenties and had worked as a cartoon animator in the Disney studios and in aircraft design with Douglas. He came home for a Christmas furlough with me to Cleveland—we went to the symphony—and the three of us spent a week's furlough (it was recognized by the command that we were leading a very stressful life and needed frequent recreation periods) in Ishpeming in the Northern Peninsula of Michigan, which was Bill's home base.

At one point we organized a formal dance, known as the "Foxhole Formal" involving ASTP soldiers and Illini coeds. (Marilyn was my date who came down by train from Chicago. My principal recollection of the event is necking with her in the lobby of the local hotel as we waited to put her on the train for her return trip.) Our pictures appeared in the local society pages, copies of which were miraculously put into my possession by Bill Markert recently when by the strangest coincidence I discovered through a mutual friend that he was alive and well and living in New Castle, Maine.

In retrospect, it scarcely seems possible that we could have been such enthusiastic fiddlers while Rome was burning. But we had collectively shut our eyes to the ongoing events of the war. My letters home during this period make no mention whatever of the remote but bloody campaigns which were taking place in Africa, Russia and the Pacific.

The ASTP French curriculum was a joke. I and a handful of others in the French program were the only ones who had an even colorable claim to fluency. (There were a few men of French Canadian background, but aside from their heavy accents being virtually incomprehensible to my French ear, *they* had trouble with English.) The emphasis was on conversational French, of course, but most of my fellow students had trouble getting beyond "La plume de ma tante." This was not helped by the fact that the basic text that was used—apparently the only one readily available in quantity—was designed for society ladies traveling to Paris and the Riviera. It was replete with wonderfully idiomatic examples of how to assure that you were accommodated at the second seating in the first class dining salon on the *Normandie*, and how to make sure that the concierge in your Paris hotel would have your chauffeur with the Rolls Royce at the front door at the right time. My fellow students found it almost impossible to mouth such words in class when we had to enact the roles of these personages in oral exercises.

The atmosphere was in fact so ridiculous that almost no one took it seriously. There was, for example, rampant cheating on tests and papers, and I'll never forget one soldier—somewhat older than most of us and with strong Protestant religious beliefs—protesting in class that his low grade wasn't fair because he was one of the small handful who had not cheated. He was booed down by the others, following which the teacher said prissily that he couldn't imagine any such perfidy among American youths. Jesus!

One very serious note was struck, however. One morning, those of us in the French program were summoned to a confidential meeting. We were not told the subject, only that it was mandatory that we be there and that we were not to mention to anyone that the meeting had been held.

It was not a long meeting. The presentation was by two young officers, a major and a captain. They apologized for not being able to tell us much about what they were up to but stated that they were interested in recruiting volunteers "with your qualifications" to participate in a program which could not be described beyond stating that it might be both difficult and dangerous. A question period followed in which no answer went beyond saying "perhaps." That, in fact, was the response to a query as to whether the activity might involve being parachuted behind enemy lines into France.

Well, if that might be in the cards, not me!

There were several guys who hung behind when the meeting was dismissed, and I don't recall whether any of them disappeared from our midst as a result of this siren song, but it was not until many years later that I learned what had been afoot.

The Office of Strategic Services, America's first comprehensive intelligence agency, had been organized shortly after Pearl Harbor, and one of the missions to which it soon directed its attention was liaison with the French underground, both as a means of developing intelligence on enemy activities in France and to encourage and plan sabotage against them. One aspect of this program was the organization of so-called "Jedburghs," which were teams of three officers and/or non-coms, one

American, one English and one French, one of whom was qualified as a radio operator. Over three hundred men volunteered for this duty and 93 three-man teams were ultimately parachuted behind the German lines after D-Day. Each wore the uniform of his country, which it was hoped would afford protection from summary execution in the event of capture. William Casey, who much later was head of the CIA (successor to the OSS) during the days of the Iran-Contra investigation, was intimately involved in the organization of the Jedburgh program, and in his book, *The Secret War against Hitler,* commented about the Jedburghs that "the uniform did offer some protection to volunteers inexperienced in clandestine work and speaking at best a barely passable French that would give them away as quickly as their uniforms."

On second thought, it seems highly likely that some of the guys in the Illinois ASTP French program must have volunteered because Casey was obviously describing our group!

I ended up spending almost eleven months in the ASTP at Illinois, and I did derive a few tangible benefits from it. My fluency in French improved somewhat, and I also did get a year's college credit awarded later on when I returned to Yale. Apart from that the experience was of little value to me and none to the United States of America.

Well, maybe it is possible that the Republic did profit a bit from my stay at Illinois. At some juncture during the period, a very bright French professor named Mossé who was teaching a course in French Civilization asked each of us to write a paper in French setting down our views as to where and when the Allies should land on the Continent. This project really interested me, and I spent some hours in the library researching the physical attributes of the French coast, weather patterns and the like. I then wrote a paper suggesting that the focus of the invasion should be on the Norman city of Bayeux, pointing out that there were good beaches on the coast both to the east and west of Bayeux, that since this locale was many miles farther from Germany and from England than the Pas de Calais, the Germans would be unlikely to anticipate an attack there, and that early in the month of June, when spring storms would have abated, would be the ideal time. Inasmuch as the actual invasion a few months later made use of both sets of beaches (Americans to the west, English to the east) and the time was exactly as I had suggested, the astute Professor Mossé obviously forwarded a copy of it to the War Department where it was quickly implemented, while giving my paper an

'A' and prudently returning the original to me to divert suspicion!

More seriously, it has always seemed to me that if the plan seemed so logical to me, a 19-year-old schoolboy, let alone the Allied high command, and indeed to General Erwin Rommel, who was in charge of the German Normandy defenses, why is it that it was so utterly beyond the grasp of Adolph Hitler, who refused to listen to Rommel? Part of the reason surely is the elaborate and fascinating propaganda hoax erected by the Allies to mislead him; it involved George Patton as commanding general of a totally mythical U.S. Army based in southeast England which routinely emitted false radio traffic and the like to make the illusion real. Though there were doubters in the German high command, there were believers enough that large panzer forces were kept in the east by Hitler until well after the Normandy landings to provide a defense against the "real" assault by Patton. It's a fascinating question on which much has been written.

In April 1944, the Wonderland illusion came to an abrupt end. We were called into an assembly at which it was summarily announced that the entire program was being canceled. No reasons were offered, but for once our attention focused sharply on the march of events overseas, where the casualties had been mounting up in the Pacific, North Africa, and in the bloody Italian campaign, which had turned out to be anything but the "soft underbelly of Europe" that Churchill had so inaccurately called it.

In addition, it was widely and correctly assumed that the invasion of France would shortly be unleashed—in point of fact the Normandy landings would take place only three months later. Bodies were in dire demand, and here was a source of 110,000 of them.[3]

And unlike the earlier stages of our country's mobilization when one might select between a number of service schools, now there was no choice at all and no chance whatever to say "Not me!"

A few days went by between the announcement that the ASTP was dead and the receipt by each of us of our mimeographed orders. The wait

---

[3] The Pentagon's manpower planners had projected that ninety infantry divisions would suffice as the basic foundation of the nation's ground forces. By April 1944 it had become apparent both that this number might be quite low (it was) and that manpower requirements to replenish casualty losses of riflemen had been grossly underestimated. These mistakes were to plague the campaign in Western Europe throughout 1944 and 1945.

was not a happy one, for we feared the worst. And while some of us—like my friend Bill Markert, for example—found something of a haven in the anti-aircraft service, the vast majority of us were headed for the infantry.

In September 1992 a letter came to light which placed these anxious moments of April 1944 in what was for me a startling new perspective. My mother died on September 2, 1992 at the age of 95. In the closing of her apartment, a small packet of letters was discovered which had been written to her by my father, who had died in 1980 at age 93. One of these, dated Sunday, April 2, 1944 was written on stationery of the Blackstone Hotel in Chicago. The letter makes clear that I spent that weekend with them in Chicago. In the course of it my mother left by train for California to settle the affairs of an aunt who had just died. My father then spent Sunday with me before putting me on the train for Champaign that evening. He then returned to the hotel to write the letter.

My parents had rarely been separated from each other during their married life and thus the main thrust of the letter was to express my father's urgent longing for her and how hard he felt it would be to pass the long week ahead before she should return to his arms. But it also contained the following paragraph:

> I had a good afternoon with Sandy. I didn't get under the surface very deep and find it very hard for me to do it with him. He seemed to feel that the war is futile—that no good will come of it, that we are in it and must see it through; that it is stupid and that there is no great principle at stake for which a man could gladly die. He also said, tho, that we have to go through with it and that's that. I could be of no help to him as I found nothing in what he said with which I disagreed. It is a very harrowing experience for a thoughtful youngster and he is that. I am satisfied that he has an active imagination and he sensibly cringes from what he sees ahead. There is nothing of the bravado in him and I know no one who can contemplate what lies ahead without fear. Those who can just don't know. Sympathy and helplessness—these are the lot of parents in time of war.

The letter and this paragraph were a revelation to me on several levels. First, I had and have no recollection whatever of the Chicago weekend. Second, it had never occurred to me that the stern parent I thought I knew could ever have been the author of the rest of its text, which can only be characterized as a passionate love letter, written as it was by an ardent 58-year-old!

But the most startling aspect of the letter concerned the openness with which we had apparently expressed ourselves to each other. In spite of his protestations to the contrary, he had indeed "gotten under the surface" and had elicited the emotions which I clearly remember but which I would normally never have breathed to a soul, let alone to him. To suffer alone and in silence was in those days an article of faith with me, especially so as regards my father, whose attitude towards me seemed stern, demanding and everlastingly judgmental and almost never one of sympathetic understanding. Yet the letter leaves no doubt that on this occasion at least not only did I tell him what was on my mind but he agreed and did sympathize!

Did I sell my Dad short? The unhappy answer is I don't think so. I don't remember—whether then or later—ever being as frank and open with him as I obviously was on April 2, 1944. In later life we were always cordial, but the communications line so briefly open on that day normally ran in one direction only and the sympathetic ear which he told my mother he had given me failed then or thereafter to become meaningful to me.

Publicity photograph for the "Foxhole Formal", University of Illinois, March 11, 1944. Author is second from the right.

The Infantry and Camp Rucker

April-September 1944

IT seemed then and still does a singular irony that so many of us ASTP-ers who had originally been recognized by Army policy as being worthy of a professional level of training, however ill-conceived, should now be dumped, as we unceremoniously were by the tens of thousands, into the most menial and dangerous branch of all, the infantry!

And that was my fate. I was assigned to the 66th Infantry Division which was in training at Camp Rucker, a resort picturesquely situated near the town of Ozark, Alabama. I remember thinking later when I was in combat in Europe that notwithstanding the danger, the fear and the terrible winter living conditions, it was on balance better than Camp Rucker.

The countryside was grim and forbidding, for starters. It was broken with hills and declivities permitting virtually no useful agriculture except the barest subsistence sharecropping. The camp itself consisted of hundreds of two-story wooden barracks arrayed in rows, each undistinguishable from its neighbors, and the rows separated from each other by parade and drill grounds on which we were constantly practicing close order drill, except of course for those periods when we were walking guard duty or "policing the area" for illegally discarded cigarette butts.

The camp offered nothing in the way of amenities except for a hard-bench movie house and a PX. The fastest-moving items of merchandise offered were piles of sateen cushion covers in garish colors with gold-tasseled fringes. They were imprinted with mawkish poems addressed in large letters "To My Mother" or "To My Sweetheart," and they sold by the thousands! The nearest town, Ozark, was a crossroads surrounded by trailers occupied by wives and various camp followers. Beer was served there on Saturday nights and was consumed by the carload. For me, it was like being drafted a second time, only worse.

It is, of course, a deliberate plank of military policy to systematically eradicate individuality or initiative in the infantry soldier, leaving only one response—instinctive discipline and instantaneous obedience to orders. That much one could at least understand if not sympathize with, but what was intolerable (though I tolerated it) was the sadistic relish with which junior and non-commissioned officers exacted the performance of unnecessary and intentionally demeaning tasks. This phenomenon was so universal that it was quickly enshrined in the G.I. vocabulary as "chicken-shit." The role of chicken-shit in the military hierarchy was to amplify the superior's status and power by making the underling grovel.

A classic example is that of the sergeant who requires recruits assigned to latrine cleanup to clean the toilet bowls with a tooth brush. An even more outrageous form of chicken-shit was when a superior blamed and punished his subordinates for mistakes he himself had committed.

For example, the captain of my 200-man infantry company was from Scranton, Pennsylvania, and a butcher in civilian life. In one memorable incident, something went wrong in the field exercise in which we were engaged. He assembled us in a wooded clearing to acquaint us with our shortcomings and after leading into his subject became progressively less and less coherent until he was screaming with rage. He finally had to be physically subdued and led away by the junior officers out of our sight to regain his composure. It was a chicken-shit scene.

That may have been the same field exercise which required us before dawn to descend into a valley, cross its floor, and move against the opposite slope to "capture" its summit, which was defended by other, equally hapless, units. The only trouble was that no one had bothered to reconnoiter the valley floor. It was composed, as we shortly found out, of a series of broken boulders six to ten feet in height, overgrown by vines. When you stepped in the dark into the spaces between them you thought you were on solid ground but you then broke through the vines and fell into the crevasse, but because our officers remained safely up on the ridge, it wasn't called off until many had been injured, equipment lost and broken, etc. It was a fiasco from start to finish and vintage chicken-shit. It was also, although I was fortunate enough not to know it, a foretaste of the quality of leadership I was to experience six months later in Europe.

Another abiding memory that I have of Camp Rucker is that of the "nine mile speed march," a staple of infantry training. It required the troops in full field equipment—rifle and 45-pound pack—to cover that distance in a two hour time period, or an average of 4.5 miles per hour. It doesn't sound like a lot, but it can't be done without dogtrotting for most of the distance. They were at least charitable enough in the Alabama summer to schedule it at night when the temperature was only 90 to 95 degrees with equivalent humidity. It was excruciating. No part of the anatomy failed to chafe against some other part. Blisters on one's blisters. We ran along the back roads, past sharecroppers' shacks and discerned through the doors and windows the soft glow of kerosene lamps, the shadowy black forms and the low voices and chuckles. They were doubtless consuming cool, sweet watermelon, and totally free of chicken-shit. How I longed to change places with them!

On balance, I would have to say, I think, that the proportion of officers and non-coms whose treatment of their men was characterized by generous doses of chicken-shit was well in excess of fifty percent. Those who felt comfortable enough within themselves to deal with their subordinates on terms of reason and mutual respect were really quite rare, and when a G.I. found himself under the orders of such a person he counted himself indeed lucky.

I should not pretend there were no positive aspects to our training. Weapons training was extensive and for the most part, excellent. We spent weeks on the firing ranges becoming familiar with the M-1 rifle, the M-1 carbine, the Browning Automatic Rifle (a light machine gun, called the BAR), the .45 caliber pistol, grenades, rifle launchers and a few others. We were taught how to "zero in" our rifles—adjusting the sights so as to compensate for differences between individual pieces—and thus to assure accuracy, under ideal conditions, to as close as one foot at a range of a quarter mile. While shooting as a sport never appealed to me greatly, I had something of a talent for it and quickly became an expert marksman in all that I was exposed to.

The regime of five o'clock reveille, followed by day-long exercises and training together with a fair amount of night time field work resulted in all of us getting in to the best physical shape of our lives. It is unfortunate that the benefits of this excellent weapons and physical training did not carry forward to Europe. That is another question to be addressed on a later page.

Oh, yes! There was one other military maxim which if mentioned before was certainly learned at Rucker. It was: "Never volunteer." It was not to be found in any training manual. To the contrary, it was a distillation of wholly G.I. folk-wisdom, meaning, in essence, "Keep your head down and don't go looking for trouble." In other words, "Not me." Its inherent truth was instantly clear to me and most soldiers, but I was constantly amazed at how regularly it was disregarded, usually to the volunteer's clear disadvantage.

The training regimen at Rucker also featured such staples of Army life as close order drill, poison gas training, bayonet drill, guard duty, KP and "short arm" inspection. It is not easy to rank these in terms of unpleasantness.

Gas training, which I confess I looked forward to slightly as novel and mysterious, involved getting familiar with gas masks and learning the names, characteristics and aromas of the various gasses (mustard gas, phosgene, chloropicrin and tear gas). This was done by donning the mask, entering a stifling hot gas chamber in a tarpaper shack and then pulling a corner of the mask away from one's face to sample the atmosphere, at which time all novelty and mystery were replaced by coughing, gagging and weeping, as we inhaled, among others, concentrated essence of geraniums and rotten eggs. This was then compounded by an exercise in which one was required to march double-time for a protracted period while wearing the mask, an experience which for me was more suffocating than inhaling the gasses. I could never have survived if poison gas had been used. (Our instructors counseled that if we were ever caught in a gas attack without masks, we should put a urine-soaked handkerchief to our noses, since urine was a source of "sterile" water which would absorb some of the poison; at the time this seemed clearly preferable to the claustrophobia of the mask.)

Bayonet drill was particularly memorable, not only because the official training regimen was explicitly calculated to elicit the worst and most bestial traits of the soldier's psyche, but also because of the particular sergeant detailed as our instructor. He felt that the essential lesson could best be imparted by contrasting the act of thrusting a bayonet into the gut of a dummy with sexual foreplay. He would lunge at the dummy, stabbing and scything the blade while roaring gutturally. He would then suddenly halt, purse his lips in obscene caricature of a kiss and simper, "This ain't like nibbling titty!" as his tongue snaked in and out between his lips. He felt this illustration of the point to be so compelling that he repeated it several times to assure that his meaning would not escape us.

I am everlastingly grateful that no bayonets ever stabbed—in my presence, at least—anything more grisly than a K-ration can.

Of guard duty and KP, little of any novelty can be said. Guard duty was mind-numbing and inescapable: Two hours pacing a designated circuit through the night, two hours off, followed by the normal training schedule the next morning. Ugh!

My memory of KP consists entirely of peeling potatoes, though I don't doubt that I also was a "pearl diver" (dishwasher), wiped tables and all the rest. The metal vegetable peeler that is now ubiquitous had not yet been conceived by the mind of man, and a good quarter of the potatoes consumed by the services during the war were for that reason converted to peelings.

"Short arm" inspection was the Army's euphemism for one of the main elements of its program to combat venereal disease. The scene that comes vividly to mind is a dawn reveille formation where it is cold and not yet fully light. Standing in formation we would be required to open our trouser flies to inspection and to expose and manipulate our genitals on command of a non-com ("Skin it back! Milk it down!") who would then stride down the file. We were assured that the symptoms of disease would be readily visible to this scrutiny. Maybe so, but I never saw anyone being sent to the medical officer as a result, and this weekly routine ranked high among the degrading features of infantry training.

Barracks life at Rucker was enlivened considerably by frictions between us ASTP refugees, on the one hand, and the substantial numbers of high school dropouts and southern rednecks, on the other. Our non-coms, many of whom were rednecks themselves, delighted in imposing chicken-shit tasks on "the college boys," while the officers, most of whom had been to college, bent over backward to avoid showing favoritism towards us. Every now and then, however, we'd have a taste of sweet revenge, as when we became so fed up with the incessant hillbilly music played loudly over a redneck's radio in the barracks that we took up a collection, bought it from him and smashed it.

A redeeming sidelight to life at Rucker was the discovery of an oasis in Marianna, Florida, about 60 miles south of Ozark, called the Hotel Chipola ("Every Room With Private Bath," according to its stationery letterhead) situated on the town square. I would hitchhike down every free weekend to enjoy the almost miraculous luxury of a clean and pleasant private room and an excellent small garden dining room which was air conditioned and served delicious southern fried chicken. My company on these occasions would be a fellow ASTP-er, either a contemporary named Art Hummel or a philanderer of advanced years (perhaps 30) by the name of Hal Pittsburg who was from Brooklyn. Marianna was the site of an Air Corps training facility and abounded with the wives and girlfriends of the cadets, many of whom seemed to be off on training missions during the weekends. Pittsburg had an astonishing success rate with these ladies. How he did it I'll never know—every weekend there would be a different one. The ways of the world were slowly revealing if not explaining themselves to me.

For my part, I was content to enjoy the food and drink, revel in the unlimited and uninterrupted sleep, and shut out from my mind all thoughts of the following week let alone thereafter.

Another bright spot was a two-week furlough back to Cleveland as our training wound down. I well understood that this trip was the last I'd see of home until I got back from wherever it was I was going.

While I was with the 66th, the Division functioned as a training unit designed to ready troops for the replacement system in Europe and the Pacific. Hence when I got my furlough orders I knew that the handwriting was on the wall. (It is a chilling sidelight that soon after I departed on my way to Europe, the 66th Division's mission was changed to that of a combat division. It eventually shipped out to Europe as a unit, and on December 24, 1944, when I was undergoing some vicissitudes of my own in Belgium, 2,200 men of the division were packed aboard a Belgian vessel named the *Leopoldville* en route from Southampton in England to Cherbourg, France, when it was torpedoed by a German submarine in stormy seas. Total chaos followed, compounded by the Belgian crew's abandoning ship and by the failure of rescue vessels in Cherbourg to respond promptly. Three hundred of the 66th's troops were killed by the torpedo and 200 more perished from drowning or hypothermia. The German submarine escaped. The pastor of the church in Cleveland who delivered the eulogy at my father's funeral in 1980 was a *Leopoldville* survivor; I doubt I would ever have heard of the disaster—it was kept secret at the time—if we had not chanced on that sad occasion to discuss our careers in the infantry.)

In any case, I enjoyed my two weeks in Cleveland, not the least of which was flying both ways on a DC-3 airliner, which was a new and fascinating experience for me. On reaching home, my mother insisted (for reasons that she never articulated, probably not even to herself) that I sit for a formal photographic portrait which shows me in summer khakis with the shoulder patch of the 66th Infantry Division. Also while I was home our springer spaniel, Burr, mysteriously contracted rabies and died. He never exhibited any symptoms of "madness" but the doctor nonetheless prescribed rabies shots for all of us—a series of injections, one per day, for fourteen days. The sites of the inoculations became increasingly sore as the series progressed, especially as each arm, leg and bun had to be used a second time. The treatment was especially debilitating for my father who became feverish as it continued and had to take to his bed. Since the disease is almost invariably fatal, however, elimination of the risk more than made up for the discomfort and the inconvenience.

And as for me? Though I was assured by the doctor that it would be altogether prudent for me to stay in Cleveland until the full course of shots had been completed and that he would be glad to communicate with the Army to obtain an extension of my furlough for the purpose, did I do so? Not me! In retrospect it seems idiotic to have ignored this advice and returned to Camp Rucker as originally scheduled, but that is precisely what I did. The only explanation I can offer is that I was so imbued with the need not to make a special case of myself or to appear to be seeking preferential or different treatment that there seemed to be only one choice: The stupid one!

Would it have made any difference? Clearly so. I would have missed the shipment to Europe that I became part of as soon as I got back to Alabama. But might I have stayed with the 66th Division and might I have been on the ship that was sunk? I will never know.

On leaving Cleveland the doctor gave me a small box about the size of a pack of cards containing ten small vials of rabies antitoxin, with instructions to deliver them to the medical officer on my arrival and arrange to be injected once a day until they were gone. The medical officer, however, said he had no refrigeration facility in his office. He suggested that I take the box to the mess sergeant of my company from whom I could then obtain them one by one. (I wondered in passing what the effect on the vaccine might be of not being refrigerated for the hours it took to get to Alabama.) The Company mess hall refrigerator, however, was a huge walk-in affair, with sides of beef hanging from hooks, lattice-work shelves, etc., with no readily discernible place for such a small box. We finally fixed on putting it on top of a grill which protected the recessed ceiling fan.

That worked fine for the first day or so, but when I went to get the next bottle of serum, you know what hit the fan, don't you? As I reached to get the box, its end tilted up, there was an instantaneous crash, and the whole box, bottles and all was atomized by the fan. A spray of serum—doubtless lethal rabies germs—was blown in a fine mist down onto a bunch of chickens, not to mention shards of glass. You can perhaps imagine the scenarios that I reeled off in my teenage mind, as I recoiled from this catastrophe: The soldiers of the Company would all contract rabies, and if I did not report what had happened, would die agonizing undiagnosed deaths. Of larger importance, I might myself do so since the last half of my course of treatment would not be injected into me. On the other hand, if I did report it, a refrigerator of food would have to be condemned, which would mean no less than a court martial, with attendant shame, humiliation, and, no doubt, discipline.

Did I report it? Not me! I did nothing. And though it took probably a week or ten days for me to be sure, nothing happened to anyone, not the food workers, or those eating in the mess hall or, thank God, to me.

One thing as I have said that I did learn at Camp Rucker was the use, cleaning and care of my M-1 rifle. Our drill sergeants were ever assiduous in impressing on us how precious the rifle was to us: "It's your wife!" "A court martial offense to fail to keep it in top condition." I learned this lesson painfully, however. After one horrendous "night problem"—it may have been the "Nine-Mile Speed March" or the "Night on the Moon Landscape"—I got back to the barracks soaking wet and utterly exhausted. And I didn't clean my rifle until the next morning. And then, my God, what happened? Though the exterior was in good shape, the interior of the barrel had become pitted by rust which, like Lady MacBeth's spot, could not be erased no matter how hard I tried. The piece was permanently damaged, just as we had been warned would happen in such circumstances.

Our rifles, as well as the rest of us, were regularly and routinely inspected by non-coms and officers, but it wasn't too often that one of them would look down the barrel. When it finally did happen, I wished that the ground would open beneath me! Miraculously, none of those who did look at it seemed to know how to focus their eyes so as to see clearly up and down the inside of the barrel. (I could; I had 20-15 vision in those days.) I'll never forget the burden lifted from me as I survived its final inspection on turning it in prior to leaving Alabama, although I did wonder what might happen to the poor sucker to whom it would next be issued.

It is curious that not one of the above incidents or events of my experience at Camp Rucker, all of which I remember with crystal clarity, found its way into the letters I wrote home during that period. I wonder why. Well, what did I write about? Here are a few examples:

From a letter dated June 11, 1944, five days after the June 6 landings in Normandy:

> The way it looks now the war in Europe will be over by the time I have completed my training here, and if I see any fighting at all, it probably will be against the Japanese... There will be another war soon, anyway, of that I am convinced. And all I want to do now is get out of the Army as soon as possible and enjoy what 'little time' may be mine.

From a letter dated June 19, 1944:

> It is evident that the men who, at the present time, track the destinies of the world are not influenced in their decisions either by what the one or the many have to say. One has trouble picking out the lesser of the two evils in the coming presidential election [Roosevelt v. Dewey]—neither one of which wants to tell anyone what his opinions are. It just seems to me that the whole problem [of governing the world] is so immense that one human brain is physically incapable of coming to a decision. The only answer seems to be that a war every 15 or 20 years is the price that has to be paid for the intervening years of peace. Why, though, why?

From a letter dated June 25, 1944:

> This basic training routine through which I am now going is really rough. The weather helps not. With the thermometer hovering at 100-102 degrees or thereabouts, cases of heat exhaustion are many, and increasing daily. Friday night we had the pleasure

of going through infiltration course [crawling under barbed wire entanglements with live machine gun bullets being fired four feet overhead]. Aside from the fact that it was hot and that I got sand all up and down inside me and that the skin got worn off both hands and knees and that the screening smoke they used was vile and made 50 percent of the infiltrators sick about half an hour later, and that I had to drag somebody else's rifle and pack in addition to my own because he didn't wait one half-hour, and that my rifle looked like it had been used during World War I and buried for 20 years and just dug up and that I had to stay up until 2 a.m. cleaning it, it wasn't so bad. [I suspect that this passage may be tinged with hyperbole. It is also worth adding that the Army's infiltration course was really just another form of chicken-shit: it wasn't really frightening because you knew you weren't going to get hurt, and thus it became just another way of making the G.I.'s grovel.]

From a letter dated July 22, 1944:

I wonder if you have heard from Nicky yet? [My older brother had just gone overseas.] It is a great consolation to all concerned that the end of the war cannot be far away. The recent German Army revolt [the reference is to the attempt on Hitler's life by his officers at Rastenburg on the 20th of July 1944], though unsuccessful is a sure sign that the end is drawing near. Perhaps not by direct revolution, but in terms of Army morale it must mean much. Here's the kid that can tell you just how much it means, too. It can't last too much longer. [My crystal ball was distinctly cloudy in writing thus; if anything the failed attempt probably prolonged the war rather than the contrary because Hitler ruthlessly executed thousands of suspected plotters whose influence might otherwise have helped lead to an earlier surrender.]

From a letter dated August 20, 1944:

We sweat and waste eons of perfectly good, never to be recaptured time playing an inferior brand of Boy Scout in the woods. We are just starting to have regimental problems—I just can't wait! The other day our Battalion Commanding Officer, a stupid fool by the name of Colonel Edwin J. Nowick, Jr., gave us a pep talk saying that there was no doubt in his mind that the 2nd Battalion would be the best, and then, obviously expecting an overwhelming vote of confidence, said 'How 'bout that, men?' You could have heard a pin drop. Two seconds later when he said 'that's all I have to say,' the house was brought down with cheers. [I have, curiously, no recollection whatsoever of this scene, but I have no doubt whatever of its total accuracy.]

It could be said of my treatment at the hands of the Army at Camp Rucker that it was both dehumanizing and contemptible, seeming as it did to elevate chicken-shit to the level of deliberate policy. My experience supplied copious evidence for the truth of such a view. We were deliberately dehumanized, but it wasn't totally without reason. The training regimens were euphemistically phrased as "military courtesy" and "military discipline," but their avowed aim was to subordinate the soldier's ego in the interest of blind obedience to orders.

Such instinctive obedience is unarguably essential to the efficient functioning of large bodies of troops in combat, and the training did accomplish that objective—to start with. But when the message was pounded home as single-mindedly and relentlessly as at Rucker, it had the not so incidental result of tending to suppress instincts of leadership, self confidence and esprit de corps. The fact was, however (although we did not understand it at the time), that we were all being groomed to be shipped overseas as replacement privates and privates first class (my then rank), rather than as an effectively functioning integrated unit. Our officers made it clear through both attitude and behavior that they had no real interest in us or our future well-being and that they simply didn't give a damn about our leadership capabilities. This, no doubt, comes as close as anything to explaining why we were subjected to such a heavy-handed training regime.

In retrospect it is more than a little surprising that some of us were later able to discover within us subconscious reserves of the very qualities which this regime had tried to squeeze out of us. We did so in spite of, rather than because of Rucker chicken-shit.

I became aware during that long hot summer in Alabama that my father was attempting to develop an alternative to the infantry for my military career. There are one or two veiled references to this in my letters home and I have a recollection of learning that he was contacting one or two friends who were officers in Washington on my behalf. There was nothing whatever that I could or did do at my end to advance this effort, but I have no doubt that I was keenly interested in it. It didn't work. I was deep in the entrails of a giant machine and there was no escaping it.

En Route to Europe

September-October 1944

FINALLY in the late summer of 1944, I departed on a long, hot hayfeverish train ride from Alabama to Massachusetts, where our detachment of replacements would await transportation overseas. I had the sensation of a noose tightening around my neck but I tried not to think about it. The stopping place was Camp Myles Standish, a sprawling temporary camp in the sandy pine barrens near Plymouth, Massachusetts. While there, I had the good fortune to be taken under the wing for an overnight pass or two by my cousin John Sheldon and his father Percy, who lived in East Milton, a suburb of Boston.

John took me in his almost new automobile to visit my Uncle Dudley Millikin and his wife Eunice, in nearby Needham. My memories of this occasion are less than detailed. At this stage of the war, booze of any kind was in short supply and good booze couldn't be found, but Uncle Dudley had plenty of it. He was both proud and jealous of it, but for a soldier on his way overseas he was generosity itself. In a letter home I said "Martinis came in bursts of six."

The results were predictable: on the way back to East Milton I managed to desecrate John's automobile and possibly also his Naval Officers uniform with waves of vomit. A mortifying performance—Uncle Percy, a dear man with a twinkle in his eye, clucked and shook his head about it the next morning but refrained from comment. This crumbled my self-respect even further as we got back into the auto (which John had now carefully cleaned as best he could but not aromatically) to send me back to camp. What a hangover!

I was now in the grips of the U.S. Army's Replacement System. This was devised as a means of rapidly re-supplying infantry divisions which had sustained battle losses with fresh supplies of trained troops. "Packages" of men, 100 to 200 in number, under command of several officers (themselves replacements, but from officer schools or other units) would be given shipping orders to a port of embarkation, such as Standish, to await the availability of a convoy or ship to take them overseas. My package consisted of about seventy-five percent former ASTP-ers. We were a group in our late teens and early twenties who regarded ourselves, no doubt a bit pretentiously, as a substantial cut above the ordinary G.I. Justified or not, we developed then and retained throughout our infantry experience a sense of identity and spirit which marked us as different.

Each package of replacements would advance as a unit through the series of replacement depots ("repple-depples" in G.I. vernacular) until it was within five or ten miles of the front, at which point the men would be dispersed among nearby fighting units. The effectiveness of this system, which was able to replenish casualties overnight, has been credited with the Army's ability to rebound from losses and continue to press offensively. It is said that the German High Command never did come to understand how the system worked and that throughout the war it continued to assume that units sustaining losses would not be able to function effectively as fighting units for long periods.

The system did have substantial drawbacks. It worked well in instances where a unit had lost a minor portion of its men, say up to fifteen percent. But where much larger losses occurred, as in the case of my own unit after its ordeal in the Hürtgen Forest and later in Ardennes, its effect was to paper over the disorganization, and sometimes the demoralization, of the supposedly reconstituted unit; bodies could be replaced overnight but not cohesion, self-awareness or the command structure. And there was little or no precedent, or "doctrine" in official military lingo, to guide the remaining leadership of the depleted units in how to rebuild that structure.

As I waited with my package to move forward in the system, I had a memorable introduction to Army poker in a game that went on intermittently for over two days. I was in and out of it during this period, never ahead or behind conspicuously, until late one night I got hot and got about $150 ahead—an enormous sum of money at the time. Quietly proud of my mastery of this virile endeavor, I announced, on winning a particularly large pot, that I intended to withdraw from the game. This produced a fiercely hostile reaction on the part of several of the heavy losers who let me know that they felt it was unacceptable that I should depart with so much of "their" money. It was even hinted that actions rather than words might ensue should I persist in my intentions. Did I leave the game? Not me! I instantly reconsidered, at least to the point of staying around for a few more hands during which I lost some of it back and the threats diminished to mere grumbles.

I finally made good my escape, and in the process learned a little about the etiquette of the poker blanket. (This account will no doubt put readers in mind of the scene in "The Sting" in which Paul Newman takes the big-time New York gambler to the cleaners on the Twentieth Century Limited.)

My cousin Sheldon, who was an officer on the staff of the Navy's Northeastern Sea Frontier, had correctly (if indiscreetly) predicted that I would be sailing on the *Mariposa*, a luxury liner previously engaged in San Francisco-Hawaii service.

Just before leaving Standish, on September 12, 1944 all of us who were to board the *Mariposa* received a complete issue of all-new equipment, including rifles and BAR's and plentiful sets of everything in the way of uniforms down to and including extra sets of heavy combat boots. These we stowed in enormous duffel bags that were equipped with shoulder straps. Thus burdened, we were required to board the vessel by means of cargo nets slung over the side to the pier below. Why on earth this means of boarding was exacted of us was not clear; it was both difficult and dangerous. The fly-weight Cliff Hackett, for example, recalls teetering dizzily 30 feet above the pier with 35 pounds of BAR and 50 of duffel bag and being almost unable to make it. The consensus was that this was one last, generous helping of chicken-shit which some stateside martinet had decided to visit upon us helpless GI's.

The *Mariposa* sailed alone, not in convoy, because of its speed. We made the trip from Boston to Liverpool, England, in something like ten days. It took longer than the standard six or seven days because of the need to zig-zag to avoid submarines.

Here is how I described the trip in a letter dated September 25, 1944 from "somewhere on the (censored) Ocean":

> At this point I am just as much in the dark as concerns my location as you are, though by the time you get this I will have long since arrived at wherever it is I may be going. The only indications one has are the weather and the direction (which is never the same the next time you look)—and both methods are far

from reliable. However, if I can't draw any conclusions from the weather I can still enjoy it, and this I have been doing. Except for the first day, we couldn't have asked for better. The water has been glassy. The sun and air warm, and the water the most heavenly shade of blue imaginable. The accommodations leave much to be desired, but as I am not uncomfortable I can't complain. We get but two meals daily, so that by the time the dinner bell rings one is so hungry that the relative quality of the food is only a minor concern. Time is my own to do with, amazingly enough, as I choose, and I am free to roam the decks or to avail myself of what few facilities have not converted into sleeping quarters. Naturally, the ship is terribly crowded and it is difficult to find squatting space, so when I find a place, I stay there all day reading and sleeping and sopping up sun and sea breezes.

An aspect of the sleeping arrangements which did not make it into my letter had to do with a running joke which got started in our cabin. Each cabin had six tiers of steel pipe bunks equipped with canvas "mattresses" attached to the pipe with rope laced through grommets in the margin. Someone early discovered that hilarious results were guaranteed if the ropes were cut, because the occupant would not be affected until the middle of the night when the rope would work loose and deposit his struggling form on the man below. As we neared England, this had happened so many times that most of the canvasses were secured at only a few places to the pipes. By this time the hilarity was considerably reduced because the buns of the guy above were in your lap, etc., etc.

An incidental benefit of the enforced intimacy of *Mariposa*'s accommodations was that acquaintances and friendships developed, some of which carried forward to our ultimate destination. One such was my friendship with Cliff Hackett, with whom I was to spend many months in combat and with whom I have recently and most happily become reacquainted. In addition, no fewer than six of us who gathered at our reunions in Minnesota in 1992 and 1994 were among those who traveled to Europe on the *Mariposa*. More of that later.

Another curious aspect of the trip overseas, also related no doubt to the crowding of the vessel, was that no effort whatever was made to keep us in physical shape. No exercises or calisthenics were prescribed, and the day was spent as described in my letter, eating, sleeping and reading.

— Not Me! —

(Some blessed soul in the military bureaucracy had succeeded in launching a program which made recent books and current periodicals available in reduced size but large quantities everywhere we went; it was an absolute godsend!) In the case of some of my fellow soldiers bridge, poker and craps went on around the clock, but I had assimilated the lesson at Myles Standish and did not indulge. But by the end of the trip we had unfortunately lost a fair measure of the physical conditioning we had had when we left our respective training camps in the states.

There was virtually no discussion of the future on the *Mariposa*. The knot of apprehension grew in my stomach notwithstanding the brief daily news reports which now were chronicling rapid advances into Belgium, Luxembourg and even Germany.

On board the *Mariposa*, September 1944.

England and an Introduction to German Weapons

October 1944

I'LL not forget our arrival in Liverpool. The *Mariposa* steamed up the Mersey River at night, and at a certain point lingered in the roadstead awaiting tugs. Longshoremen had come aboard to handle hawsers and the like, with one of whom I fell into a conversation. After weeks and months of uninspiring Army life, hillbilly songs on the radio in Alabama and largely arm's length social relationships, I was eager for more uplifting and refined conversation. But I could scarcely believe my ears! Not only was the accent so different from the cultured English of the movies that I could hardly understand it, but when I did grasp the drift, I discovered to my surprise and horror that every other word was "fookin'." It was only after careful analysis of how this word was used in context with others that I realized that it was a word which was in my vocabulary, though pronounced very differently. Curiously, the meaning conveyed by the speaker appeared to be identical.

It's amazing that this conversation with the Cockney longshoreman could have shocked and surprised me so profoundly. How naive I was!

Things looked up briefly when we were put on a first-class railway carriage for the trip to our next destination. Frosted glass partitions, lace antimacassars, and pictures of pastoral English castles and other tourist destinations were on the bulkhead. At least I hadn't been totally misled by the cinema!

The first of our overseas "repple-depples" was a camp outside of a beautiful small town which was known to the GI's as "Chocolate Park," but which I think was more properly spelled "Chalcote Park." Here we were given very memorable demonstrations on the appearance and firing characteristics of various captured German weapons, including especially two variations of German machine guns which were later to become extremely familiar to me.

The difference between the German weapons and their American counterparts could not have been more marked. As I was later to learn, the clear superiority of the German machine guns was not an anomaly. To the contrary, it carried virtually through the whole gamut of weaponry. The German machine guns, particularly the MG 42s, were lighter in weight and fired at many times the rate of their American equivalents. The latter fired at approximately the same rate as a woodpecker does when he goes at a tree—distinctly separate sounds, at 500 rounds per minute. The German ones, by contrast, sounded as though someone was ripping a huge sheet of canvas, and fired at a rate of 1,200 rounds per minute. Our instructors in England tried to minimize their superiority by asserting that they were much less accurate than ours. My subsequent experience was altogether to the contrary.

The German artillery was also superior to ours. Especially was this so in the case of the famous 88-mm cannon, which had originally been designed as an anti-aircraft gun, but later became both an artillery and an anti-tank weapon and was mounted as well on many of the German tanks and tank destroyers, which were tractor-chassis mounted like a tank but with minimal armor protection for the crew. It could knock out an American tank, that is pierce the tank's armor and kill the crew inside, with great ease.

American weapons typically had not advanced much in design since the First World War, one exception being the M1 or Garand rifle. Among the American automatic weapons, the "Tommy Gun" famed in Chicago Prohibition gang warfare and the Browning Automatic Rifle ("BAR"), were in common use. The former was not a bad weapon (more on it later) but it used a .45 caliber bullet, the same as the standard automatic pistol, and it was not a very effective weapon beyond 50 feet. The BAR seemingly weighed a ton (it was 16 pounds versus the M1's 9 pounds) and was an ordeal to carry around. The German Schmeisser machine pistols were like today's assault rifles (e.g., the AK-47), light, hard hitting and with a much longer range than the Tommy gun and a higher rate of fire. And while we finally did get some good heavy tanks towards the end of the war (the "Pershings") the earlier ones, largely Shermans, though faster and more mobile than German tanks, were inadequately armored and had lighter cannons which had difficulty penetrating German armor. They were also called "Ronsons" by the tankers because being gasoline rather than diesel driven, they caught fire readily when hit.

The unfavorable comparison was less the case with aircraft simply because in that department there was no choice but to build designs in keeping with the civilian technology which had advanced enormously during the period between the wars. But in the U.S. at least, there was no "civilian technology" in respect of ground-based weapons. The military was starved for funds by a Depression-conscious and isolationist Congress, and there was not enough time to catch up. It was a source of sore trial to us infantrymen throughout the war.

One further word on the German 88. It was a cannon which propelled a shell at a velocity much greater than the speed of sound. This meant that it came at you in a straight line, rather than in a parabolic arc, and it arrived before you had any warning of its coming. For the most part, our artillery was of the "howitzer" variety, meaning that the shell was lobbed up in an arc, like a snowball. You could hear it being fired and then the whooshing sound that one knows of from the movies. If you happened to be looking at its source when fired, you could even follow its flight with the naked eye. With a little practice, you could easily distinguish those that were over, short or coming close to you, and you even had a few seconds to find protection, if not to change your underwear.

No instructions were ever given us about these distinctions, and I can't imagine why. I learned from painful experience that when someone fires a rifle or machine gun at you, those bullets, like the 88, travel well over the speed of sound. The result is that the first sound you hear is that of the projectile breaking the sound barrier (this phrase didn't exist at the time, but the phenomenon was plain enough) overhead or nearby giving you no clue as to its source. However, if you listened closely a fraction of a second later, you could hear at a distance, the much less noticeable sound of the muzzle blast of the weapon which fired it and in that way get a fix on the bastard that was out to get you. A very valuable lesson.

I was captivated by England. From a letter dated October 1, 1944 datelined "Somewhere in England":

> Of course I can't tell you where I am, but I see no objection in saying that it is a very beautiful spot. Big trees and country lanes and thatched cottages abound. I have really fallen in love with it. I have never seen trees and grass as green in my life. The whole

country is just so different from the States that my fascination could not be more complete. Everything is so clean and tidy—there is none of the litter anywhere that you find at home. I hope that I'll be here long enough so that I'll be able to see some more of it.

Alas this was not to be. Our package of replacements was soon en route by train to Southampton on the English Channel, to be loaded on a nondescript English freighter named the *Cheshire* manned largely by East Indian sailors. We were crammed into freight decks reeking of rancid food and/or the Indian crew, it was not clear which. The food was standard English "other ranks" quality—inedible—and we were required to sleep in hammocks. It is, of course, only a few hours' sail across the Channel but in October of 1944 there was still risk of submarine and air attack so that our ship waited at anchor in the Solent—the sea approach to Southampton—for two or three days until a convoy could assemble.

The War is Being Won Without Me I Land in Europe

October 1944

AS I made my way forward toward the battle front, great events had meanwhile been taking place in various parts of Europe and the world. The D-Day landings had, of course, taken place on both sides of Bayeux on June 6, 1944 (just as I had recommended in the paper submitted to Professor Mossé in Illinois months before), but the Allied forces had been penned up in the difficult "bocage" country there for almost two months. Allied planners had failed to foresee what formidable obstacles the hedgerows would be nor had they planned for the high casualty rates which they would cause. American losses alone by the end of July came to 30,000 men before the engineers were able to devise means for our tanks to break open the hedgerows and advance into the more open terrain beyond the original bridgehead. After expensive thrusts at St. Lô, Avranches and Caen, enormous advances were possible, both by the British on the east flank and the Americans, particularly General Patton's Third Army, on the west and south. Operation ANVIL, the invasion of southern France by a combined force of American, British and French troops, made rapid progress and joined with the northern invaders near the German frontier in October.

Meanwhile, General Dietrich von Choltitz, the German in charge of Paris, unexpectedly and against the explicit orders of Hitler, withdrew his forces from the city and threw it open to the Allies, by whom it was immediately taken on August 25th. Unbeknownst to me, my future division, the U.S. 28th Infantry Division, was designated to parade with the Free French Forces down the Champs Elysées, to the accompaniment of the tears, hugs, shouts and tumult of hundreds of thousands of ecstatic Parisians.

In Italy, Rome had fallen, while on the Eastern Front, the Russian armies were winning enormous victories in tank battles around Warsaw, Poland. In one of the war's more brutal and shameful phases, the Russian High Command abruptly suspended these efforts when there was an uprising in Warsaw of Polish partisans whose leadership was not acceptable to the USSR. The Germans took full advantage of the opportunity thus deliberately presented to snuff out the rebellion, which they did at the cost of many thousands of lives, whereupon the Russians, their political opponents having been eliminated, resumed the offensive and shortly "liberated" the city.

In the Pacific, the island-hopping campaigns led by General MacArthur and Admiral Nimitz were moving slowly forward, but there was every evident prospect of a long-sustained conflict in that theater.

The only aspect of these great events which had any real meaning for me, of course, was what was going on across the channel in France. The stunning success of the summer campaign there gave rise to hopes by many that the war in Europe might be over before winter set in.

None of my letters home give any indication of how I was reacting to these events. I was now overseas, the opportunities to write were fewer, and when one did write it had to be shorter. Moreover, all mail was now censored, which meant that consciously or subconsciously, the writer curtailed his expressions on almost every subject. I am sure, however, that my emotions had not given away at this point to unmitigated optimism. It is more likely, I think, that I blocked the subject out of my mind, inasmuch as I was powerless to affect the course of events.

In any event, our convoy at last gathered and, in the calmest of weather (if it had been rough it would have been horrendous because we were not allowed out on deck) our convoy maneuvered toward France.

We at last came on deck on a clear sunshiny October day off the coast of Normandy. We were to land at Omaha Beach.[4]

---

[4] As previously noted, Cliff Hackett and I disagreed as to whether we landed at Utah or Omaha Beach. He remembered it as Utah, and I recall seeing a light ship anchored off the beach with the word "Utah" in large letters on its side, but a letter I wrote home on May 15, 1945, clearly says "Omaha." The doubt was set to rest by the unanimous agreement of those attending our Minnesota reunions, and by my visit to the scene on August 21, 1990. My recollection of the "Utah" lightship, I think, means only that we approached Omaha from the west. (See the entry for that date in my Journal, excerpts from which are at-
continued...

Omaha Beach had been one of the two landing sites for the American forces on D-Day, June 6, 1944. Utah, which was the smaller of the two, lay to the west at the base of the Cotentin Peninsula, at the northern tip of which is located the port of Cherbourg. Omaha, to the east, featured a broad gently sloping beach over five kilometers in length and easily 200 meters wide at low tide. Some 7,000 American troops who gave their lives in the assault on the beaches in June 1944, are now interred at the strikingly beautiful American cemetery just above Omaha Beach at the town of St. Laurent-sur-Mer.

In June 1944 the beaches had been naked to the sea; there were no dikes or other protections, natural or artificial, to shield the approach of our troops, and substantial casualties occurred not only from enemy action, but from the capsizing and swamping of landing craft from the action of the waves. (Eisenhower had almost postponed the invasion due to concerns regarding weather.)

Now, however, in October 1944, all was serene. In the interim about forty ancient vessels of all sizes and shapes had been sunk in a line parallel to and about 500 yards off the shore. This was truly an astonishing sight! We were told that these vessels, the aggregate length of which was over two miles, and no two of which were the same, had been filled with concrete and sunk in place, thus replacing in very *ad hoc* fashion the prefabricated artificial port, or Mulberry, which had been towed to the site and sunk soon after the landing. Unfortunately it had been destroyed by a vicious spring storm from June 18 to 22 which caused more damage to Allied supplies than had been inflicted on D-Day. But the line of sunken ships had worked well, and in October, virtually all the supplies for the entire Allied expeditionary force, which numbered well over a million by this time, were still being brought in over the Normandy beaches. It would not be until early November that the British would finally clear the approaches to the Port of Antwerp in Belgium to relieve the burden on the beaches.

On the day of our landing, the only means of access from ship to shore remained the same one used by the troops on D-Day: descending over the side of our ship down rope netting to LCIs (Landing Craft, Infantry) tethered alongside. Although the day would be classified as

---
...continued
tached as Appendix I to this memoir.)

"calm" in mariners' terms, the LCI was pitching and rearing in a moderate three- to four-foot chop, and it would rise and fall away under one's feet while threatening simultaneously to catch a leg between it and the side of the ship. I had a hard time to keep from thinking what must have been going through the heads of those who landed on D-Day.

The entire beach teemed with activity. Dozens of small vessels were plying back and forth between the shore and the ships in the roadstead, while others, like LSTs (Landing Ship, Tank) with shallow enough draft to approach the beach but still large enough to cross the channel, were off-loading their vehicles by means of bow ramps lowered to the beach. The LCIs were the smallest of the lighters, being no more than 40 to 50 feet long. We came ashore without incident, although we did, like the famous picture of General MacArthur going ashore in the Philippines, get our feet wet.

We did not tarry long to observe the spectacle but immediately marched inland. Here the Army sprung a welcome surprise on us. At the top of the bluff we came abreast of a Quartermaster depot where we learned that the many duplicate items of uniform and equipment that we had laboriously heaved up the sides of the *Mariposa* and through England were now to be turned in. It had been the Army's way of transporting surplus gear to Europe. And so we unceremoniously dumped all of the overcoats and extra pairs of shoes in unsorted piles and went on our way, now with a much reduced and more realistic kit. Though we did not know it then, it would again be drastically reduced one month later as we marched across the frontier into Germany.

My emotions on first touching the soil of France were complex. Consider that I had devoted a substantial share of my recent educational attention to French language, literature and culture, and I was now in France! Every sight, sound, and odor was of intense interest: The outline and distinctive script of the road signs and the billboards, the blue denim work clothes and wooden shoes of the farmers working in their courtyards and fields, their faces and figures, ruddy-hued and shorter in stature than Americans, and the unique hedge row configuration of the fields which had caused so much anguish and grief to our troops in June. And of course the physical appearance of the hamlets on our line of march.

There was evidence of damage, but since the Germans' line of resistance had not stiffened until several miles inland, there were many houses and farm buildings which had remained untouched. Their simple architecture, warm stone walls and red tile roofs were precisely as they had been depicted in the *National Geographics* I had read at home.

— Not Me! —

Photograph from which a commemorative stamp was taken. 28th Division, Champs Elysée, France, August 29, 1944. Men of Baker Company of the 112th Regiment identifiable on the left side of the front rows.

Enlargement of U.S. commemorative postage stamp. Note aircraft overhead—an after-the-fact figment of Post Office imagination.

Carentan, France
I Meet Rene Bucaille and Family

October 1944

OUR immediate destination was the small Norman farming community of Carentan, about 20 kilometers from the beach and home to several thousand inhabitants. Carentan had sustained a fair amount of damage, but again, many of its homes and buildings, including its memorable Cathédrale de Notre Dame, remained functional. Our unit bivouacked in a large, gently sloping field located just south of the center of town where we pitched our pup tents and laid out our gear to air in the early fall sunshine. In the late afternoon of our first day there, a French workman in blue overalls and carrying a wooden tool box, made his way down the pathway through our encampment. Eager to attempt communication, I said "Bonjour, monsieur," and a conversation ensued which to me seemed a minor miracle. I could actually say things which he readily understood and vice versa.

He turned out to be René Bucaille, a carpenter, who, as a result of the June events, was one of the busiest men in town.

In short order, he had invited me to come for dinner the next evening, and I walked home with him so that he could show me where he lived at 16 rue Sébline. On return to our encampment I found myself to be a minor celebrity. It apparently had occurred to very few of my compatriots that any business of consequence could be transacted with a mere "Frog," but after I had recounted the results of my conversation with René, I was deputized to negotiate purchases of food, hard cider, and even, in the case of one sergeant, to accompany him to the cathedral to ask the curate to say a Mass for his mother. (I vividly recall standing before this worthy in the cool and fragrant interior, totally tongue-tied because as a non-Catholic, I could not think how to translate this request into understandable French, when suddenly it came to me: "M. le sergent demande si vous voudriez bien prononcer la messe pour sa maman," to which he readily assented.)

At their home the next evening, René introduced me to his wife Suzanne and their children, a son Michel, about 12 and a girl of about 8. The evening outstretched my fondest imaginings. René's workshop behind the house had been badly damaged during the invasion, but their tidy stone house was fully intact and filled with delicious aromas which emanated from a copious rabbit stew which I remember to this day. It and its bountiful accompaniments were complemented by hard cider and the whole was topped off by a memorable "marc de calvados," a clear apple brandy which smelled of apple blossoms and which René had carried on his back from a town near Tours, where the family had taken refuge until the fighting in Normandy was over. But the evening was even more memorable for the atmosphere of warmth and friendship which was unique in my 19-year-old experience.

We tarried in Carentan a few days before moving on. The weather remained warm and our hillside sunny. It was actually pleasant airing out our gear and I enjoyed wandering around town, frequently in the company of Michel Bucaille who was a bright and curious lad. I visited with the family several more times, one being a trip to a movie theater the damaged roof of which was partially open to the skies. I have long since forgotten what the film was, but never will I forget trying to retain my composure and carry on an elevated conversation with Suzanne while René and Michel, indulging in what was clearly an unexceptionable rural practice, paused in the amply lighted street on the way home to urinate against the wall. If my bladder had been bursting, I could not have brought myself to join them.

The recounting of these few bare facts regarding Carentan and the Bucailles does not begin to convey the importance which the visit carried for me both at the time and later. Here was a family with whom I had formed a friendship wholly apart from the Army, wholly apart from any of my own family connections, and entirely because I was able to communicate fairly fluently in French. The relationship was instantaneous, two-way and intense. Our views on most subjects discussed were altogether harmonious, and nowhere more intensively than in our feelings for the Germans. Their hatred for them was implacable. They recounted instances of hostages taken and shot, and of course they had been forced to flee their home and town ravaged by the invasion, but they had enthusiastically welcomed it and blamed it on not on the Americans but on the "sales Boches." While I could not for want of the experience share fully in the intensity of their emotions, I had some of my own arising from my present status and the unknown events which loomed before me. If I had been able to foresee the future, our empathy would have been total. Their vision of my future was probably a good bit clearer than my own, but of course we did not discuss it.

As we prepared to depart they plied me with delicacies well beyond my capacity to carry, but to avoid seeming ungrateful I took them all including the liquid ones and parceled them out among the guys, who were glad to get them, and Suzanne and I held a long embrace before we parted, and we resolved to write and keep in contact. We did correspond over the next year or so but little did I dream that our next visit would be delayed by forty-eight years or that it would be every bit as moving and even more surprising than that of 1944. Readers wishing to learn the details of that long-delayed sequel are invited to turn to the entries for Tuesday and Wednesday, August 21-22, 1990, which will be found in Appendix 1.

Through the Repple-Depples
Verviers
Christine

October-November 1944

OUR progress now continued on its way through the repple-depple system. In normal times, the transportation system in northern France consisted of an excellent network of highways and railways but both of these had been heavily damaged, and what remained was now greatly over-burdened. It had to convey all necessary supplies from Cherbourg and the Normandy beaches over distances of 200-300 miles to meet the needs of the northern Allied Expeditionary Force. Shipping priorities were accorded to the various commodities in heaviest demand, those being food, gasoline and ammunition. Generally speaking, these moved up towards the front over the highways in 2½-ton trucks organized into what was known as the "Red Ball Express" (a name which survives to this day, I believe, as an interstate trucking company). There was no west-east artery in northern France which was not continually crammed with truck convoys. The set of roads with the best bridges was dedicated to one-way west to east traffic, with secondary roads devoted to the east to west traffic of returning empties. The "front" had now reached and somewhat stabilized along the western boundary of Germany and the trucks' destinations were supply depots and ammunition dumps in Belgium, Luxembourg, Holland and eastern France.

Our trip to the front was broken up into a number of segments, the first of which took us south to a small town near Le Mans, already then known as the site of the 24-hour road race. We bivouacked there in open fields and I had additional opportunities to exercise my linguistic skills, mostly to slake the appetites of my colleagues for food and drink. And then we were off in what seemed an interminable train ride toward the east.

Replacement troops apparently carried a low priority, for we were assigned to railway transport, the equipment for which had not changed an iota since the first World War. It consisted of the same "forty-and-eight" box cars (forty men or eight horses) which my father had ridden in in 1918. If the eight horses were one half as uncomfortable as the forty men, there would have been grounds for an animal rights activist protest.

I must have spent almost two weeks in forty-and-eights during the period from October 1944 to June 1945, and I can thus qualify, I believe, as an expert in this form of travel. It was excruciating! However adequately a forty-and-eight might have accommodated forty French soldiers in 1916, in 1944 they were torture devices for American GIs who must have been several inches taller than the poilu and probably 20 pounds heavier. Notwithstanding this difference, there were still forty of us assigned to each car. We sat with our backs to the outside walls and feet toward the center. During the day we could achieve a tolerable level of comfort by pulling our knees up, and if the weather was decent, by having as many as possible sit in the doorways facing out. But at night it was miserable. The doors would be closed to preserve warmth, and sleeping soldiers would slump down, extending legs even further toward the middle. One would be awakened in the dark hours by a cry of anguish from the soldier whose feet had finally reached the bottom of the pile and who could no longer stand the pain of the weight on top of him and would wrestle and strain to remove his feet from the bottom, to place them as gently as possible on top. There a short period of blissful relief would be enjoyed until the painful process repeated itself.[5]

Information in the wartime was disseminated only on a "need to know" basis. Though that phrase was not then in vogue, the effect was the same: the lowly GI was virtually never told where he was going, what was in store for him or even where he was. His information on

---

[5] Uncomfortable as we felt we were in the forty-and-eights, the experience was nothing compared to the torture visited upon the many thousands of American prisoners of war captured by the Germans during their Ardennes offensive two months later. There were many instances in which they were for days packed in so tightly they had to stand up with no food, water or toilet facilities.

these subjects came, if at all, from rumor which circulated incessantly (and turned out to be true often enough that they could not be routinely dismissed), or from what inferences he himself could draw from observations of his surroundings. Notwithstanding our seemingly aimless shunting by train in every conceivable direction, there did come a time when we knew where we were. This occurred when the train came to a sudden stop in the fall sunshine and I came to the open doors to behold off in the west the distant silhouettes of the Eiffel Tower and the Basilica of the Sacré Coeur on Montmartre. The train was to be stalled here for the better part of a day, and it seemed almost intentional that these magic talismans of Paris, the City of Light, of which I had read and heard so much, should be so near at hand and yet be so utterly beyond my reach. I would eventually get there, but it would not happen for many months, and as I gazed out from the train, it was far from certain that I would ever see them. A sudden lump grew in my throat and my eyes filled with tears: I was actually acutely homesick for a place that I had never *been*. I had to jump down to the railway embankment with my back to the train to wipe my eyes and to escape the wiseacres on the train.

I have reproduced text from my letters home in earlier chapters with the comment that they rarely seem to discuss any of the events or experiences which have survived in my memory. I do so again here with several more caveats. While my letters from Europe do seem to move in a track more synchronous with my memory, there are clear indications that I was doing my best within practical limits to commit to paper what my stateside audience was most likely to find palatable. In other words, I downplayed whatever might be found unduly alarming, and also avoided subjects that would be hard for my readers to understand. It also should be noted that items would continue to appear in my overseas letters of which I have no memory at all.

This is from a letter dated 28 October 1944:

> I am able to tell you that I have seen Carentan, Caen, Argentan, Alençon and some more, the names of which I don't remember, the most enjoyable of which was, by all means, Carentan. It is a town of some 2,000 inhabitants, a large proportion of which are prisoners in Germany, in the French Army, or were killed in the American bombings right after D-Day. It was nowhere nearly so hard hit as were Caen and St. Lô, however, the former of which

has but one habitable room left standing. But there are plenty of bombed out houses anyway, and the Cathédrale de Notre Dame had been pretty well shot up. The main line of German resistance was, from what I could gather, some miles south of the town, closer to St. Lô. But naturally, by the time we got there things had returned as nearly to normal as possible under existing conditions. The food situation was not bad, and most everyone looked healthy if not fat.

I may be somewhat prejudiced, but I certainly noticed a marked difference in the attitudes of the English and the French towards the Americans—there may be several explanatory conditions existing. All I know is that the French couldn't possibly under any circumstances have been any nicer to me than they have been. I have been wined and dined, invited into their homes, been given all sorts of whatever goods remain to them, and have everywhere had my money given back to me. Nothing seems to be too much. I have tried to repay them for their hospitality with such items as cigarettes, soap and coffee which are in great scarcity over here, as far as civilians are concerned. I was really a little homesick when we had to leave Carenten, for in the short time I had been there I made as many friends as I ever have for a corresponding period.

All they can talk about is "Les Boches" or "ces salauds d'Allemands." After hearing some of the tales they tell I am willing to believe anything anyone may say about the Germans. During the occupation, atrocities weren't just something that would make the headlines occasionally, they were an everyday occurrence. Apparently they were polite to the point of punctiliousness, but what they did through official channels in the way of reprisals, etc., would fill many a grisly book.

Most of the kids have parents or uncles who have in some way been permanently or impermanently removed from the family circle, and if you can make them smile, you have accomplished a major victory.

But one of the things that impressed me the most was the fact that they have snapped back to the old way of life as though nothing has happened. The bombed-out families have moved in with their neighbors and everything continues as before. Everybody confidently expects to see another war in another twenty years—just as they have seen them in years past. War seems to be an accepted hazard to living, not an exception to a rule.

As for my present position—we are still far from the front, and I imagine it will be a month or so before anything develops. Til then we will enjoy a scenic trip through sunny France (I wish it was sunny)—seen from the door of a forty and eight—wonderful accommodations.

Our railroad destination turned out to be the small Belgian city of Verviers, which is about 20 miles east of the larger city of Liège and about the same distance from the German frontier to the east. There our package of replacements was lodged in the gymnasium or play room of a parochial elementary school which was situated on a hilly city avenue traversed by clanging tram cars.

The treble sounds of city traffic were now punctuated by a thunder-like rumbling from the east. It emanated from artillery fire at the front no more than 20 to 25 miles away.

As a city in southern Belgium, Verviers was located in the "Walloon," or French-speaking area of the country, to be distinguished from the Flemish-speaking portion of the country to the north. The Walloons of Verviers made no secret of their distaste for the Flemish, who represented two thirds of the population and thus were politically and economically dominant.

During the week or so that our package spent in Verviers, I was taken instantly under the wing of the family that served as custodians of the parochial school. It consisted of a mother and father and their twenty-year-old daughter, Christine. She was as pretty as she could be, slight, blond, blue-eyed, unmarried and about eight months pregnant.

Since there was virtually no military training or activity required of me, Christine and I became inseparable companions, going to the movies and a restaurant and also sharing her family's mealtimes. If the fare was simple, the hospitality was warm.

The ambiguity of Christine's circumstances seemed more than a little curious, both then and now. The family were without question devout Catholics (else how could they have kept their job), yet there was no censure in their attitude towards their daughter, whom they clearly loved, nor about my relationship with her (although that was totally above board). On the contrary, they actively encouraged it.

Christine never talked about the identity of the father of her child-to-be, though I have a dim recollection that he may have had something to do with the Belgian underground. (Like the Bucailles, Christine and her parents made no bones about their contempt and hatred for the Boches.)

She loved to laugh and joke and we delighted in each other's company. There was, however, a distinct undertone of wistfulness in her attitude as she awaited the inevitability of motherhood, and as she wondered, I am sure, about what the future held.

I was powerfully attracted to her, and under other circumstances, I would without question have been more demonstrative about my feelings for her. But as a sheltered nineteen-year-old it never occurred to me to deal with her other than with affectionate respect. We did, however, hold hands in public, and I wasn't even slightly concerned about what the burghers might think about it.

Here is what I wrote home from Verviers on 6 November 1944:

> I am really developing into a somewhat of a globe-trotter, am I not? A Cook's tour in high gear and with lousy if interesting accommodations. It certainly is an understatement to say that this is the most interesting experience of my life to date! And tho I might have wished my arrival on the continent to have taken place under different circumstances, the combination of being regarded as a liberator and being one of the few liberators who speaks the language of the liberated is an accident that happens once in a lifetime.
>
> ... Right now I am sitting in a nice warm Belgian kitchen chatting cozily and occasionally writing a line—not a very rapid way of getting a letter written, but certainly pleasant. There is the cutest blond-headed little baby playing on the floor [I don't remember whose the baby was except that it was not Christine's], and I plan to have a fast game of backgammon when the "patron" [this would have been her Dad] arrives home from work. We are not doing much right now—for about the fifteenth time getting all our clothes inspected, and being issued the shortages we have cataloged sixteen times—and mainly waiting for further

orders. Very enjoyable, except that for some insane reason we are kept restricted without passes.[6] A little annoying when I could have the key to this wonderful Belgian city merely for the asking. The police commissioner, for whom I had done some "work" with the American officers [I haven't the slightest memory of what this might have related to], had invited me to dinner but we left almost before I could say thank you—I wonder what he thinks of me?

... [N]ow we are living in what used to be a gymnasium attached to a parochial school—the family in whose home I am now adjoins the building and can be arrived at without having to pass any guards.

Another item of interest—buzz-bombs go over at the rate of about five or six a day making a noise like a motorcycle without a muffler and going like bats.

All for now—pass this letter around—I love you.

There's not one word of Christine, but how was I to explain her situation (which even I didn't understand) to my parents?

The V-1 buzz-bomb was really a small airplane carrying a 2,000 pound package of explosives. There were two short stubby wings amidships and a tail assemblage at the rear surmounted by a "ram-jet" engine rigged somewhat in the manner of the tail engine of the DC-10 airliner. The operation of the engine produced a very characteristic and unmistakable sound on the order of the putt-putt-putt of a one cylinder gasoline engine. The V-1's were never a problem at the front lines, although we grew used to seeing them flying overhead at about 2,000 feet and perhaps 300 miles per hour. Once launched, the only remaining control over their destination was the amount of fuel on board. The original design was conceived by the Germans as one of their much-vaunted "secret weapons" to turn the tables on Britain, and a great shower of them was launched against London in the early months of 1944. On arriving over the city, the fuel would exhaust itself and an automatic mechanism would

---

[6] I am not sure how to square this statement with my clear recollection, mentioned above, of having escorted Christine on excursions into the town. One could exit to the street from her family's front door without passing the guard at the gym door. I suspect that this is how we did it.

point the machine at the earth, where a devastating concussion would ensue. By the fall of the year, however, counter-measures mounted by the British consisting of re-deployed anti-aircraft and fighter planes, had all but eliminated them as a problem in England, with the result that the Germans were now using them as a much shorter range weapon, targeting such cities in Belgium as Antwerp, Liège and Verviers.

To be in the target area of a V-1 bomb was an unnerving experience. So long as the "putt-putt" could be heard they represented no threat, but the abrupt cessation of the noise would be followed by a hair-raising silence prior to the thundering detonation. The tension was intensified as it became clearer that Verviers had become an intended destination of at least some of the missiles: You knew the engine might well stop but would it do so when it was over your head?

During the day, as soon as the distant noise was detected, all activity and conversation would stop and all would race for a window or other vantage point to follow the path of the marauder. It would proceed arrow-like on its way, the motor would stop, everyone would hold his breath and a few seconds later the earth would reverberate with a huge explosion. At night the evil bird was invisible, and you never could be sure until the sound started to fade into the distance that it might not quit altogether and end up with your number on it.

Though the V-1's caused hundreds of random deaths, they almost never fell on any military targets, and hence their strategic importance was nil. Hitler is said to have been mesmerized by the concept of the secret weapon, and it was through his personal intervention that large quantities of matériel were diverted from conventional warplanes to the V-1's and the later V-2's, a blunder which only served to enhance the Allies already large air superiority. The V-1's only real impact was in terms of frayed nerves and lost sleep amongst civilian populations, and this too, in the last analysis, was negligible.

In March 1945, I was able to return to visit Christine on the occasion of a three-day pass from the front. Such passes were supposed to be spent at R-and-R centers in large hotels commandeered by the military a few miles behind the lines, but I had no interest whatever in squandering the time in regimented association with other soldiers, and hence hitched a ride to the town of Eupen, located a little to the east of Verviers near the German border. Christine had written me that she and her parents would be visiting relatives there, and I found them in a substantial stone farmhouse abutting a main highway on the outskirts of the town. By this time she had had her baby and mother and child were the source of much admiration on the part of an extended family gathering of perhaps fifteen people.

I vividly remember being one of the guests at a long dinner table on what was clearly a festive occasion. Another of the guests was a young, handsome Belgian whose sleeves were rolled up to display sinewy biceps and forearms. His relationship to the family, if any, was never made clear to me. It was known, however, that he had been a member of the resistance, and he spent the entire evening trying to overcome Christine's. This he did by making continuous and explicit references to her evident physical charms, which made everyone else at the table laugh uproariously and made me squirm with a complex amalgam of jealousy and embarrassment. She resisted these clumsy tactics through reddened cheeks and downcast eyes, but a hint of a smile could be seen at the corners of her lips, and it was apparent to me that his attentions, though crude, were not altogether unwelcome. Adding to my confusion was the possibility— never expressly negated by anyone including Christine—that the young man might have been the father of her child. I did not know what to think!

It was on the occasion of this later visit that I asked Christine if she would sew my newly-won sergeant's chevrons onto my jacket and overcoat. She happily agreed, but voiced the opinion that they should be higher up the sleeve than seemed right to me. Unfortunately, I persisted, and it was not until I returned to my unit and was faced with the jeers of my buddies, some of whom were now subordinates, that I discovered that she was right and I was wrong.

At the time I started to compose these lines, I had probably not thought of Christine more than once or twice in forty-five years. Yet the memories of her flood back vividly and as I think of her now, I am left wondering how it can have been that all memory of her last name and her address—not to mention any desire to see her again—could have vanished so completely from my head and record as they most surely had by the time I emerged from OCS four months later. Did my newly-exalted status blind me to my earlier relationship, or was the matter compounded by the unanswered questions surrounding her? I can only wonder, because it is altogether clear to me now that we represented very vital psychic lifelines to each other at a difficult time for both of us.

My last letter home from the repple-depple system was from just inside the German border and much closer to the rumble of artillery. It contained news and also a socio-political treatise:

> Somewhere in Germany. As you can plainly see, I am losing no time in getting up into the middle of things. And though I am not there yet I am near enough to being there to wish I was back where I started from.
>
> But miracle of miracles, I am as close to being physically comfortable as I have been for quite some time. and the closer we get, the less "GI Nonsense" [a euphemism for you-know-what] we encounter; a distinct relief I can tell you. We are left, at this stage of our journey, pretty much to do as we please for a couple of days...
>
> In the winter it is cold in Germany, lest you believe otherwise. Right now there is a layer of snow under foot, making it most uncomfortable walking in the water-and-cold conducting GI boot. But we are promised overshoes in the very near future, necessities even without the snow. [We didn't get overshoes until much later.] You must have seen enough pictures of the western front to know that it abounds in mud.
>
> It was indeed very sad when it became time to leave Belgium. Although we weren't there for long, I know that if and when I get a chance to go back, I'll have several places to stay, and excellent company to take my mind off my troubles.
>
> I was able to visit the city of Verviers, Belgium (I think the censor will pass that) (though it gripes me to have to be so vague about everything), and if the inhabitants of the town are any indication of the people of Belgium's character, I am certainly going to include it on my post-war itinerary. It may be that they haven't seen enough of the American soldier to have the novelty wear off, but whatever the reason, they couldn't have been nicer...
>
> [F]or example: I had two batches of laundry done without even asking, and had payment refused in such terms that there was just nothing I could do to make them accept it. At the same time, most of them don't have enough money to buy what food is available and pay the monthly rent.
>
> Since I've been there, I have less respect than ever for the

Occupation-exiled Belgian Government, which was sheltered for so long under the wings of the Messrs. Churchill and Roosevelt—and which hasn't permitted one election to be held since it has been back—already a matter of some three months or more. The people seem to suffer from what approaches a national inferiority complex, and said complex seems to be of such long standing and to have become so oppressive that I wouldn't dare predict what the people might do to manifest their discontent. It is true that I came in contact with only one class, and that was the working class, where such points are apt to be sorer than elsewhere. Consequently, I can't say just how widespread it is; but everyone I talked to, when the conversation veered towards politics as it usually does, either turned out to be a self-admitted Communist or to have plans to escape to the Belgian Congo or go somewhere, possibly even America, to avoid the uncertainties of living at home. But for all that, there isn't one person to whom I talked of whom I can say that he was unfriendly or uninteresting or not a real individual. The national level of good taste, if there is such a thing, was many cuts above that of the U.S., and the people were ten times better informed and better educated, though they might not have spend as much time in school as the average American.

A powerful emotional undercurrent which marked our progress through the replacement system was the ever-heightening sense of foreboding. It was not anything anyone talked about; indeed, one did one's best not to think about it, let alone discuss it. Nonetheless, it was inescapable. Unlike those in the path of an advancing hurricane who know there is at least a chance that it will veer away, the specter of combat for an infantry replacement was inexorable. Our forward movement conveyed its own message, but if one needed a reminder, it was amply provided by the artillery, now no longer like distant rolling thunder, but clearly identifiable as distinct individual explosions.

I Join the 28th Division in the Hürtgen Forest

November 11, 1944

ON November 8th or 9th, 1944 we embarked on the last leg of our Cook's Tour of Europe which finally took us into Germany. The trip started by forty-and-eights, north through a corner of Holland and the town of Maastricht and thence east over the German border to the outskirts of the city of Aachen, known in French as Aix-la-Chapelle. Aachen was a city rich in history, having been the capital of Charlemagne's Holy Roman Empire. It had also been a city of architectural treasures. But as we drove through it in 2½-ton trucks to which we had transferred, all there was to see was devastation. We did not know it then, but the city had been besieged by the American First Army for two solid weeks in September. It was the first military objective within the Reich to be attacked, and although efforts to surrender it intact had almost succeeded, the German general who had hoped to do so, a native of the city, was relieved before he could carry out the plan, and, on Hitler's direct order, it was then tenaciously defended, with the result I now saw.

In my travels through France I had seen many badly damaged towns, but they were nothing compared to this. The destruction there was nowhere nearly so widespread and much of it had already been cleared up and repaired. This, by contrast, was total. It was as though a wrecker's ball had been loosed with the objective of flattening everything! Skeletal remains of walls were left to show that in the center of the city, the buildings had been four and five stories high, most now leveled in disorderly heaps of masonry rubble bleached like animal bones. The sight and smell were nauseating.

We had passed a night or two en route, and it was now November 11, 1944, the twenty-sixth anniversary of November 11, 1918, World

War I's Armistice Day. We were told that this was to be the day that we would finally join a combat infantry division at the front. The irony escaped none of us.

We were again aboard a truck convoy moving forward cautiously through an inky night, with the many starts and jerking stops that were seemingly unavoidable in the blackout. The artillery detonations grew louder and soon were accompanied by ever-brightening flashes of white light which tore at the night sky. The muzzle blasts were ever louder until we could tell that they had passed *behind* us!

In the back of the truck no one spoke and each of us was alone with his thoughts. Mine were chaotic, but dread was the overriding emotion, as I asked myself, "How in God's name could I have let this happen to me?" I reflected back on the efforts while I was at Rucker to try to wrangle a transfer to a more palatable assignment and wracked my brain why I had not myself done something to improve my situation. My fellow frequenter of the Hotel Chipola, Hal Pittsburgh, had brown-nosed around, as the current saying had it, and had talked his way into a berth as company clerk in the 66th Division. It wasn't the Pentagon but neither would Hal be patrolling beyond the front line. I had turned up my nose at his ploy at the time, but I envied him now.

The convoy ground to a final halt, and we fell into extended march formation at the side of a muddy road. After a wholly superfluous admonition to make no unnecessary noise, we started to move forward, each with his everlasting 45-pound field pack, rifle and ammunition. No audible orders were given; if we stopped, it was because we ran into the man ahead and were in turn run into by the man behind. The night was starless, but there were looming shadows on both sides of the road and the consciousness of being in a deep forest was confirmed by a damp pine aroma.

After about an hour's march, we were met by guides who led us with hooded flashlights to a clearing in the forest where someone with a hooded flashlight and clipboard called the roll of the new arrivals and assigned each of us to accompany a non-com to the bivouac area of our new unit.

Twenty yards deeper into the woods my guide halted and introduced me to a shadowy form told me that he and I would now be partners, sharing the same foxhole. We said hello, and in a terse and muffled exchange, he told me that we were supposed to stand guard duty, two hours on and two hours off, and that if there was any incoming artillery, I should duck into our nearby foxhole, which he now showed me, suggesting that I should stash my gear and take the first two hours watch. When I had done so and he had given me the password and response for the night, he promptly dove into the hole. With this scant indoctrination, I was on my own.

That first night of guard duty beneath the snowy, dripping boughs of the Hürtgen Forest was one of the nadirs of my combat experience. It was absolutely pitch black. I did not know where I was. I did not know the soldiers I was with or even where they were. I did not know where or how far away the Germans were or in what direction, and I hadn't the slightest idea of what to expect or what was expected of me. I felt stupid and was scared silly, and it seemed impossible I would survive the night.

First there was artillery. I had been hearing its noises from varying distances as we had been nearing the front, but now I was in its midst, and what had been distant rumble and reverberation now was totally transformed because it was aimed at *me*! Nothing I had been taught or heard prepared me for it. I barely even knew what the word meant!

First came the report of the firing cannon, distant and muffled. This would be quickly followed by a sibilant rustling the first hint of which was easily mistaken for the wind whistling through the pine trees—and vice versa. I dove headlong into my hole a number of times, terrified and completely at sea, before I began slowly to be able to tell the difference.

The rustling then grew to a roar and was followed by a blinding overhead flash of light and an ear-splitting detonation, very staccato, as though some giant had taken a half dozen large trees and snapped them like match sticks inside my head. These overpowering jolts were followed by the whine and scream of the fragments of shrapnel hurtling down from the overhead boughs, and the final echoes of the tumult resounding from the nearby hills, until—after many seconds of quiet—it seemed safe to unwind from my fetal position in the bottom of the hole to see if I was still in one piece.

There were perhaps a dozen more or less similar occurrences during the course of that first two hours. I was experiencing "harassing fire" and tree bursts, as I later came to learn. Harassing fire was intended not so much to cause casualties as to keep those at whom it was aimed nervous, awake and uptight. It sure did the job that night! Tree bursts meant that the artillerists had set the fuses of the shells so that they would detonate on slightest impact, as by grazing a tree branch. This was intended to shower the troops below with the scythe-like action of shrapnel from above, on the theory—an entirely accurate one, usually—that more damage would be done that way than if it struck the ground, to be muffled by earth and snow.

But thanks to the excellent foxhole in which I found myself, I managed to survive to the end of that first watch, when I roused my colleague and dove into its sanctuary like a hibernating bear, avid to savor its comparative warmth and security and to shut my ears, eyes and mind against the fearful chaos outside. Emotionally and physically exhausted, I was instantly in a coma, which was just about as long as it seemed until I was being jostled awake for my next stint.

At the end of that one, which was no different from the first, it had begun to dawn on me that my hole represented virtually complete protection against any artillery barrage save perhaps for a direct hit on the hole itself, which didn't seem very likely because all the shells were bursting overhead in the trees. The hole was about four by eight feet in area and about five feet deep. Three quarters of the area was overlain with heavy timbers which were in turn covered with dirt removed from the hole. The interior beneath this two-foot roof provided a protected if sodden sleeping area, while the space open to the sky served as the sentry's station.

Eventually a milky gloom began to replace the blackness, and I found I not only had survived but I had begun to be able to tell when the shells were going to fall nearby and when they would go harmlessly over or short. The learning process was extremely rapid, and I found to my astonishment that my angst had significantly receded!

I now found that I was in a forest of mature conifers a foot or so in diameter, thirty to forty feet high and planted in geometric rows about twenty feet apart. There was snow on the ground and in the upper tree branches, but it did little to relieve the murkiness that pervaded the place even at midday. The sky was gray and the temperature was about freezing.

Campfires burned during the day, but they were of limited value as heat sources both because they were hard to get and keep going and because a blaze big enough to impart warmth also had the not-so-incidental effect of melting the snow on the overhead boughs, with results both predictable and profane. Again to my astonishment I found myself reacting with muted glee the second or third time I saw clumps of snow cascading down on to groups of GI's trying to heat coffee over their meager fires.

Daylight also brought with it an opportunity for me to find out a little bit more about where I was and about my new unit.

The 28th Division Through Hürtgen

MORE fully stated, I was now a member of the Second Platoon of Company B of the First Battalion of the 112th Infantry Regiment of the 28th Infantry Division. You may ask what all that means. Here is a brief primer.

The American infantry division in World War II was organized on what was called a "triangular" basis, that is, each larger unit was composed of three units of the next smaller size. From the bottom up, the structure looked something like this:

Unit	Components	Number of Men	Commanding Officer
Squad	11 Riflemen, 1 BAR Man	12	Staff Sergeant
Platoon	3 Squads	40	1st or 2nd Lieutenant
Company	3 Platoons	190	Captain
Battalion	3 Companies	830	Lieutenant Colonel
Regiment	3 Battalions	3250	Colonel
Division	3 Regiments	12,000	General

In addition, at each level there were auxiliary units (each rifle company, for example, had a Heavy Weapons platoon with 60mm mortars and .30 caliber machine guns), and medical, administrative, artillery, tank and other units at the various higher levels.

Farther up the line, two or three divisions were usually organized into a Corps, and two or more Corps could constitute an Army or an Army Group. At the very top was "SHAEF," or Supreme Headquarters, Allied Expeditionary Force, commanded by General Dwight D. Eisenhower.

The 28th was the infantry division of the Pennsylvania National Guard. That is, its cadre of officers and non-coms had been members of the division prior to the start of the war, having participated in the peacetime weekend exercises and summer maneuvers which were the basic elements of National Guard training. Its units had then been filled out with draftees prior to its initial baptism of fire in Normandy in late July 1944. It was at just about this time that the Allied Armies finally succeeded in breaking through their encirclement by the Germans at Avranches in Normandy, and the division had then participated in the pursuit of the retreating foe across the breadth of France. There had been many casualties and hair raising times during the months prior to Hürtgen, but clearly Hürtgen was far and away the division's most gruesome experience.

There was, however, one short interlude which loomed large in the memories of the few who had lived it and still survived, that being the division's participation in the parade on August 29, 1944, celebrating the liberation of Paris. For them, it was one of the most emotional moments of the whole war. (I missed it since I didn't join the division until two months later.) The civilian population had been under the heel of the occupying Germans for four long years during which an upswelling of underground resistance had developed. The Germans had reacted with brutal reprisals, and the long-standing hatreds between the two countries had greatly intensified.

Now at last the horror had ended, and the joy of the Parisians was boundless. Every illustrated history of the war displays pictures of the men of the 28th swinging down the Champs Elysées with wreaths draped about their necks, bottles of champagne held aloft, while being hugged and kissed by pretty French girls. Conspicuous in many of these photos is the red "keystone" divisional shoulder patch of the 28th.[7]

Momentum carried the Allies swiftly eastwards after the August 25th liberation of Paris. On September 13th, the U.S. First Army crossed the

---

[7] At our company's 1994 reunion in Minnesota, I was shown a U.S. postage stamp which had been issued commemorating the liberation of Paris. It was a miniature reproduction in khaki of a photo of the parade showing a head-on view of many men marching down the Champs-Elysées. The image of the stamp was of course tiny, but it was a miniaturization of a photograph of the parade which was the frontispiece of the 28th Division's official history of World War II. By curious happenstance, the photo showed men from Baker Co. in the front row on the left-hand side. Thus my colleagues at the reunion were actually able to point to and name the names of some of the men appearing on the postage stamp!

German border and penetrated the homeland. And now for the first time since Normandy German resistance stiffened.

An early manifestation was the failure of an Allied airborne offensive in late September known as "Operation Market-Garden," commanded by British Field Marshal Montgomery. Its objective was to establish a bridgehead over the Rhine River at the northern extremity of the front in Holland. Some of the parachute and glider troops were able to land without much opposition, but the ground forces trying to make contact with them could make little progress, and the operation ended with the destruction and capture of many of the airborne units and 12,000 Allied casualties. The operation was to be memorialized in a book and movie entitled *A Bridge Too Far*.

Stiffening German resistance was not the only complicating factor. Throughout the summer and fall, the entire enormous job of supplying the Allied expeditionary force, consisting now of almost two million troops, was conducted through round-the-clock use of the port of Cherbourg and the Normandy beaches.[8] By the time the front had reached the German frontier, its supply lines had extended to several hundred miles, and a larger and larger proportion of those supplies was necessarily expended in transport activities and supporting the troops doing the transporting (collectively known as the "Communications Zone" or "ComZ"). Hence, gasoline and ammunition were both in short supply.

As a result, it was warmly debated amongst the commanding generals, as subsequent histories have revealed, as to whether a delayed "full court press" all along the line should be the strategy, as favored by Eisenhower, rather than a more immediate and concentrated thrust in the North (favored by Montgomery—it was his zone) or in the South (favored by American General Patton—that was his zone). The quarrel, which was an acrimonious one, was finally resolved by Eisenhower in favor of a compromise full court press, which meant that pressure would eventually be maintained along the line but that a "limited" offensive would meanwhile be mounted in one area, that being in the U.S. First

---

[8] The Allied invasion of southern France, delayed by landing craft shortages, had finally taken place on August 15, 1944 with the amphibious landing of the U.S. Seventh Army. It made rapid progress northwards and also opened Marseilles, Toulon and other French ports, which were soon handling a full one-third of Allied logistical needs. The increased supply, however, was more than consumed by the larger forces and greater distances.

Army's Hürtgen Forest sector, where the mission was to achieve the first rupture and penetration of the formidable line of concrete fortifications which ran the length of the German frontier. It was known to the Allies as the Siegfried Line and to the Germans as the West Wall.

The Battle of the Hürtgen Forest has never become as well known as the later so-called "Battle of the Bulge." There are two reasons. First, the battle was restricted to a relatively small and inaccessible area which attracted little attention from war correspondents. More importantly, however, it was an unmitigated disaster, and hence one that none of those responsible wished to publicize. The Bulge involved enormous losses but its end result was to finish off the Wehrmacht's offensive capability, so in the end it was a victory. Hürtgen, in contrast, accomplished nothing, and into the bargain involved enormous American losses.

The effort extended from September 1944 to February 1945, during which period large numbers of American units were involved. The 28th's active participation in the Hürtgen battle covered the period from November 2-10, 1944, and I joined Baker only at the very end of that involvement. Because I was not a participant in any of the hard fighting there the battle is beyond the scope of this memoir, but in recent years it has undergone extensive analysis both in the military literature and in army staff schools, and the full scope of the disaster has come to be recognized. There are three books in particular which have brought it into focus. They are *Follow Me and Die* by Cecil B. Curry (Stein and Day, Briarcliff Manor, New York, 1984), *The Battle of the Hürtgen Forest*, by Charles Whiting (Orion Books, New York, 1989), and *A Dark and Bloody Ground* by Edward G. Miller (Texas A&M University Press, College Station, Texas, 1995).

All three books are bitterly critical of the command decisions which led to and extended the campaign. They suggest that the planning for it was both cursory and slipshod and that the generals responsible, including Maj. Gen. Norman D. Cota, Commander of the 28th Division, sacrificed thousands of lives based on third hand information unverified by personal visits to the front.

Even more telling is their analysis of the strategic aspects of the battle. Early broad brush histories of this part of the European campaign suggest that the objective of the Hürtgen offensive was to capture several large dams to the south of the forest which impounded the headwaters of the Roer River, a tributary of the Rhine across which the Allied Armies would eventually have to attack to reach the German "heartland." If these dams were left in German hands while the attack was in progress, so the argument goes, there would be an unacceptable risk that the dams could be "blown," with the result that downstream bridges would be taken out, valleys flooded and many Allied soldiers drowned.

The more careful recent analyses are to the contrary. After research of contemporaneous records and accounts, they conclude that the planners gave no attention whatever to the threat represented by the dams until the end of November and express doubt as to whether the generals were even aware of their existence until then or even later. Had they focused early on the dams as the strategic objectives of true importance, the obvious course would have been to bypass the Forest altogether. Instead they appear to have fallen into the error of designating highway junctions shown on a map as objectives and to have persisted beyond reason in capturing them in spite of the impossibility of their terrain and their relative insignificance. General Major von Gersdorff, Chief of Staff of the German 7th Army commented after the war that, "The German Command could not understand the reason for the strong American attacks in the Hürtgen Forest... [T]he fighting in the wooded area denied the American troops the advantage offered by their air and armored forces, the superiority of which had been decisive in all the battles waged before."

Whatever may be the correct view as to the strategic planning, there can be no doubt that in its result, Hürtgen was a virtual abattoir. During the first two weeks of November the 28th Division had been given the mission of taking the three small farming towns of Vossenack, Kommerscheidt and Schmidt, all located adjacent to the forest and about 15 miles inside the German border. Just beyond were the pillboxes of the Siegfried Line. Over a period of four or five days repeated efforts were made to capture these objectives. Several were temporarily successful but the German defense was formidable, including armored counterattacks and intense artillery concentrations which threw the unprotected infantry back with huge losses. The 28th suffered casualties of over 200 officers, some of them majors and colonels, and 5,000 enlisted men. In the 24-hour period ending at midnight on November 10, the day before I joined the division, my 112th Regiment lost 558 men (killed, wounded, captured and missing) and 34 officers. And these losses were only a small fraction of the American army's in the Forest. The division, in a word, was torn to shreds and was completely demoralized.

Almost nothing of the foregoing was known to me and my fellow soldiers when I joined Baker Company. What we did know was that the company's strength had been reduced from its normal 190 to only 30 men and that there were no officers left. We knew that 150 of us GI's and a whole new complement of officers (some with experience from other outfits but most as new replacements) had joined the company.

The appearance of our new confederates was as disquieting as their pitifully small number: they were filthy, disheveled, exhausted and despondent. None of them was happy to see us because the clear message of our arrival was that the company would soon be ready to be sent back into the line. Few of them were willing even to speak with us or answer our questions, saying "You don't really want to know." Though many of them had just been promoted to replace the non-coms who had become casualties, the usual satisfaction occasioned by promotion was nowhere evident.

It was only over a course of several days, as they recuperated and became a little better acquainted with us, that we began to learn a little of what had happened to them. We heard hair raising tales of being pinned down by enemy mortar and artillery fire with no opportunity to dig in. We heard how the weather had deteriorated and how the one supply track into the steep Kall River gorge had become impassable because of mud and artillery craters, resulting in tanks and other tracked vehicles tumbling into the deep valley. And we heard how many casualties had to be left behind, while the litters of the few who were evacuated had to be hand-carried for miles from an aid station behind the enemy lines through the mud at night to avoid observation by German artillery. It was also at this time that we learned of the division's nickname "The Bloody Bucket" (a reference to the red keystone shoulder patch) which clung to it like glue throughout the war.

We were naturally terrified by these accounts, and it was altogether fair to say that those who lived to tell us about them were "demoralized." But the effect on us replacements was different. We had not lived through the horrors, but it had a lasting impact on us anyway. Throughout our remaining time in combat, we would all remain aware of how our force had been betrayed in Hürtgen and what that meant as regards the quality of our division's leadership. Our expectations would thus be permanently polarized and we never would regain confidence in it. For us replacements, however, the realization was a gradual one, and in the days immediately following our arrival we were nervous and tense and full of anxiety as to what lay before us and whether we would be able to successfully cope with and survive it, and our focus was largely on these personal concerns. None of us gave a moment's thought to whether we needed to be "reorganized" or otherwise fortified. That, however, was what was shortly to be undertaken on our behalf.

In the remaining few days of my stay in Hürtgen, I continued on the crash course of learning how to survive in winter combat in Germany. I had already absorbed much on my first night of guard duty and this tuition continued. Learning to gauge the nuances of arriving shells was a very rapid process, and it was not long until the guffaws with which the veterans had greeted my panicky dives into the nearest hole at the slightest sound were no longer heard. I too had sensed how to discriminate between the ones that would fall harmlessly (to me anyway) nearby and those which presented real risk.

The pattern of the first night was little changed in subsequent days. We remained in the same nameless stretch of woods. The company's motorized kitchen was able to deliver hot food to us once a day. We started to get to know the new officers and non-coms, to whom we were as new as they to us. I remember only two of the officers, one being a Lt. Russell Farrar, who would later become commanding officer of Company B. The other was a blond 2nd lieutenant named Peetz, who was our platoon leader or assistant platoon leader. Those elevated to sergeant had been promoted more or less arbitrarily because the new officers who made these promotions had no first hand knowledge of their abilities. Several of them were extremely memorable characters who are vivid to me even today. More of them later.

More on Hürtgen

November 1944

A couple of other vignettes filter back through the years as I think of Hürtgen. On one occasion, another soldier and I were detailed to accompany an artillery forward observer ("FO") somewhere in our battalion's sector. The FO was a lieutenant who was accompanied by a radio operator with an SCR 300 radio, a battery-operated transceiver weighing about 35 pounds and which could be carried on a man's back. The four of us installed ourselves in assorted foxholes on a high bluff at the forest's edge overlooking a valley below where we spent the better part of the day observing the scene before us. For once the mists had cleared and there was a distant view.

The time passed without incident so far as our personal safety was concerned, but since I had never heard of a forward observer and had no insight whatever into how artillery operated, the day was fascinating in the extreme. (It seems in retrospect incredible that in my infantry training at Rucker we should not have been afforded some minimal or at least theoretical exposure to artillery, but to the best of my recollection there had been none at all.)

To my untutored eye, there was little to be seen in the vista before us save the unbroken contours of the cultivated forest that stretched down the valley and up its opposite slope to the horizon. The lieutenant, however, appeared to make some sense of it, and dovetailing his observations with those from a Piper Cub plane droning overhead, he transmitted messages to the artillery battalion to our rear, giving map coordinates and specifying the type of fire which he was requesting. As a means of zeroing in on a particular target, he would call for a single round and then would adjust as necessary to bring the fire to the desired location. He would then call for "fire for effect," whereupon a barrage would be laid down for the purpose of destroying or preventing whatever enemy activity was taking place.

It was a very informative day, not only providing precious instruction as to the sights, sounds and workings of field artillery but also giving me an abiding sense of respect for the courage and usefulness of the FO's job. By its very nature, it required the observer to be at the very edge or even in advance of the front line. And the enemy, of course, knew that our observers would be out there, and was aware of the topography which suited their needs. Accordingly there would often be German artillery fire brought to bear on suspected FO locations, and infantry patrols would sometimes be sent out to deal with an observation post which had proved to be particularly effective. This, of course, was why my companion from Company B and I had been assigned to accompany him.

A footnote to this experience relates to the personality of the particular FO with whom I spent that day. Though chicken-shit pulling of rank was conspicuously less in the front lines than in the rear areas and the U.S., the caste division between officer and enlisted man was nonetheless fairly rigorously maintained even in the foxholes. It was a rare occurrence when an officer would unbend to the point of sharing with a dogface information of the sort I learned that day. So it was a memorable day from that point of view also. I was impressed with the man and—never dreaming that he might serve as a model for *my* future conduct—I began to understand that it was not only possible to treat subordinates with respect and consideration, but that that style of leadership could be truly inspirational. Unfortunately, I don't remember the man's name and I never saw him again.

On our way back to our unit my buddy and I encountered a Red Cross canteen in a mobile trailer at a busy road junction. A quagmire of mud rutted by heavy military traffic had turned the roads into foot-deep gumbo. We stopped for a few minutes to partake of coffee, doughnuts and cigarettes. (It took a very short time for most soldiers, including myself, to become sickened by the taste of doughnuts, but I hadn't gotten to that stage yet.) The location was near enough to the front that outgoing artillery could be heard passing overhead, and yet here were conversing—no doubt about the weather—with two young American girls as though we were at the corner drugstore.

I'm not sure how significant a contribution the Red Cross made to the American military effort in the war, but it seemed to me both heartening and extraordinary to find its female representatives at this bizarre time and place doling out coffee and doughnuts. Red Cross girls were plentifully in evidence in the rear echelons, but I don't remember ever seeing such a sight again at the front in my five months there.

Hürtgen also provided my indoctrination into the Army's field rations. When the kitchen was not available, we survived on "K" and "C" rations. The former were packed in a box somewhat smaller than, but the same shape as, a Kleenex box. They contained a can of meat or cheese the size of a tuna can, a bar of chocolate or dried fruit, crackers, four cigarettes, coffee and that vital indispensable, toilet paper. The "K" was designed for use when troops were on the move and there was no opportunity to prepare anything hot.

The "C" consisted of two soup-sized cans, one of which contained a protein food, such as pork and beans or corned beef hash, which could be heated, while the other can had the miscellaneous items found in the "K."

There was an inevitable progression in relation to these rations to which virtually every GI fell victim. The protein items (I remember especially pork-carrot loaf that was a constituent of the "K") seemed quite tasty at first bite and the greenhorn would quite happily consume not only his own portion but those cast aside by the veterans. As a result, he quickly became sated with the product and after only a few days could no longer abide it. The objective of providing a balanced diet to troops in the field proved for the army to be an impossible one.

It may seem odd that I have such vivid and enduring recollections of my few days in the Hürtgen Forest. Indeed, they are lodged in my head much more fixedly than those of many later events which were much more dangerous and dramatic. Even today, for example, the appearance and aroma of a snowy winter woodland will evoke a Proustian reverberation of Hürtgen.

The explanation, of course, is that I arrived at the front having only the vaguest notion of "what it would be like," but at the same time with a cumulative and certain dread that it would be ghastly and with the gravest doubts as to my ability to survive it. Hence every nerve and fiber of my being was open in those crucial hours and days to absorb the slightest scrap of useful information.

I was extremely fortunate that my period of crash indoctrination occurred as it did: there were no further casualties, and apart from artillery we were not molested by nor did we even see any Germans. At the end of those few days, I had developed—somewhat miraculously as it seemed to me then—a sense that it just might be possible to minimize at least some of the risks at the front by careful and intelligent attention, and that I might even develop skills which, if I was also absurdly lucky, might see me through to the end of the war.

My Second Phony War

November 16-December 16, 1944

I now embark on an account of the five months which I spent as a front-line combat infantryman with the 28th Division. My recollections of this period will never be other than fragmentary and kaleidoscopic, but they have nonetheless been greatly clarified, supplemented and chronologically ordered by the contributions of Cliff Hackett, who became company historian after the end of hostilities, Charlie Haug, who in 1949 himself recorded his recollections of his wartime experiences under the title *Courageous Defenders: As I Remember It*, and the many and varied remembrances of the other survivors of Baker Company who convened at our reunions in Minnesota in 1992 and 1994. I continue to stress, however, that unless I have noted otherwise, what I have written remains what I remember and believe to be true.

On November 15, 1944 the 28th Division moved south from the Hürtgen area back through Aachen and Maastricht, Holland, and thence into southeastern Belgium. The move was accomplished by a night-long convoy of 2½-ton trucks (they would be called "ten-wheelers" in today's CB lingo), which were the workhorse of the Army's transportation system. They featured a ribbed canvas covering over the rear deck with room for about sixteen soldiers each. It was cold, and though the distance could not have been much more than 100 kilometers, the trip seemed interminable.

The movement of a 10,000 man division required many hundreds of trucks provided by transportation companies which existed for this purpose. Their drivers were no doubt well trained in the necessity of maintaining a constant speed and uniform intervals between each truck, but all it took was a moment's inattentiveness to unleash an accordion-like compression effect throughout the convoy, resulting in crash stops, and sometimes crashes, involving the vehicles towards the rear of the procession. Since the benches in the trucks ran fore and aft, this meant that the men in the rear would be catapulted towards those in front. I am not sure which contingent had the worst of it, but the air would be blue with obscenities each time it happened.

The immediate destination of Company B turned out to be the small farming town of Weiswampach at the northeastern tip of Luxembourg. There we were deposited with all of our gear and equipment as dusk gave way to a pitch dark night. Although no one told us so, we were about to march towards the east to relieve another division (the 8th) which had been on line just over the German border, which was five kilometers distant.

Weiswampach is situated in the midst of the Ardennes which are usually characterized as "mountains," but which, in this area, are more on the order of a high, rolling agricultural plain, 1,500 feet or so above sea level, interspersed by the deep and steep clefts of river valleys 500 feet below.

Weiswampach was on the crest of a ridge, and the first few kilometers of our march took us down a steep country road into the valley of the Our River and the town of Ouren, which is situated at the junction of the frontiers of three countries: Belgium, to the northwest, Luxembourg to the southwest and Germany to the east. (At the time of this march, I was aware of none of the geography; I later made it my business to acquire maps and know their contents, but on this night all I knew was what my immediate senses told me, and that the German frontier and army were nearby.)

Even though the first few kilometers were all down hill, the burden of our 45-pound field packs and related gear began to take a toll. It had now been a good two months or more since we replacements had had any serious exercise. We had sat in indolence and idleness on the train from our stateside training camp, played poker at Camp Myles Standish, read books on the Mariposa and sat in forty-and-eight's or repple-depples while in England, France and Belgium.

The field pack which each of us was carrying consisted of the following: two wool blankets (or blanket and light sleeping bag), complete change of winter clothing, one or two day's rations, mess kit, toilet articles and personal belongings, entrenching tool, rifle or BAR, bayonet, cartridge belt with ten clips of .30 caliber ammunition, additional bandoleers of cartridge clips, canteen full of water, shelter half or tent, a grenade or two and a gas mask. In addition, we wore boots with canvas leggings or combat boots, long wool winter underwear, a heavy wool olive drab uniform, a sweater or two and field jacket and/or a heavy woolen overcoat, topped off by a plastic helmet liner and steel helmet.

We had been schooled in the sanctity of this equipment, and in the need to care for and preserve it. It had also long since become second nature to us that we should at all times be "in uniform," meaning that each of us in a unit should wear precisely the same prescribed items of clothing as every other man and no others.

I had noted in Hürtgen that not one of the company's veterans wore precisely the same uniform as any other. I had assumed that this was because the men had probably not been issued the same items as we had or because of losses during the holocaust of Hürtgen. Now, however, we began to learn differently.

As we progressed on our march, I became aware of items of gear underfoot and along the wayside. I was preoccupied by the anguish of my own aching muscles, however, and gave them little mind.

The company paused in the murk of Ouren to link up with guides from the 8th Division who would lead us to our new positions.

As we marched into the town, we for the first time heard from the men of the 8th a refrain which we would later come to recognize as the standard GI greeting from troops at the front, ecstatic at being relieved, to the men who were about to replace them. There were two elements to this welcome: "Go back! Go back!" uttered in doleful and falsely solicitous tones (as if any of those arriving could possibly do so), and "You'll be sorry!," this drawn out in a sing-song chant with the first syllable of "sorry" given heavy stress. We would later come to relish the times when we, too, would be able to utter these calls to those relieving us, but the first time we heard them as we walked into Ouren not only was the humor lost on us but we found them most unnerving, which was of course exactly what was intended.

The rest in Ouren was a godsend. Very soon, however, the word came down the line: "Move out!"—a phrase that then and later never failed to send a spasm of dread down my spine. It always meant departure from a known place of relative calm and safety—in an invariably forward direction—towards one of risk and danger.

We were on our way again and this time it was straight uphill. (In August 1990 we drove up this road and it could be surmounted by our sedan only in lowest gear.) Gasps and moans of distress were soon heard on all sides. Beads of sweat poured down my face. Before long there was a veritable cascade of equipment falling to the roadside, not to mention soldiers who—to the tune of muffled curses from the non-coms—simply sat down to rest. For a time I shrank from discarding any gear. I could not imagine that our officers would condone this wholesale abandonment of government property. But eventually it became clear that they were unconcerned (indeed none of them was in any kind of "uniform"), and so I began to unload too.

The first thing to go was the gas mask. It weighed several pounds and was carried in a separate canvas bag with a shoulder strap. Some of the veterans, I had noted, used the bag in lieu of the canvas field pack as a place to stow essential gear, so I kept the bag. Other items soon followed—anything that weighed a little and that I could conceivably do without. I don't doubt that some items were shucked that I later wished I had back, but the anguish was great and the restraint of discipline had for the moment conveniently evaporated.

Cliff Hackett's memory of the march up from Ouren is as vivid as mine. In the Army's inscrutable way, he had long been designated as a BAR man, though he weighed no more than 135 pounds. A "partner" had been designated, however, whose job it was to share with the operator the carrying of the weapon. Cliff's partner obstinately refused to do so, to the point that Cliff at last could stand it no longer and cried out "Won't somebody please help me carry this goddamn weapon?" It wasn't until the next day that he discovered the savior who lifted the load from his back and carried it the rest of the way was Lt. Farrar.

I often wondered in subsequent days whether any effort was made to gather up the stuff that had been dumped that night on the way up from Ouren, to, as it turned out, the German border town of Lutzkampen. (Indeed, I wondered whether we might not be ordered to stand inspection with note being taken of the missing items.) I never found out, but the winnowing of equipment turned out to be permanent; never thereafter were we required to be "in uniform," and (with the exception of rifle, helmet and entrenching tool) each man was left to his own devices when it came to deciding what clothing and equipment he would keep and what he would do without.

My own kit ultimately consisted of helmet, rifle, cartridge belt and ammunition, mess kit, canteen and canteen cup, bayonet, entrenching tool, two sets of long underwear, three shirts worn on top of each other, field jacket (more waterproof and lighter than the Army's woolen overcoat) two pairs of woolen pants, combat boots, sleeping bag and extra blanket, and toilet articles and personal items stowed in the gas mask pouch. (I often found entertainment in later years in Hollywood's depiction of ETO combat soldiers in movies: they were usually shown with full regulation field packs marching in file and cadence towards the front. That was simply not the way we looked or acted: no two soldiers dressed identically and we never "marched" anywhere. And notwithstanding the legend that General Patton always required his troops to wear neckties, careful scrutiny of some of the pictorial histories of his Third Army will demonstrate the contrary.)

There was little else about that march that was remarkable. If there was any artillery, it could only have been the distant rumble which I had now for many days been used to. We toiled up the farm lane to the top of the hill and eventually arrived at an isolated farmhouse which was to become our company command post ("CP"). There we again were met by guides, and now each platoon, and each of its three squads were separately led to their new locations.

That of my platoon was to be in the company "reserve" position; that is, a location a half kilometer or so behind the positions of the other two platoons, which were "on line." (It was a characteristic of infantry tactics in static positions that two of the three sub-units of each larger one would be on line, with the third one held in reserve.)

The reserve position which we gratefully inherited from the 8th Division's departing company—we did not have to dig new foxholes—was situated in the northeast corner of a woods which in turn was sited on the top of a north-south ridge just to the east of the Our valley. From the foxholes where our men were to stand guard the view was across open farmlands sloping downhill to the east and towards other woods uphill to the north. We were fortunate that this woods was deciduous in nature. It was thick enough to cover our movements in the daytime, but it had none of the claustrophobic setting of Hürtgen, with its low-hanging coniferous boughs making it so dark that one could not even read in the daytime.

Although I did not know it at the time, this position and one or two others in the company area were to be my home for the next month.

As already noted, the generals in charge of my fate had decided immediately after the division's mauling in Hürtgen that it should be relieved and put in a "quiet" section for reorganization and training. It would have been wonderful if we had known this, but of course we were totally ignorant and only came to discover it bit by bit over the next month.

In a document entitled "Training Memo #1" dated 11 November 1944 (the exact date of my arrival in the 28th) which I found in a repository of the National Archives in Maryland, the division had promulgated a schedule of six hours per day, six days per week of training, including calisthenics, military discipline and courtesy and road marches! The memo, of course, antedates by several days the orders moving us into our new positions in the south, but whatever may have been the intentions of the brass regarding our rehabilitation at that moment, virtually none of this absurd regimen was ever carried into effect so far as I can recall.

I eventually came to discover that our situation at Lutzkampen was more or less typical of the foxhole dweller's lot throughout the war. The emotional furniture which we had all been conditioned to expect and to rely on from childhood—almost as basic as gravity or air to breathe—was suddenly gone. We were in a sealed balloon or vacuum in which the only information available was what we could grasp through our five senses. We knew almost nothing as to how our balloon fitted in with even our nearest neighbors, let alone the rest of the world. We learned almost nothing regarding what other units, U.S. or German, were nearby or what would be happening in even the next five minutes. The vacuum of fact stirred a constant swirl of rumor, but because rumor was untrustworthy (and known to be so) it only served to remind us of how little we knew and thus to intensify our anxiety. Like untrained mutts at the end of a leash, we were subject to being wrenched from where we were to somewhere else—always in our balloon of ignorance—without the slightest notice or explanation. There was in a word an almost total absence of emotional continuity of the sort which is the normal expectancy of everyday life and which was readily available to soldiers only a few miles to the rear. The change imposed a heavy and cumulative psychological burden which many found difficult to sustain.

In any event, we now settled into an almost seamless routine which lasted for the next month. As before, activity centered around standing guard at whichever of the company positions we happened to be occupying at the time. In the reserve position which we moved into on the first night only a few guard posts were manned, and the rest of us were able to sleep pretty well through the night, and the two-hours-on, two-hours-off routine was somewhat relaxed. While there were a few sunny days—much relished of course—the skies hung low and were mostly gray, with rain or snow from time to time. It grew colder as the season lengthened into winter.

Endless time was devoted to keeping warm, fed and dry, though very little could be done about keeping clean. The company kitchen was elsewhere. (I have a recollection of being fiercely jealous of those who were at the company CP; they were indoors and had hot food, even though the CP was a little closer to the Germans than were we in our foxholes. But there would soon come a time when I would be grateful that was *not* my assigned billet.)

The heating of C rations at our campfires was a lengthy and complicated task which I never satisfactorily mastered. They would get too hot and burn, but be cold in the middle, but no matter how long you took, you still could never get them evenly warm.

Preparing a cup of coffee was different; it was a ritual one object of which was to take as much time as possible. Correctly done, it could take as much as an hour, at the end of which it would be time to start on the next cup. Heating the water—I'm not sure I ever got it to boil—would take a half hour or more with the canteen cup teetering over the campfire and sometimes falling in. The cup was made of a coated steel which imparted a hideous metallic taste to whatever it contained, but the ritual of preparation and the pleasure of consumption of the coffee was a very real solace to the foxhole dweller!

At first we were circumspect about movements in the daytime because we were in view of the German lines on the opposite ridge line a kilometer or two distant, but in the woods of the reserve position, we could move about freely. GI instinct under all circumstances was to stay in the sack as much as possible, since activity quickened during the night. It was then that supplies would be brought in, movements of units from one position to another would take place and patrols would be run.

There were essentially two kinds of patrols: liaison patrols to our neighboring unit to the north and reconnaissance patrols toward the front. While in company reserve, we carried on both types.

As it happened, our company was the northernmost unit of the division. When we arrived, the unit on our left was the 23rd Infantry Regiment of the 2nd Division, the southernmost company of which was as much as a kilometer away. To maintain contact between the two units and to assure that there was no German infiltration during the night, a detail of three or four men under a non-com was assigned to climb over the wooded ridge to our north and there rendezvous with the nearest unit of the 23rd Regiment. On alternate nights, the 2nd Division's patrols would come to us. The trips were fast, furtive and frightening.

It was night for starters. We were in woods where it was even darker. And we had to clamber along a narrow path with only masked flashlights for illumination, and that only intermittently. In spite of the clamorous beating of our own hearts, we strove for silence. Twigs would crack. Was them or us? Every sense strained at complete attention. But so far as I know, there was never any real incident connected with liaison patrols for the month of our tenure on the line at Lutzkampen. Enormous relief would always be felt when the password would be exchanged after contact had been made. (The passwords were changed daily and were usually pairs of words known to Americans, such as "Betty Grable/Harry James"—they were married at the time—or "Ford/Chevrolet," etc.)

Reconnaissance patrols were an entirely different commodity. They were even more nerve-wracking and often terrifying. The town of Lutzkampen, abandoned by its inhabitants, lay between us and the Germans, quite a bit closer to us than to them. It consisted of perhaps twenty farmhouses, barns and outbuildings grouped around a crossroads town center. Our purpose was to make sure that there were no Jerries in the town—there were rumors that they, too, patrolled the town—and that all was quiet. But it was never *really* quiet.

These patrols were a little larger, up to a squad of men. We would assemble in the CP (oh, blessed warmth!) to plan the excursion. Someone—usually with a little experience—would be designated a "point man," and he would lead the group into the town, with the next men slinking into the village at intervals of five to ten yards on alternating sides of the street. A couple of others would be outriders, walking parallel in the adjacent fields. We would try to be sure that only one man would move at a time so that the others could cover him in case of trouble. The non-com would be in the middle of the group, giving direction with hand signals if a clear night, otherwise by muffled whispers to runners who would carry the message to its destination.

My heart would be in my throat the entire time. A barn door would creak in the wind and bang shut, and it would leap into my mouth. There were cows and other livestock which had been left behind, and the first time I heard one of them emit what was clearly a human sound, I was sure the end had come! It would take two or three minutes of total silence and immobility before the thundering of my heart would subside.

Once more, I never heard of any violent incident occurring during these probes into town, and after a couple of weeks some of the guys started exploring for edibles and souvenirs in the houses. Nothing of any real value was ever found, but I did discover a carbide lamp and a portable cooker that were items of army issue to the German troops and which I used for a time. The lamp was well-made of brass. Small lumps of carbide mineral were placed inside on which drops of water could be made to fall. This produced acetylene gas which would burn with a bright white light, much superior to the candles which were standard for us. But the German lamp corroded quickly, and, of course, I had no supply of carbide, so that ended that. The cooker was collapsible. When opened up, a canteen cup would be placed on it and a heating "pill" was placed inside and lit. It was vastly superior to the GI system, which relied on waxed ration cartons and candles for these functions.

After an hour or so in the town, sometimes going to its east end to make sure all was well, the longed-for word to return to our lines would come and—at a rate much more rapid and less cautious than when we had come—we would retrace our steps.

I had learned that that it was as much as a kilometer between the left flank of our company (and the division's) and the 2nd Division to the north. It was also the fact that though I did *not* know it, the 28th Division's full front covered over 25 miles, and the spread between units at our end of it was replicated all along the line. Even within our company, the positions of the other platoons were so far to the south that we never saw any of them.

The only position other than the reserve location in the woods with which I had anything to do was a line of foxholes dug into a small bluff a half kilometer east of the woods. The bluff ran north-south in an open field and stood about 20 feet above an open draw which ran towards the east. This was our platoon's "front line" position, and each squad would man it in rotation with the others for three or four days at a time.

The drill was very much the same as I have described in Hürtgen: two hours in the covered foxhole sleeping and trying to keep warm, and two hours maintaining vigil towards the east and being cold. It was a mind-numbing routine, of course, and after a week or two of it the tendency and temptation was to slumber in both locations. I could never shake the awareness, however, that I was the eyes and ears of the American Army in Germany and no matter how many uneventful nights slid by, there was at least no conscious relaxation of watchfulness. On a clear moonlit night the dim outlines of the woods and slopes could be discerned, shapes were silhouetted by the snow and attention could somewhat abate—I knew that a grenade would not arrive in my foxhole without at least some advance warning. But when it was cloudy and windy or snowing, it sometimes seemed as though my eyeballs would burst from straining to see what was out front.

In the early evening, alertness was regularly assured by the passage overhead of a German reconnaissance plane known to all GI's as "Bed-Check Charlie." I never could quite figure out what the purpose of Charlie's nightly mission was. He always showed up shortly after dark at fairly low altitude, paralleling the front line, either north to south or south to north. Since none of us had to be told of the importance of total blackout, it wasn't clear what useful information he hoped to gain. All the same, we didn't trust him and sighed in relief as he droned away.

The nighttime landscape would occasionally burst into brilliant light when a star shell would appear in the sky. These were white parachute flares which could be launched by artillery or mortars from behind the lines. They seemed to come more from the German lines than from our own. There would be a detonation, not especially loud, and one's eyes would immediately sweep to the location of the noise where the pinpoint of incandescence would burst forth, dangling from its small parachute. The light would last for about 30 seconds, during which I would struggle against the normal instinct to crash to the ground in order to take cover. That, however was exactly the wrong thing to do. Because of the great contrast between horizontal surfaces illuminated by the overhead light and the total blackness of all others, objects took on an appearance wholly unlike that in daylight. Hence it was almost impossible to recognize familiar forms unless there was movement. A man could be standing in the open twenty yards away and be invisible if he remained motionless, but the slightest movement would be immediately apparent. Ernie Pyle, the famous newspaper chronicler of the U.S. infantry in the war, described the sensation experienced when a flare would finally go dark as "a great welcoming privacy." But during the lifetime that one remained lit, it was imperative to remain motionless and to scan feverishly with eyes only to detect movement anywhere else.

But nothing ever happened! We never saw any Germans, either up close or at a distance. We never heard any artillery except far away to the north (possibly from the Hürtgen area, since as I now know, the fighting was still going on there full tilt). If there were Jerry patrols into or near Lutzkampen, I had no firsthand knowledge of them. And although we knew that the Siegfried Line lay to our immediate front, the only conspicuous signs of it were the rows of "dragon's teeth" to the east of Lutzkampen. (By the time we visited in 1990, the dragon's teeth had been mostly removed and all that remained were a few hunks of concrete with no traces at all of any pillboxes or fortifications.)

Cliff Hackett's account of our time near Lutzkampen says:

> For almost a month, Company B enjoyed the comparative security and quiet of a static holding position. Training was carried on and slowly we replacements were transformed into a more dependable unit which began to resemble a fighting force, but which was totally untried and lulled into a false security.

It would probably be wrong to deny that training took place. I certainly don't remember any, but that is not saying that it didn't happen. We must, of course, have cared for our weapons and we could conceivably have had some very informal tactical discussions, but there was certainly nothing like the military courtesy/discipline/calisthenics items shown on the November training memo; none of us—officers included—would have tolerated such a regression to stateside chicken-shit if indeed the tactical situation would have permitted it, which it didn't!

Cliff is altogether right, however, in his observation that we were untried and wallowing in a false sense of security. We had been subjected to no real stress (although we thought we had), and there had been virtually no opportunity to test anyone's reliability or good sense.

On the other hand, we had been "on the front," had survived for a time and had experienced the trappings of combat, if not the reality of it, and I clearly remember thinking that if this is all there is to it, hey, it's a cinch! How little I knew!

My second phony war was punctuated after two or three weeks by a trip back to the town of Clervaux, Luxembourg, where a rest camp was located. The purpose was to take showers and get clean clothes and a hot meal. Why do I remember that, you ask. You wouldn't have to if you had been living outdoors in a foxhole in winter for as long as we had. It was simply the most delicious, sybaritic experience of my young life! The showers were outdoor portable canvas affairs and not much to look at, but to luxuriate under unlimited hot water and for once be entirely warm was pure heaven. And the sensation of being totally clean in body and attire was not far behind. It was like being under water and close to drowning and suddenly being released into the open air—exhilaration beyond measure!

One item in the "training" category which cried out for attention and never got any was an opportunity to zero in our unfired M1 rifles.[9] Each rifle had adjustable sights, both for the purpose of adapting fire to conditions of wind and distance, and also so that the idiosyncrasies of each weapon could be compensated for. For example, if a particular piece fired high and to the left when the sights were centered, the rear sight would then be adjusted down and to the right to compensate for the flaw. Since manufacturing variances between weapons could be substantial, this was no minor oversight. What it led to, as I was soon to find out, was a reluctance to fire at any but the nearest targets because of the chance—really the probability—that the bullet would go wide while an alert enemy would observe the location of the firer and thus suddenly have a large advantage.

I can only speculate at the reason for this omission. Did no one happen to think of it? Such things were all too readily possible in the army. Or was it because rifle range facilities were not readily available? If the latter, it was an egregious mistake; otherwise why design the rifles as they were and train us in the importance of zeroing in?

Another aspect of life at my peaceful front deserves comment. It was very early in my first days in the reserve position in the woods that I awoke suddenly from deep slumber and dashed out the door with my clothes in disarray. Sanitation was accommodated in the field by what

---

[9] George Knaphus, one of our survivors, believes that our M1's were issued at Chalcot Park in England and that we did indeed zero them in on what he describes as a 1,000 *inch* range (i.e., 83.3 feet). I have no recollection of such a procedure. It may well have happened but it is clear that it failed to assure me of the distant accuracy of my weapon after a trip of 300 miles over two months later.

was known as a "slit trench." It was just that: a trench a foot or so deep and wide and three or four feet long. This would be used by a small unit for a few days, at the end of which it would be filled in, and if still in the same location, a new one dug.

I never made it that night, and thus began a months long intimacy with diarrhea, and its close and malevolent cousin, dysentery. I don't think I ever shook them altogether, and there was no remedy for them that was more than palliative.

It never was very clear to me why the ailment was so hard to avoid in the field. In garrison with communal mess arrangements it would sometimes reach epidemic proportions, as it had in St. Petersburg, but when each of us had his own hermetically-sealed ration, it should have been minimized. It never was, and the culprit probably was water. We were issued what were called halogen tablets, one or two of which were dissolved in a canteen of water and which were supposed to make almost any water potable. The halogen impaired the taste of the water and especially of coffee, which was the one creature comfort of the foxhole, and rationalizing that our coffee water was boiled (which it almost never was), we were slipshod in our use of halogen, and the "GI shits" were the result.

Foot care presented another source of perpetual difficulty. There was a long period during which we had no overshoes (and in addition overshoes were heavy and tended to get lost when they weren't really needed), and GI combat boots, while well-designed and utilitarian, could not be made waterproof. The Army supplied cans of something called "dubbing," a petroleum product which was supposed to help. It didn't, and in addition made the boot seem colder. The result was that our feet were forever cold and damp or wet. My own method of trying to deal with this problem was to have four pairs of wool socks at all times. One set, consisting of two pairs, would be on my feet while the other two were nestled inside my shirt. The warmth of my body would dry them out there in short order, and I would try to change them at least once a day. This worked fairly well, but it didn't entirely solve the problem. Towards the end of the winter I had developed a moderate case of trenchfoot, which was characterized by a loss of blood circulation to and diminished feeling in the toes, and inability to ever get my feet warm. Many soldiers had to be invalided out because of trenchfoot and there were even cases where amputation became necessary. In my own case, it was many years before full sensation returned to my big toes.

It's hard to recreate how we filled our days during our time at Lutzkampen. Bill Kleeman, who was not with us there but who returned later to resume his job as one of our platoon sergeants, remarked at our first reunion that the addition of us ASTP-ers gave the company "whole new character" (a comment intended to be complimentary, I think), adding that on his return from a wound recuperation in England in January 1945, "Ah could scarcely believe mah eyes; there was GI's a-sittin' in foxholes a-playin' *bridge!*" Though I have no recollection of it, I could easily have been one of those who had so scandalized Bill.

Of course, one thing we all did was think, dream and talk about home in all its aspects. One colleague who was married, had survived Hürtgen and was not an ASTP-er, never tired of describing for us the most intimate details of sexual intercourse with his wife. ("What I love best is getting almost ready to come and then just letting her soak!") But for most of us, and certainly for me, the daydreams were private. In my case they took the form of elaborately imaginative encounters with one or two girls whom I knew well back home but neither of whom could be described as a "girlfriend." Or, more prosaically but a great deal more plausibly, of picturing in as much detail as possible exactly how it would be when I returned home: arriving at the railroad station, greeting my parents, opening the front door, how the front hall would look, and sleeping in my own bed. More often than not this film would become blurred and fuzzy and sputter out, possibly from overuse. Other common reveries, usually enthusiastically vocalized, were about food: steak, ice cream, you name it.

I have very little memory of any individuals dating from this period. There were any number of ASTP refugees who had been my fellow-passengers on the *Mariposa* and who had joined the company with me as replacements. They included Cliff Hackett, Emerson Hazlett from Kansas, Walter "Gus" Gustafson, Bill Gibler and others, but my concrete recollections of them are mostly connected with our later experiences. No doubt the reason is that each of us was by the nature of our isolated activities largely kept separate from the others throughout the period. Still, I don't remember who my squad leader was, and can't even recall the man with whom I shared my foxhole.

One guy I do remember vividly was one of our platoon sergeants. Until our June 1992 reunion in Minnesota, I remembered him only by the nickname "Slick," which was what everyone called him. At the reunion, however, Bill Kleeman, who was platoon sergeant of the Third Platoon and who remembered Slick as well as I did, said that his name was Marvin Lefler. He was from West Virginia and looked, acted and talked like an illiterate hillbilly, which is precisely what he was. The appearance, however, was very misleading. Bill Kleeman recalled that Slick was one of the tiny handful in the company who survived from beginning to end, and he didn't do that by being stupid. Right after Hürtgen he was offered a battlefield commission to replace one of the officers who had been killed, and although all in the platoon urged him to accept, he never gave it a moment's thought. He said, "Me an officer? Who you kiddin'? I ain't gonna be no fuckin' lieutenant and get my ass shot off leadin' the parade when I can stay at the rear of the platoon and be *safe*!" Of course, he was being funny—he was a very funny man and loved to guffaw—but only partially so. It was true that the book expected platoon leaders (lieutenants) to be near the front of an attacking platoon and that they thus incurred the highest casualty rate in the Army, whereas platoon sergeants normally followed behind where they could keep the full platoon in view, but Slick clearly saw that he would be a total misfit as an officer. He couldn't walk, talk, dress or act like an officer (let alone read or write) and he didn't want to try. We all respected him even more for his decision.

In spite of his unpolished ways, he could deliver a polished lecture on technical military subjects and did so often when the division was in training in England, according to Bill Kleeman, who also ventures the view (colored by modesty perhaps) that if there had been an award for the Most Outstanding Enlisted Man of Company B, it would certainly have been Slick.

Although no one at the reunion could recall Slick's coming to any grief during the war, neither could anyone shed light on what might have become of him. I hope he survives; he was neat!

I must have written fairly frequently during this period, but curiously only one letter survives, written on December 9. It comments on my brother's comparative safety in the field artillery, on letters received and packages therein stated as being on the way, but says virtually nothing about my activities other than that I was "dry and warm." Obviously, strong censorship measures were in force, both official and otherwise. I might have said more but did not know how to.

Towards the end of our inactive idyll, about December 10, we became aware that the 2nd Division to our north was being replaced by a brand-new unit, fresh off the boat, the 424th Infantry Regiment of the 106th Infantry Division, whose shoulder patch was a golden lion's head on a blue background. I remember feeling no small lift from the brief contacts we had with them, because now they were the ones who were nervous and apprehensive, and we were the calm, experienced veterans. Their behavior was in marked contrast to the seasoned 2nd Division guys whom they replaced: they were clumsy, noisy and unsure of themselves. The fate of the two northern regiments of the 106th was to be an unhappy one: within a very short time their commanders would surrender them en masse to the attacking Germans and they would spend the rest of the war in awful captivity. As to the 424th the story would be very different; its fortunes and those of my own 112th would be closely intertwined in the events about to unfold.

The Ardennes Offensive
The Strategic Background

July-December 1944

HAVING seen what life was like during this peculiar interval of alleged combat, it may again be appropriate to stand back and look at the larger strategic context of which I knew nothing but against which my ant-like role was now to be played out.

In light of the onslaught about to be visited on the Americans in the Ardennes, one may ask—and many have—how it came to pass that this area of the front was so thinly defended. As has been noted, the 28th Division's front was over 25 miles, four or five times more territory than was deemed strategically ideal, and it was the same or worse both north and south, where the 106th and 4th Divisions and the 9th Armored Division were similarly scattered along the line. All in all, the three infantry divisions covered a total distance of 88 miles.

There were several answers to this question. First, as we have already seen, the Allied forces were undergoing a period of consolidation as supplies were accumulated. The great port of Antwerp, which British Field Marshal Montgomery (preoccupied as he was with "Market-Garden") had failed to clear when he should have, had finally been opened on November 2 to supplement the strained resources of the Normandy beaches, but until stockpiles of ammunition and gasoline reached adequate levels, there had to be a general marking of time. Secondly, there was little in the way of strategic military objectives to the east of the Ardennes (and their German counterpart, known as the Schnee Eifel), as contrasted with the industrial Ruhr to the north and the Saar Basin, rich in coal and iron, to the south. Thus, those were the areas in which our troops were concentrated. Thirdly, the difficult topography of the Ardennes, marked as they were by many steep river valleys, rivers and bridges, and a narrow and twisting road system, all seemed to suggest that the enemy would think long and hard before any significant initiatives would be launched there. But the final and by far the most important factor was the perception of the Allied generals that the German war machine was beaten; it had lost so many men and so much matériel that it could no longer mount an effective offensive.

Notwithstanding all of the above, the area had historically been the focus of two other successful German attacks, one during the Franco-Prussian War of 1870, and the second in the more recent past when the world was startled by the success of Hitler's "blitzkrieg" into France in the spring of 1940. Then the German tank columns had smashed through Ardennes—likewise lightly guarded because of the seemingly minimal risk—and brought about the Dunkirk evacuation of the entire British expeditionary force and ultimately the fall of France.

It is said that all of this was known to the generals concerned, principally Generals Eisenhower and Bradley. There are records of their having specifically discussed the subject and having reached the conclusion that though there was a risk, it was a slight one,[10] and that in any event the worst that could happen was that whatever attack might come through would be pinched off at its shoulders by counterattacks from the north and south. There was a most important additional factor: the Allied war effort was reaching the bottom of the manpower barrel; there were very few infantry divisions left in the pipeline and Air Corps and anti-aircraft units were being cannibalized to provide desperately needed replacements for the units already in the field. Hence it was thought unnecessary and wasteful to deploy battle-worthy units in quiet sectors.

On the basis of this reasoning, the Ardennes front was deliberately kept thinly defended both in its forward positions and with respect to reinforcing units, such as tanks, tank destroyers and artillery. Indeed, one reason we had heard so little artillery at Lutzkampen was because our division artillery units had extremely limited supplies of shells and were "rationed" in their use, with disastrous later results, as we were soon to discover.

The Germans, of course, were well aware of the distribution of the Allied forces. The probable shape of the Allies' strategic planning was

---

[10] Bradley is said to have replied, "Let 'em come!" when warned of a possible attack by a clairvoyant intelligence officer from SHAEF.

likewise quite apparent. And the evidence is that as early as the end of July, not long after the unsuccessful attempt on his life at the "Wolf's Lair," his eastern headquarters, on July 20, 1944, Hitler was already beginning to think about an aggressive attack in the west. Planning for such an offensive started shortly after that and really got moving in early September, when a very limited group of senior staff was brought into the effort after having been sworn to secrecy on pain of death.

One thing had been made crystal clear by the assassination attempt: there would be very little delegation of strategic decision-making in the future; from now on both planning and final decisions would be reserved only to Hitler. On September 25, he directed his staff to prepare detailed plans for an offensive through the Ardennes, the objective of which would be to cross the Meuse River behind the Allied lines, and then turn north to retake the port of Antwerp. The ultimate goal of this endeavor would be to sow the seeds of discord between the U.S. and England and impel them to sue for a separate peace.

The generals responded with a comparatively modest plan with limited geographic objectives, but this was quickly cast aside by Hitler, who insisted on an enormous effort involving three separate armies and thirty divisions, of which ten were panzer, or armored divisions. Other units were cannibalized to create these forces, and secrecy measures were extraordinary. Five hundred train loads of men, equipment and supplies had to be moved into position notwithstanding continuing bombardment by the Allied air forces, and it was essential that these preparations remain undetected. Movements were strictly limited to nighttime hours and all activity was to cease or be carefully camouflaged during the day. Orders were even issued that the tires of vehicles found on the road in daylight were to be shot! Horse-drawn vehicles, which were still the principal transport equipment of the German Army, were muffled by tying straw to the wheels, and even horses' hooves were straw-padded.

One aspect of the planning that was to have enormous importance for me took place at a conference between Hitler and his generals in Berlin on December 2, 1944, two weeks before the event. One of the principal commanders of the attacking forces, Generalleutnant Hasso von Manteuffel, had reconnoitered the western front, and had even visited the areas opposite the 28th Division's positions. He had disguised himself as a colonel in order not to draw attention to himself. There he had been told that the Americans went to bed an hour after sunset and did not mount guard again until an hour before sunrise. On the strength of this information (which was certainly false so far as our company was concerned but was apparently true with regard to our sister regiments to the south where the line was even more thinly held and at greater distances from the Germans), Manteuffel was bold enough to argue with Hitler at the December 2 conference that it would be a mistake to give warning of the attack with an artillery preparation; it would be silly to wake us up, he reasoned. And so Hitler, who was a firm believer in the efficacy of artillery as a result of his trench warfare experience in World War I, permitted an exception to be made in the case of Manteuffel's part of the front, and no artillery was ordered. There is no way to know, but this decision probably saved my life, because the locations of our defensive positions at Lutzkampen had not changed in a month and they would without question have been brutally punished by the enormous barrage which the GI's suffered both north and south.

At the same conference, it was agreed at Manteuffel's suggestion that large numbers of searchlights would be amassed and that they would be aimed at the bottoms of the clouds overhead, the notion being that the reflected light would furnish illumination for the final troop movements on the night before the attack without revealing what was about to occur. Hitler is said to have asked Manteuffel how he knew there would be clouds, to which he replied, "Mein Führer, you have decided everything on the prospect that the weather will be bad." That was indeed a basic premise of the offensive because everything depended on Allied air superiority being eliminated by the bad weather which generally prevailed in the area in December. Things turned out exactly as planned: the weather for the first week was terrible, and the attack was a complete and utter surprise.

— Not Me! —

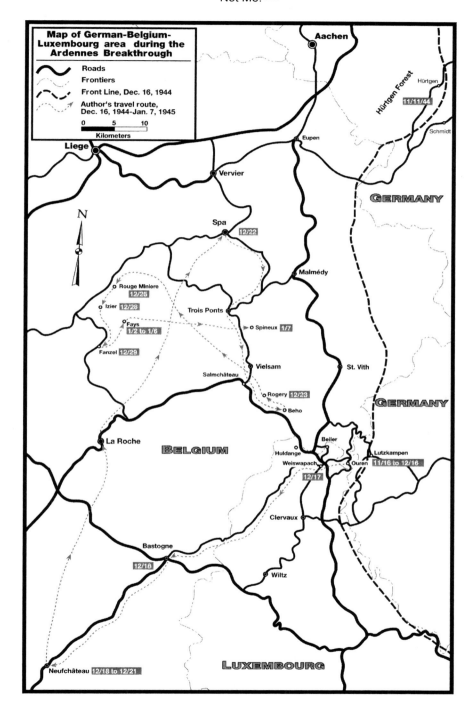

The Ardennes Breakthrough

December 16, 1944-January 16, 1945

It is customary to refer to the German Ardennes offensive of December 1944 as the "Battle of the Bulge." This is not a name which has ever appealed to me. The name was obviously coined by someone whose familiarity with the event was limited to visualizing it on a map, rather than on the ground, and in addition, it sounds more like someone's struggle to stay thin than a reference to warfare. Hence, it will be known here as the Ardennes Offensive or Breakthrough.

This is what Cliff Hackett's account says about December 16:

> The night of the 15th was extremely quiet. Not one shot fell and no gunfire was heard. At 0530 hours many searchlights came on, illuminating our position and plying the sky like a Hollywood premiere! A puzzled company watched these lights and then proceeded with their usual duties. At 0600 hours, the Germans struck Outpost 88, knocked it out and stormed the 1st and 3rd Platoon CPs. Captain Stanley Dec, the company commander, was killed in the first few minutes of fighting. In the ensuing battle, some of it hand-to-hand, the Germans lost approximately 150 men, with 73 captured and an unknown number wounded. Baker Company lost 95 men killed, captured or missing. Tanks attacked at 1600 hours—we had asked for tank destroyers, bazookas or any back-up, but nothing was available. At dusk, remnants of the 1st and 3rd Platoons, holding outpost positions, retreated to Ouren, [Luxembourg].

This account is more complete than my recollection could ever be, since in the nature of things, I saw only a fragment of the battlefield and never had access to any of the company records which were available to

Cliff in later months. But there is nothing inconsistent between the two.

The problem is that so many things now started to happen—all of them horrendous and many of them at once—that it was no longer possible to assimilate them even in the short term, let alone to piece together a chronological account at this remove. My only recourse now in attempting to recount the events of the next hours and days is to string together the recollections which I do retain in the hope that they will somehow convey an impression of the reality. Here is what I remember:

The wee small hours of the night of December 15-16 announced themselves quite early as being out of the ordinary. I was in my hole in the platoon's forward position. The night like most others was cold, dark and overcast. My hole-mate and I began the night as all others, rotating guard on the usual two-on two-off basis. During one of my stints, I became aware of a growing rumble—clearly not artillery—emanating from the east. It soon grew loud enough that I woke my buddy who grumbled his way out and we both took matters under advisement.

The volume of the sound continued to grow, but neither of us was sure what it was. It was continuous and sounded like motor noise, but it seemed louder and somehow deeper and more guttural than motor noises we were used to, and as it kept on we even talked about whether its source could be some kind of loudspeaker setup that the Germans had rigged up for purposes of psychological warfare. The fact of the matter was that we were so inexperienced (and the Army had so neglected our training) that we hadn't the faintest idea what tank engines sounded like. Our learning curve was about to become very rapid.

But for the moment, our perplexity was further confounded by the appearance of a glow of light streaming from the clouds above the eastern horizon. There were no clearly defined beams which would have served to identify the source of the light as searchlights, which in any event would also have been foreign to our experience. We were totally mystified!

Somehow we managed to get a message to the company CP to make sure these manifestations—which were so obvious as to be inescapable to anyone outdoors—had reached the attention of our superiors in the warm farmhouse. The response was: yes, we've noticed, and the implication was: don't bother us with such foolish reports. We continued to watch and listen.[11]

We remained in our holes until well after daylight. The motor noise had grown extremely loud, but it did not seem to arise from any discrete location. On the contrary, it seemed to be everywhere in front of us, while staccato reports of small arms fire could be heard from the middle distance. In the middle of the gray morning I became aware of shouting and loud voices somewhere to our right, and someone directed us to leave our holes, to move south towards the Company CP and to take up a new, largely unprotected position at the edge of a field looking to the east along the road towards the town. We had not been there long when from the corner of a hedgerow 200 yards away the air was torn by several frantically fast bursts from what I immediately recognized as a German MG 42 machine gun, the same one we had seen so impressively demonstrated in England. It was firing tracers at a target to our right, and following their path, I was horrified to see a number of GI's who were running for cover crumple and fall to the ground.

I could scarcely believe that I had seen this happen! Until mere seconds before I had not been aware of either the gunner or his targets and suddenly they were dead or wounded and he was right there in front of us!

Now I *really* looked at that hedgerow. Shadowy figures, hunched over, were moving behind the branches to the left of the machine gun. Suddenly, one of them stood up and I could see the clearly-limned silhouette of a man wearing a coal-scuttle helmet. He was giving orders in a rasping, shouting voice. The staccato German syllables came clearly across the snow to us. The man was outraged because his orders were not being obeyed, or not quickly enough. His voice was hoarse, guttural and full of urgent purpose, and it struck terror into my heart. A hatred of the brutal-sounding German language instantaneously arose within me which I haven't shaken to this day.

---

[11] George Knaphus' vivid memory of the wee small hours of the 16th has Baker's respected 1st Sergeant Ralph McGeoch ("McGyew") stopping by his post at 3:45 a.m. and asking, "How's it going, Cornbelt?" (George was and is an Iowan); he replied, "Awfully quiet." McGeoch said, "How quiet?" "Nothing, no mortars, no machine gun, no artillery." "How about the guy before you?" "Same thing; no activity." "They're up to something, I'm alerting everyone," and he did. As noted, from where I was, there was no need to be alerted by any one else.

— Not Me! —

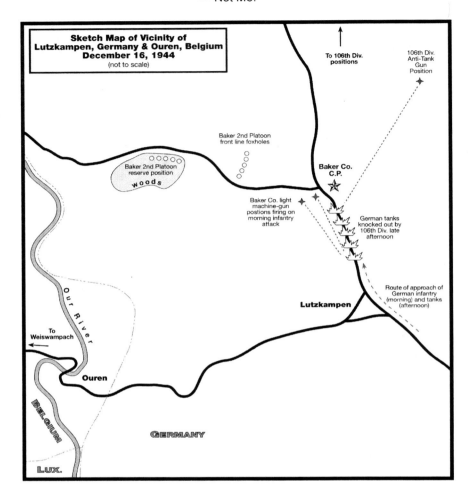

Somebody shouted "Let's get 'em!"—I think it might have been Gus—and before I knew it, the cold stock of my M1 rifle was recoiling against my cheek as it erupted and kicked back. I had never fired this rifle before and knew it might not be accurate, but the others around me were also firing and it was no secret where we were, so I had nothing to lose.

But my God, look! The instant I fired the man who had been shouting crumpled and fell to the ground! I had taken out a German soldier! But it was as though I was at a movie and it was happening to someone else. The paralysis of terror gave way to astonishment. *I* had made this happen! But then there was miraculous relief: the fire from our small group had been intense, and it had silenced ghastly machine gun and the enemy detachment were withdrawing to the rear! Whew!

I cannot from personal knowledge integrate this episode with the other events that happened during the morning, but nearby, a large column of German infantry had approached towards Baker's positions on the road leading out of Lutzkampen. What happened to them was seen by a number of my colleagues in Minnesota. A written account prepared by George Knaphus, who would later become the company's communications sergeant, provides detail:

> About 900-1,000 German soldiers emerged from the town of Lutzkampen. There was considerable shouting which surprised us. While there were only 150 of us, we had some advantage in that our two .30 caliber light machine guns were able to fire directly up the road into the mass of German soldiers. In addition, our first and third platoons (about eighty men) were also in position to fire from the right side as well as directly at the front of the advancing column. The killing and wounding were incredible. We did not count bodies, but a very conservative estimate would be 200-250 dead Germans. A group of four Germans overran one machine gun manned by Pfc. Robert Vanderford and he played wounded and when they passed by he shot them from behind ...

Cliff Hackett recalls what was apparently a different column of German infantry, but the results were quite similar. He and his assistant BAR man (he had a new one) were in their foxhole and saw the formation moving towards them up the open draw ahead of him in, of all things, close order march formation and with the men counting cadence. He unlimbered his BAR and unleashed a punishing automatic fire against the attackers from the cover of his hole, aided by his buddy with his rifle. The column idiotically kept coming forward notwithstanding the bodies—ultimately estimated at 30—that had accumulated before them. Cliff recalls that the men in the foxhole next to him were totally unmanned by fear and cowered helplessly in the bottom of their hole while this was going on. Many months later, he was awarded the Bronze Star for his actions on December 16.

No one knows for sure how many casualties were suffered by the

German infantry that morning, but they were huge. Nor can it be understood why the attack was so ill-planned or why it persisted so long. If they had had accurate intelligence as to our positions or had preceded it with artillery we would have lost many more. Even as things stood I had seen many of our guys crumple and fall.

Finally at some point during the morning the Germans regained a measure of sanity, broke off their attack and withdrew into Lutzkampen. A merciful period of relative calm followed, but for me it remains a blank. The onslaught had been so sudden and unexpected that I was emotionally devastated. I had never seen real combat before, and nothing had prepared me for its noise and chaos, let alone carnage on this scale. I was terrorized, bewildered, and at a loss to know what to expect next, but it would be worse.

At some time during the afternoon, well towards dusk, some very particular motor noises detached themselves from the general growling that had been going on all day and at last it was possible to identify them. They were the huge, black, obscene shapes of German tanks, and they approached up the road from the middle of Lutzkampen towards one of the farmhouses used by the company. There was a spattering of small arms fire in the area (I was a couple of hundred yards away to the west) and all of a sudden there was a horrendous detonation from the cannon of the lead tank and the house collapsed and fell inward on itself in a shower of sparks. A flame-thrower on the tank spouted a jet at the ruins, which burst into flame, and then at some GI's in nearby foxholes. It was inconceivable that anyone in the house could have survived. How fortunate I had been spared the luxury of its warmth!

But then, suddenly, there was a loud explosion at the side of the lead tank and it was on fire. For years it was my belief that it had been hit by a bazooka from one of the men in the nearby foxholes. (A bazooka was a rocket-propelled high explosive charge with which an infantryman could knock out a tank, but its maximum range was only about fifty yards.) It was not until our 1992 reunion in Minnesota that I learned what really had happened. The tank I saw hit was one of five that were destroyed by American counter-fire that afternoon at Lutzkampen.

It was our consensus in Minnesota that the immediate credit for the deed probably belonged to elements of the 106th Division to our north, but no one could supply the answer in detail. However, in the weeks following Charlie Haug pursued some leads by correspondence, and the blanks began to be filled in. Here is what we all found out.

The unit of the 106th that was to our immediate north was Company F of the 424th Infantry, two of whose members were Milton Schober of Skokie, Illinois, and Malcolm Lord of Denton, Maryland. The men of F Company were deployed in foxholes in the fringe of a woods overlooking and about a mile from both Lutzkampen to the south and the town of Grosskampenberg to the east. (Company F was clearly the unit to which we had been running our nightly liaison patrols.) At the edge of the same woods was dug in a 76mm (3-inch) anti-tank gun belonging to the 820th Tank Destroyer Battalion. The 820th had been in its position since before the 106th had relieved the 2nd Division. One of its members was Herbert J. Novatney of Stevensville, Michigan.

While the accounts from these men vary somewhat in their details, they are remarkably uniform in their explanation of what happened that afternoon. The anti-tank gun was manned by a crew which included a gunner named Paul C. Rosenthal, who drew a bead on the column of tanks as they headed west out of the center of Lutzkampen towards our positions. Rosenthal opened fire shortly after the lead tank had destroyed the farmhouse. Although the range was almost a mile, he hit the lead tank with his second shot, and then, to prevent the escape of the others, fired at the rear vehicle. Again his aim was deadly and in short order and with great coolness he had knocked out five of them.

Malcolm Lord recalls having talked to the Rosenthal the night before to try to persuade him to fire on a hay mow in the middle distance from which F Company felt sniper fire might be coming, but he refused to do so saying that he had been ordered to save his newly arrived, British made and rocket propelled ammunition for German tanks only. Says Lord, "Boy, were we glad he did!"

It is hard to overestimate the importance of the morning's slaughter and of destruction of this tank column, which belonged to the 116th Panzer ("Greyhound") Division. Not only were they knocked out but they then blocked the road for the approach of any others, and the presence of dragon's teeth to the north and south made the Lutzkampen road the only one for miles affording passage to the west for Manteuffel's armored units. It was a real coup, for it set back the timetable of the German attack by two full days and thus afforded the Allies vital breathing space to assess and prepare to meet the threat. Moreover, there was at the time absolutely no other way the panzers could have been stopped. As Cliff's history reports, there was no response to frantic calls from Baker to the rear for support from our own artillery or tank destroyers: there simply were no reinforcements or artillery shells available.

To the west of the smoldering CP was an open pasture which sloped towards the valley of the Our River three kilometers away. Somewhat later a group of us were being assembled there when we heard the usual warnings associated with incoming artillery, followed instantaneously by the most intense barrage which I would ever experience. Dozens of shells arrived virtually simultaneously to land within ten to thirty feet of me. Some of them were the dreaded "Screaming Meemies," the rockets known to the Germans as Nebelwerfer which made a terrifying howling sound in their approach.

It was already mostly dark, and the appearance of those shell bursts will never leave me. They were evil orange flowers with black smoky centers and tendrils of alternating white and black radiating from their centers. They were everywhere! We were in the open and totally unprotected. Instinct, instantly obeyed, had us hugging mother earth. I have no idea how long the barrage went on. We were obviously clearly visible to whoever was directing the German fire, because he had us dead to rights, and there were many who did not arise from the pasture.

That I managed to escape is mostly the product of dumb luck, but there may have been two other factors. First, an ability to communicate directly with God suddenly and miraculously arose within me and an urgent one-way conversation ensued. I don't doubt that many of those who did not walk away that afternoon must also have been on the same crowded wavelength and that at least some of them were more accustomed than I to contacts of the kind, so I don't really suggest that this was an operative reason for my survival. But I thought I'd at least mention it.

The second factor that may have proved somewhat more potent in promoting my salvation was my legs. Notwithstanding my terror and the multiple bursts close by, I managed to keep enough wits about me to tune in to that other wavelength: the rustling and whistling of shells that were on their way. After an eternity their intensity seemed to abate and there was enough interval between them to permit gauging their arrival. When the moment seemed right, I was up and away down the draw in the fastest crouch on record, interrupted more than once by clutching dives at the earth. Nor was I alone. Others were obeying the same impulse as I.

It was thus that a handful of us, still with rifles and at least some gear, were able to make our way down to Ouren, panting, bedraggled and emotionally spent. We reported in to our battalion headquarters and were detailed to some manner of guard duty overnight.

I have very little recollection of the next 24 hours. Apparently some portion of our company remained in the vicinity of Lutzkampen, because there is record of further tank attacks there on the morning of the 17th. Ouren remained comparatively undisturbed overnight but the next day orders were received at 1st Battalion headquarters to fall back the 4 kilometers to Weiswampach, which we did by riding in some of Baker Company's vehicles.

Meanwhile, notwithstanding the delay of the German timetable, the entire American First Army front was coming unraveled. The immediate objective of General Manteuffel and his Fifth Panzer Army, using the 560th Volksgrenadier Division as well as the 116th Panzer, was to force a penetration through our positions around Lutzkampen towards Ouren, where there were two stone bridges over the Our River which were deemed essential to permit his tanks to streak westwards toward Bastogne, a vital road junction on the way to the Meuse River. Other armored spearheads to the south had the same objective, and by its third day, the attack had cut our division in two. The 112th Regiment was shoved northwards against the 424th Regiment of the 106th Division, while the other two regiments, the 109th and 110th, were moved southwards. The result was that the 112th ended up playing a very different role over the next days than did its sister regiments.

For me, events took a most peculiar turn. According to a letter I wrote to my parents from OCS in France on 23 May 1945, after censorship had finally been lifted:

> The next afternoon [the 17th], we had to fall back to Weiswampach Lux., about 7 or 8 [sic] miles behind Ouren, where we spent the night. The next morning, the whole place was in a complete state of confusion, and after sweating out interminable hours in a foxhole, we finally got an order from our drunken S-3 [the battalion operations officer] to try to save the battalion vehicles.

Most of the details of what was obviously an angst-filled day at

Weiswampach have—mercifully, no doubt—been strained from my brain. I do have a memory of the captain who was the operations officer stumbling with a drunken grin out of a cafe, wiping his mouth with his sleeve and telling everyone within earshot to get in the vehicles and "Let's get the hell out of here," to which absolutely no one objected. With four or five others, I was ordered to get into a jeep trailer as a small convoy—six or seven jeeps and small trucks—headed back up the hill towards Weiswampach. At first I did not dare to believe it but we were actually heading due west, and the agonized tension that had gripped me for the past two days gave way gradually to intense relief as our small convoy distanced itself from the sounds of battle.

A bizarre safari then ensued. About fifteen from Baker and other units of the Battalion with my Platoon Leader, Lt. Peetz, were in the convoy. It was my lot to occupy the left rear corner of the trailer, a two-wheeled vehicle about four feet by five feet in size with sidewalls of about 18 inches, with no shelter whatever from the winter winds. Five or six other men shared this cramped, uncomfortable and frigid space as we drove through intermittent snow flurries for five days, our only shelter being ice-encrusted GI blankets held overhead to break the wind. Never mind! We continued to put distance between ourselves and all the noise and horror!

At about nightfall on the 18th we arrived in the snow-swept town of Bastogne, which was shortly to become famous as the scene of the encirclement of the 101st Airborne Division. That would not occur until just before Christmas, but the booming of artillery to the east was growing and to those of us who had experienced first-hand the devastating impact of the German tank columns, the night was a very uneasy one.

It was, however, a relatively warm one. After unfolding our stiffened bones from their contortion, we somehow found a corner of floor in a house on the town square (which I remember clearly but could find no likeness of in 1990), and managed to pass an uneventful night.

With the light of hindsight, I now know that there was logic in what seemed at the time mindless idiocy. The 112th by now had been attached to the 424th Infantry and other remnants of the 106th Division (the two northern regiments of which had meanwhile been surrounded by the Germans and which, with almost no resistance, surrendered) on the northern flank of the German penetration, and it was the aim of our hegira to circumnavigate its westernmost extreme and then to turn back east to reunite the company with its vehicles and men.

I did not know anything as to the whereabouts of the rest of the regiment, but I did pay close attention to our route of travel. On the next day, December 19th, we continued southwest to Neufchâteau, Belgium (which was the town to which the 28th's division headquarters had by that time retreated), and then hit the road again on the 22nd, each of us docilely taking the exact same location in our vehicles and traveling through Marche, Belgium, and then, turning ominously east again, just south of the large Belgian city of Liège, arriving at dusk at the town of Spa, having covered a distance of perhaps 150 kilometers.

Spa was a hot springs resort in the time of the Romans whose name has became generic for that type of center. It also served as the headquarters of the German Army and Kaiser during World War I. We spent a peculiar night there.

Until December 18th, it had been the headquarters of the American First Army, commanded by Lt. Gen. Courtney Hodges, to whom eight divisions including the 28th reported. Partially influenced by a false report of Germans in the area, the general had that day moved his headquarters (at the army level, quite a luxurious setup, usually) back about 25 kilometers to Chaudefontaine, so that when our ragged group of 112th Regiment stragglers arrived on the 22nd, all of the lush billets of First Army had been freshly vacated and were available for the taking.

One would think that this would have been a godsend to a shivering group of dogfaces. Well, it was better than a foxhole, but not a whole lot. First Army headquarters had been billeted in a château at the top of a low ridge which paralleled the main street of the town. My memory of it is distinctly Charles Addams-esque: dark crenelations of spiky stone looming against the night sky and cold and cavernous apartments within. The eerie motif carried through to include the inhabitants, as well. I was pressed into service to try to communicate with the chatelaine, a skeletal women of sixty years who looked down her nose at having to converse with a mere enlisted man and was in addition intolerant, insensitive and inhospitable. She at first refused to let us occupy her aerie. When it was made plain that this stance was unacceptable, we were grudgingly granted admission, but we could use no furnishings, would have to sleep on the floor, etc., etc. Her husband, a shriveled meekling, trailed behind trying unsuccessfully to execute her orders. We suspected, but found no proof, that they were German sympathizers. If they were, it would have been very atypical for the French-speaking Walloons of the region. In any event, we spent a cold and cheerless night there, for her attitude succeeded in making me, at least, feel uncomfortable. I found myself wondering whether my grandmother, who lived in a somewhat similar fortress of black stone and who shared our hostess's stern and humorless outlook on life, would have behaved similarly to men who had traveled half a world to liberate her country. I did not think so but was not entirely sure.

The encounter was, however, an eye-opening one for me, and its lesson valuable. It was my unfailing experience both before and after—and it applied even when we got back into Germany—that the farmers, peasants and townspeople who had the least to give were invariably the quickest to offer to share it, often eagerly and without having been asked. It took me a little while to understand that those who have little often instinctively recognize the need for their common good to share their meager belongings with others, even items as basic as food and shelter. On the other hand, while it was unusual for us to encounter privileged civilian personages, when we did we could almost count on being snooted by them in one way or another. We weren't even officers, after all!

We remounted our conveyances for the last time on my 20th birthday, December 23, 1944, and finally rejoined the remains of our company at midday in the small town of Beho, Belgium, about 20 kilometers northwest of Ouren. There we found that even when augmented by our fifteen-man force, Baker Company's strength had been reduced to about thirty-seven men and two officers.

Charlie Haug's 1949 memoir recounts in chilling detail how this had come to be. While we had been gallivanting around Belgium by jeep, the rest of the company (or what was left of it) had been pushed back to the northwest from the Our River and had been seared by encounters with the Nazi panzers in the towns of Beiler and Huldange, Luxembourg, losing many killed, wounded and taken prisoner. Only twenty-two men and one officer thus remained. Their fragment of Baker, together with other remnants of the 112th, had been successively attached to the 424th Infantry Regiment and then to the Seventh Armored Division, eventually ending up near the town of St. Vith, which would deservedly turn out to be almost as famous as Bastogne as an American defensive bastion.

During my six-day absence from the company, the extent and nature of the German penetration had gradually become apparent to the Allied command. While there had been one or two intelligence reports suggesting that the Germans might be plotting some sort of countermeasure, the tremendous successes of the summer and fall and the enormous German losses had so pervaded Allied thinking that these were brushed aside. A colonel who had a suspicion about what was about to happen was told he had been working too hard and was ordered to go on leave to Paris. Montgomery had been given Ike's blessing to go on a golfing holiday to England.

Not only was the offensive a complete surprise, but it was a day or so before SHAEF could be persuaded that anything more that local skirmishes was afoot. (If I'd been asked I could have told them!)

But by the twentieth, its scope and objectives had become fairly clear and countermeasures were initiated. Among these were a diversion of some of Patton's Third Army forces in the south from their eastern push, to strengthen the southern shoulder of the penetration; the release by Eisenhower of the only reserve forces in the theater, the 82nd and 101st Airborne Divisions, to help First Army fortify the northern shoulder; and finally, the issuance of a directive by Ike on December 20 that all U.S. forces on the northern shoulder should for the duration of the threat be transferred from the command of Bradley's Twelfth Army Group in Luxembourg City to the south to Montgomerey's 21st Army Group on the north.

Many chapters have been written about the scandalized reactions that this order provoked among the American commanders who were affected, principally Bradley and Patton, but the practical effect of it, so far as I was concerned (who of course knew nothing of it), was that the 112th Regiment was now under British command, rather than American, and my fortunes for the next few days would be very directly affected by a debate which was taking place between Monty, on the one hand, and his new American subordinates on the other.[12]

---

[12] Bradley blew his stack both at Montgomery's "tidying" comment (see below) and at the implication that he couldn't handle the situation. The controversy boiled on for a number of days and was not resolved until Ike forced Monty to apologize and Churchill spoke on the floor of the House of Commons to give full credit for the ultimate Ardennes victory to the Americans. It is just as well that we in the foxholes knew none of these goings on. Our reactions would
continued...

There is considerable controversy, some of it not resolved to this day, as to the wisdom of Montgomery's decision that the American defense of the town of St. Vith should be abandoned and that the units which had tenaciously provided that defense, which included the 7th Armored Division under Generals Robert Hasbrouck and Bruce Clarke, the 424th Infantry Regiment of the 106th Divison, and my own 112th Regiment, should be ordered to fall back to the north and west.

Monty first visited First Army Headquarters and, with the prickliness that always seemed to characterize relations between British and American brass, managed to offend the latter with his apparent arrogance, stating that he wanted the American forces withdrawn for the purpose, as he put it, of "tidying up the line." General Hodges and his staff at First Army, and Gen. Matthew Ridgway (destined for later fame in Korea and elsewhere) vigorously opposed any such withdrawals, taking the view that the forces that were in place around St. Vith were adequate to contain the Nazis. Monty at first permitted himself to be persuaded, and thus the effort to retain the town continued for a couple of days after the night of the 20th. On the 22nd, General Ridgway, an airborne commander imbued with the macho notion that ground once taken should never be yielded up, issued an order that the forces around St. Vith should permit themselves to be surrounded if necessary, and should then form a "goose-egg" defense. On receipt of this order, Gens. Hasbrouck and Clarke, whose forces were exhausted, did exactly as ordered but acknowledged to each other that what they were facing was clearly a "Custer's last stand," because fresh German troops, including the Hitler Begleit ("Escort") Division, were now known to be reinforcing Manteuffel's forces.

A fascinating insight concerning these high-level machinations—of which, I cannot repeat too often, I knew nothing at the time—has recently come to my attention in the form of a reprinted review of a biography of General Clarke published in 1974 under the title *Clarke of St. Vith*. The book quotes from a letter of that year from Hasbrouck to Clarke as follows:

I find it difficult to refrain from expressing my indignation at

---

...continued
without question have been disgust and blasphemy.

Hodges and Ridgway and my appreciation of Montgomery whenever I talk about St. Vith. It is my firm opinion that, if it hadn't been for Montgomery, the First U. S. Army, and especially the troops in the St. Vith salient, would have ended up in a debacle that would have gone down in history.

The book further quotes from an unpublished handwritten note from Montgomery to Clarke which says:

> I, personally, did not visit the Seventh Armoured Division; the situation in which the division was placed was reported to me by one of my liaison officers who had been there and had talked to Gen. Hasbrouck. As soon as I heard about the division, and about Ridgway's order, I went at once to the headquarters of the First Army, discussed the matter with Hodges, and ordered the division withdrawn. I instructed Hodges to inform Ridgway that I had canceled his order and to tell him I was not prepared to lose a very good American division because of the sentimental value of a few square miles of ground; men's lives being of more value to me than ground which is of no value. Ridgway never forgave me for canceling his order—so I was informed. His philosophy was that American troops never withdraw.[13]

And thus, the order had come down at the moment of my rejoining Baker for the 112th to withdraw behind the Allied line to the west. But there had also been a crucial footnote: the 112th and another unit were designated to serve as rearguard protection for the other troops that had been at St. Vith and who were to withdraw first. Even had I known of Monty's solicitousness for our well-being (which indeed appears to have been characteristic of the man and by no means limited to this one instance), I am still not sure that I would have been grateful to him, because the day which was now about to unfold and the rearguard activity which it would require of us turned out to be anything but a relief. Cliff Hackett's terse account puts it as follows:

On December 23rd, the company was on the road out of Beho

---

[13] *The Bulge Bugle*, Volume XIII, page 9.

when orders came to return and act as rear guard. We were deployed to guard three railroad bridges and the roads out of town. At about 1200 hours, the company received orders to move the road block to Rogery, Belgium [about 4 kilometers west of Beho]. While en route, we were fired on by German tanks and machine guns. The jeep was hit and [various named individuals] wounded and captured.

On arrival in Rogery, part of the company was deployed in the town and part dug in on the hill overlooking it; but our foxholes were barely started when a German spearhead, led by three tanks and command cars with motorized infantry approached the town. Because the Germans were wearing American uniforms and had some American vehicles, we were unable to identify the enemy until they were actually in the town. There was quite a bit of action in the street and then the tanks fired point blank up the hill, wounding half a dozen men. With nothing heavier than a BAR, which was no match for the tanks, our company was soon in wild retreat.

The events of that day are etched indelibly into my head. The only thing is, they don't match anyone else's recollection or the physical facts, and I was for a long time at a loss to reconcile the two. Here is what I remember:

We marched amid falling snow through a series of Belgian hamlets. Visibility was poor, and though the sound of small arms fire and cannon could be heard near at hand, I couldn't see much of what was happening, but it was clear that we were under hostile small arms fire; through the curtain of falling snow I could see men in our column falling to the roadway. There was considerable back and forth movement resulting from the countermanding of orders that we unhappily were used to and hated. At last the snow tapered off, and with the clearing of the atmosphere, the confusion seemed also to subside. We were in a substantial town, not merely a farming hamlet like those through which we had just passed. Cliff Hackett, Gus Gustafson (who was later to be promoted to sergeant and become the assistant squad leader of my squad when I became a staff sergeant and its leader) and I together with others were ordered to dig in to protect two bridges in the town below.

I can see the panorama in my mind: we were at the north end of a north-running ridge which sloped away before us to the junction of two rivers below, one of which ran north in the valley to our left, and the other of which joined it from the west in front of and to our left. Coming from the east, crossing a bridge over the first river before us and then running west along the north side of the second river was a highway. In the immediate foreground and to the right atop our ridge was a château, monastery or other substantial building which overlooked the town, just as we did. The distance from us to the road was perhaps a quarter of a mile, a long shot for a rifle. With us on the hill, however, was a 57mm anti-tank gun, a small artillery piece designed to be towed behind a vehicle, and we had been detailed to serve as infantry protection for it. (On the presence of this weapon my recollection, which is quite clear, differs from Cliff's, who states that we had nothing heavier than a BAR. The key to me is that it was the presence of the 57mm that drew the fire that was to come.) While the piece was denominated "anti-tank," it had long since been demonstrated that it offered very little threat to the huge and heavily-armored Tiger and Panther tanks of the Wehrmacht. It was in this situation that the Nazi column began to move from right to left along the road in front of us.

Our ignorance about what tanks sounded like—an ignorance which the army had done nothing to dispel in our stateside training—was by this time long gone, and so we had for some minutes been aware that armored vehicles were approaching from the east which were blocked from our view by the large building in the right foreground. We were naturally apprehensive and our eyes strained in the direction of the sound to assure we would identify its source the moment it came into view. And so it was with considerable relief as the column emerged from our right that we observed the familiar American logo on the side panels of the vehicles: a white star enclosed by a white circle. There was nothing about this column that led any of us suspect that they were not friendly forces. So we went on digging.

The first part of this column, after crossing the north-flowing river, turned left to enter the town while the balance of it continued westward along the road to our front. When the first group came near the men who were stationed in the town, the latter discovered the deception and immediately began firing. Those of us on the ridge followed suit forthwith, as did the anti-tank weapon, aiming at the column across the valley.

The anti-tank gun had fired no more than two or three shots in that direction when the German column let go at it—and us—with their cannons. The effect was frightening, concussive and disorienting. We were lifted from the ground and thrown back upon it, literally not knowing where we were, and certain that we were gravely wounded. And indeed, many were, those that had not been killed. The 57mm had sustained a direct hit and been torn to pieces, and its courageous crew, who doubtless knew that the odds were stacked against them, were all killed. Those of that survived were completely panicked, and large number of Baker men, totally lacking any effective deterrent to the Nazi armor, took cover in all directions as best we could.

The above account comes solely from my memory, unrefreshed by any extraneous sources. I have encountered two problems in squaring it with the topography of this part of Belgium and standard historical references covering the Ardennes Breakthrough.

First, the location and layout which I so vividly remember simply do not exist in or near Beho or Rogery. In 1990 (and certainly thus in 1944) neither of these bucolic hamlets was anywhere near as large as the one I remember as being spread out before me in 1944, nor was there any large landmark building, either. And finally, the lay of the land is totally dissimilar: while both towns are in rolling territory, it is open farmland without the ridge and valley topography which I have described.

Secondly, the standard historical references make no mention of a column of German armor disguised with American equipment being anywhere near Beho or Rogery on the 23rd of December. The two recognized texts, John Eisenhower's *The Bitter Woods* (Putnam, New York, 1969), and Charles MacDonald's *A Time for Trumpets* (Morrow, New York, 1984), both identify the attacking force as the Führer Begleit Brigade, an elite unit which had been responsible for guarding Hitler's eastern front headquarters, the "Wolf's Lair," but which was released for duty in the Ardennes when the Russians got too close to the Lair and Hitler moved his headquarters to Berlin. MacDonald goes into considerable detail in itemizing the Führer Begleit's equipment and says nothing about any American equipment or uniforms.[14]

There is plentiful documentation, on the other hand, of other uses by the Germans of American equipment and uniforms, and of English speaking troops so equipped, during the Ardennes attack. One such, a

---

[14] See MacDonald, pages 469-70 and 484; Eisenhower, page 358n.

Hitler brainchild, was the 150th Panzer Brigade, whose commander, also named by Hitler, was Lt. Col. Otto Skorzeny, a daredevil and charismatic leader who had caught the dictator's eye as the result of earlier escapades, most notable of which was his rescue of Benito Mussolini, the erstwhile Italian dictator, after Italy had capitulated. Skorzeny had organized and led a daring airborne capture of Mussolini from his Italian guards on a mountaintop redoubt where he had been held prisoner.

The masquerading unit's mission, again conceived by Adolph, was to attack in conjunction with an airborne force which was to be dropped behind Allied lines at the start of the offensive with the purpose of sowing distrust and confusion. As it happened, the airdrop portion of this scheme quickly went awry, and Skorzeny's force became a part of the conventional armored attack, still decked out as Americans.

There seems to be no question, however, but that the attack by Skorzeny's force had sputtered out two days earlier well to the north and east of Beho and Rogery.[15] Skorzeny himself was wounded on the 21st and invalided out.

I haven't the slightest doubt that my memory of the topography is a real one. (We were later, though I've not been able to pinpoint just when, at the town of Trois Ponts, which is on the Salm River a few miles to the north; both the features and the very name of Trois Ponts—three bridges—conform to my memory.) What seems to have happened, doubtless caused by the trauma of the event, is that my clear recollection of what happened in one act of the drama has been superimposed against the scenery of a later one. This at least is the best I can do to come up with an explanation.

On the question of the attack's being spearheaded by American equipment, however, there can be no doubt or confusion of any kind. There was general agreement on this in Minnesota. It is also supported by other documentation which has recently come to light.

One is in the form of the typescript of an interview with an officer of Company A of the 112th which was recorded on May 4, 1945, about four months after the event, at a camp for the American POW's in Moosberg, Germany. The officer in question, 1st Lt. Francis C. Smyson, stated that on the 23rd at "1630 an armored column approached Rogery from the southeast. Through field glasses it looked like an American column since

---

[15] See MacDonald, page 453, and Eisenhower, page 353.

it was led by a jeep and two American half-tracks." Smyson's account goes on tersely to refer to the fire fight which ensued and to his having been taken prisoner a few hours later.

Equally persuasive is the inferential support of a journal of the campaign compiled by the commanding officer of the Führer Begleit Brigade, Generalmajor Otto Ernst Remer. In his entry for December 22, he states that about twenty American tanks were put out of action and captured some of them "still completely intact" at Sart-lez-St-Vith, a few miles to the east. He also documents the loss of several of his own tanks and vehicles and complains of the lack of fuel because unexpected delays had led to its being consumed at a rate three times more rapid than had been anticipated. What could have been more natural than to make a virtue of necessity by replacing his own losses with the American vehicles which may even have had full gas tanks? But since masquerading as the enemy could raise grave questions of violation of the Geneva Convention it would not be something which an intelligent commander would ever commit to paper in his journal.[16]

Cliff Hackett's entry for December 24, 1944 states simply:

---

[16] Following the clash on December 23 involving my unit, the Begleit Brigade continued on to the west where it was involved in the fierce fighting to the west of Bastogne which continued for many days after the U.S. garrison there had been relieved by Patton's Third Army from the south. I have found no record of its having employed American equipment during this period and hence conclude that Remer found it convenient to rid himself of the incriminating evidence along the way.

A startling insight into Remer's character is provided in a book entitled Quest (Melchior and Brandenburg, Presidio Press, 1990), the account of an investigation conducted in the early 1980's by a twenty-year-old German student named Frank Brandenburg into the whereabouts and current status of prominent former Nazis. Brandenburg interviewed Remer at his home in Bavaria where he denied being one of the conspirators who had plotted Hitler's failed assassination on July 20, 1944, as was widely reported by other sources. To the contrary, Remer claimed proudly to have been among the first in Berlin to have talked personally with Hitler right after the event, to have been promoted to colonel in that phone call, and to have promptly carried out Hitler's order to round up the conspirators and hasten their executions. His vigor in doing so, he said, led later to his further promotion to general and to the command of the Begleit Brigade. This history seems altogether consistent both with Remer's illegal use of American vehicles on December 23, 1944, and with Brandenburg's revelation that in 1982 he was still an unrepentant Nazi and active as an organizer of a neo-Nazi political party. Quest, pages 83-95.

— Not Me! —

We split up into small groups and wandered through the woods and fields until, on December 24th, contact was made with the 82nd Airborne at Salmchâteau, Belgium.

That tells what happened, but even though my memory of those next thirty-six hours is far from complete, there is still a good bit more to tell.

The attack on the ridge was in full daylight, but it must have been late in the day, both because so much had happened earlier and because my next recollection is being in a woods at night. Cliff Hackett, Gus Gustafson and perhaps one or two others of us held a council of war to dope out the best way of regaining friendly lines now that we were behind the German advance. The armored column had not been further interested in us and had continued off towards the west and disappeared. We were all of us Pfc's, the lowest of the low, and there was no obvious candidate to serve as the leader of our group.

The plain course was to head west and perhaps somewhat north. We had no idea how close the nearest friendly forces were, but they had to be in that general direction. It also seemed prudent to try to travel at night rather than in the daytime to avoid as much as possible encounters with enemy forces. While this tactic would have the disadvantage of slowing us down, it had several compelling pluses.

First, none of us had retained a weapon; the onslaught on the ridge had been so sudden and the surprise so total the only instinct had been rapid escape, with the least possible encumbrance. Thus to be seen in daylight by any enemy force would be to put us at risk of being fired upon with no means of retaliation. Secondly, none of us had any very sanguine expectations of what a German prison camp would be like; it might be a lesser of evils but none of us wished to invite it. Finally and by far the most important consideration was what had happened in the previous week at Malmédy, Belgium, 25 kilometers to the north. I doubt that we were then aware of any of the details, but I know we had heard of the Malmédy Massacre, in which about 150 American prisoners of war had been herded into a field by a German SS panzer column and systematically mowed down by machine gun fire. It was thus imperative that the likelihood of contact with the enemy be reduced to the absolute minimum.

Moving through enemy-held territory at night was a new experience. True, we had run patrols at night in and about Lutzkampen, and they had served to sharpen certain skills, but we now reached new levels of heightened and intense awareness. I had a sense of becoming almost painfully conscious of all the data being transmitted by my sensory neurons: the sensations from my feet—was the ground hard or soft, was it snow, gravel or pavement? The wind and the odors carried by it—was it pines or farm aromas or wood smoke, and which direction was it coming from? The sounds—could they be identified, and were they hostile or friendly, near or far? And what was there to see in the sky and on the ground—if there were glimmers at ground level, might they mean Germans, or perhaps a Belgian farmhouse, where the probability of strict blackout might be slightly less?

All of this information was filtered through my super-honed senses, and almost without my being aware of it, various possible courses of action would be evaluated and the least threatening alternative would become clear. For example, the decision might be, "Let's move single file along the edge of that woods; be careful not to let yourself be silhouetted against the night sky; at the corner of the woods let's halt and see if we can figure out if there's anyone in the buildings that seem to be just beyond."

Something of that general nature is what actually did happen that night. We persevered for some hours, but of course we had little if any food and we were dead tired from the harrowing events of the long day. And so it came to pass that I found myself an advance party of one in the small hours of the morning to scout out the situation in a farmyard just below such a woods.

I crept forward as quietly as possible through the snow towards the entrance to the walled farmyard where I paused to try to decipher the meanings of the signals emerging from the courtyard. The aroma of the farmer's "fumier," the cherished manure pile which in those days was a measure of his prosperity, dominated all others. But there were sounds of movement too, and murmured voices. I strained to make sense of these and thought I could detect something that sounded like French. It was hard to be sure, because there was noise of beasts snorting and there is in any event enough dialect to rural Walloon to make it hard to understand.

There was nothing, however, which suggested any German presence, and thus emboldened I walked into the courtyard and said, "Je suis un soldat américain; y-a-t'il des Allemands dans l'environ?" What ensued took me totally by surprise.

— Not Me! —

The person I was addressing turned out to be an elderly Belgian farmer, short of stature and deep of voice. He refused to believe I was American, protesting that he had fallen for that kind of thing before, only to learn that it was a German way of finding out the sympathies of the populace and visiting retaliation on those who seemed too anxious to welcome "les Amis." He completely refused to be persuaded of my good faith.

It wasn't until his wife, who had been lurking in the shadows and now emerged, came to my assistance that the situation was resolved. She was much younger and cannier and could not have been quicker to offer the hospitality of her house to me. I told her there were others outside but that we would welcome any shelter whatever during the coming day. She took all this in stride and said we could bunk down in the hayloft above the stable.

I went to fetch the others and we all straggled into the courtyard and then, at Madame's invitation, into her kitchen for some rough, chunky brown bread and cheese and what passed in wartime for coffee. It would be scorned today, being made of acorns and God knows what else, but it was hot and delicious! After a few minutes, the guys went off to the barn and were instantaneously asleep in the hay.

I stayed behind to learn whatever I could about Germans in the vicinity. Madame was clearly the smartest of the four or five in the household, but as she stayed at home all day, her information came from her husband and a second older man, both of whom seemed to understand only dimly what had been happening in the last few days. All they seemed to know was that "C'est la guerre!"

Eventually I was able to distill that there had been many "Boches" and "chars" (tanks) earlier in the day but they had now all drawn off to the west and disappeared. Madame thought we would be safe in the loft through the day and if anything unusual occurred she promised to wake me immediately. With that, I too climbed up the ladder to the loft to the welcoming hay and the reassuring bovine and equine sounds and smells which filtered up warmly from below.

Although I seemed unaccountably to be in charge of our group, the thought of mounting guard did not occur to me, and as though I had been clubbed, I was asleep.

When we awoke, it was already late in the day. There was some additional palavering with the family, from whom I learned that there were thought to be some American troops across a broad river valley which lay to the west. Indeed, the shoulder patch worn by these men was described to us as being two large A's against a blue background. We knew what that meant. They were part of the 82nd Airborne ("All American") Division!

The U.S. Army in Europe had three airborne divisions, the 82nd, a parachute outfit, and the 17th and the 101st, which were partially equipped with gliders. As elite units, they brought a certain reputation and esprit with them even before they had entered combat, but both had been enhanced by their participation in the D-Day landings and in the airborne offensive in September, even though that had not been successful. They were an all-volunteer force (not me!) and were known to mere mortals like us as tough and aggressive and likely to shoot first and ask questions later. We were heartened to hear that there were friendly forces nearby, but extremely edgy at the prospect of having to cross their lines.

Madame had given us directions as the route best calculated to get across the river without having to expose ourselves. At the end of a north-running ridge we would come to a small hamlet and a bend in the river where it might be possible to cross unobtrusively.

After profound thanks and warm good-byes—Madame and I exchanged a hug and a kiss—we set off again through falling snow and gathering dusk along the low ridge toward the north. It took us several hours to cover the ground because we proceeded with the utmost caution, stopping every few moments to take our bearings.

There were only two incidents. As we approached the hamlet of which Madame had spoken we suddenly found ourselves on a hillside above but very near a semi-ruined farmhouse. The flickering light of a single candle was visible at eye level a few yards away through a shattered second floor window where a wisp of curtain was blowing out in the wind. Within, I caught sight of a scrawny old crone sitting up in bed and wearing a white nightgown and nightcap. I can see her to this day, with two strands of white mucous trailing from her nose to the bed covers, back-lit and shining in the candlelight. This pitiful sight stopped me in my tracks, but there was nothing any of us could do to help her and in any event we had our own compelling priorities to pursue. We moved on through the snow without a word, and I don't think she was even aware that we had passed.

We forded the river—it turned out to be the Salm, which was not deep, it had been too cold for that—and mounted the opposite bank. If we had been going slowly before, it was now at a snail's pace. I heard a clinking of metal a few yards to our front, and then the command: "HALT!" You can believe we did so! And then: "Password!" You can also believe I then did some fast talking: we were from the 28th Division, there were five of us; we had been cut off by a tank column the day before, etc., etc. Our interrogator listened to this with suspicion and then followed with some quick questions: Where do the Dodgers play? What date is Independence Day? And the like. Evidently we responded satisfactorily because the airborne soldier said they had been told to expect some of us. We were quickly hustled back to a battalion headquarters where the S-2, an intelligence officer, cross-questioned me for about five minutes about where we had been and what we had seen. Having satisfied himself, I was dismissed, and the five of us were sent back to a farmhouse where I wrote the following letter to my parents:

Dec. 24

Dear Mum and Pop,

Luckily I am able to write a V-Mail [a small photostat used by the Army to reduce shipping space] just to reassure you and let you know that "so far so good." The last week has been a hair raiser, but censorship rules that nothing can be told for two weeks, so you'll just have to tune in this time next week. Anyway I'm still eating three meals a day when I get them and am of sound mind and body. There isn't much I can say that might cause you to stop worrying, but let it be said that if I have gotten thru this far I can coast the rest of the way! I'm fairly sure the worst is over.

Your twenty-year old son feels it would be a little ironic to say Merry Christmas under the circumstances, but by the time this arrives, Happy New Year will be much, much more appropriate, n'est-ce pas?

I well remember the circumstances of the writing of that letter. The remaining fragments of Baker were at last in a position to savor the rest which had been promised by Montgomery. (We never knew that he had done so or that he had tendered his "Congratulations for a job well done" to those who had helped to hold the perimeter at St. Vith.) I was in the farmhouse behind the lines of the 82nd Airborne, tired but feeling warm and safe, which was a sensation both novel and luxurious. I wondered long and hard before I wrote it what I could say that would be truthful but not unduly alarming. But I hadn't the slightest inkling of how important that letter was to become to my parents.

Unbeknownst to me, and for reasons never satisfactorily explained, I had by this time I been reported "Missing in Action." I am not sure precisely when the telegram to this effect was received by my parents (according to one of my Minnesota colleagues who also was reported MIA, the telegrams were sent on December 17 and received on December 19), but the news was not printed in the Cleveland newspaper until Sunday, January 7, 1945. Its publication begot a flurry of no fewer than sixty-seven letters of sympathy mailed to my parents, which says a great deal more about them than it does about me, since I was personally known to only a very few of the writers.

Whatever may have been date of receipt of the telegram—it no longer exists—the date stated in it as that of my disappearance must have been December 23rd or earlier, because it was the receipt of my letter of the 24th which first gave them tangible evidence I was alive and well. But that letter did not arrive until about the thirteenth of January, and in the interim they were frantic with worry. My father contacted the army's Adjutant General's office, and even wired Col. Gustin Nelson, Commanding Officer of the 112th Regiment, to learn my status, from whom a favorable response was ultimately forthcoming, but not until long afterwards.

A peculiar wrinkle in regard to these inquiries, and perhaps a partial explanation of why I was reported missing in the first instance, is that they brought to light that throughout my army career to that time I had been using an incorrect serial number, 35543159. When my father used that number in asking about me, he was told that there was no record of any soldier having that number, and since virtually every personnel record in the Army was keyed to number, rather than name, tracing my whereabouts proved most difficult. It was not until February 23, 1945 that I learned that my correct number was 35055274. In a letter of that date reporting the correction I told my parents, "Changing serial numbers in mid-career is unheard of in the Army—you should have seen the startled expressions on the faces of the Co. clerks and officers."

An equally bizarre aspect of my "MIA" episode is how I first heard about it. Amazingly no one in the company ever told me I had been so reported. About February 2, 1945, when we were fighting in Alsace, I got a letter from John Ivan Sloan, my Cleveland dentist, who had seen the newspaper announcement of my disappearance and wrote to express his confidence that it would find me alive and well! In a letter home on February 6, I said to my parents:

> I broke half the furniture in the place getting closer to the light when I started to read Dr. Sloan's letter—it startled me so! I will write to him at the same time I write this to thank him, for it is a rare man who will write to somebody who probably isn't there.

As mentioned it appears that there were three of those who attended our 1992 reunion who were also reported missing at the same time I was, apparently on December 17. This suggests that every man in the company who was not physically present at the company's headquarters that morning—according to Cliff Hackett, ninety-five men—must also have been so reported. If this is the way it actually happened, then it is clear that the reporting procedure was both hasty and ill advised. Still, it seems odd that I recall no talk about it in the company in February when I first learned that it had happened to me.

It was in the February 6 letter that I referred to the regimental commander's having wired my parents that I was safe and well, for which I complimented him, adding, however, that "he is too bloodthirsty for my pacific temperament." I don't remember ever encountering Col. Nelson, but this characterization of him leads me to an observation concerning the hazards of life in the infantry. It was the universal viewpoint of every dogface GI that the dirtiest and most dangerous missions would invariably be assigned to his unit. It was always his squad (or platoon, company, battalion, regiment or division) that would have to take a patrol or lead an attack while the other squads (or units) were in reserve, or were given first crack at passes to Paris or whatever else was the cushiest deal at the moment.

The reason, it was widely believed, was that the "can do" unit was the most reliable, while the less effective outfits were allowed to sit on their asses! Loud protests and cries of anguish to this general effect would invariably be heard every time a risky mission was announced no matter to whom it was given. The times that one's unit was given easy jobs were regarded as only its just due and were thus immediately forgotten.

In the interest of completeness rather than that of flattering the writer, I quote here from the text of an undated "Certificate of Merit" awarded to S/Sgt. Alexander H. Hadden "In Recognition of Conspicuously Meritorious and Outstanding Performance of Military Duty" near Rogery, Belgium. This document came into existence long after the event and perhaps even after the war in Europe had ended. It reads:

> On December 20, 1944, when his unit was subjected to a vicious enemy attack, S/Sgt. Hadden with five other men were cut off from friendly lines. S/Sgt. Hadden immediately took charge and ordered his men to remain still. They stayed in their position until darkness and then S/Sgt. Hadden led them through the enemy encirclement until they located a friendly unit. No casualties were suffered to either S/Sgt. Hadden or his men, due to S/Sgt. Hadden's coolness and leadership ability. The courage and devotion to duty displayed by this soldier reflects the highest credit on himself and the Armed Forces of the United States.

The certificate was signed by the selfsame Col. Nelson. It contains three errors: first, the date should have been shown as December 23, not the 20th; second, at the time I was a mere Pfc., and finally, it is a considerable overstatement to say that I "immediately took charge." Apart from that, dispassionate analysis would have to conclude that it says very little more than that I was adept in beating a retreat, which Î would be the last to deny. It was eventually sent to me with the explanation that the text had been sent to higher headquarters in the hope that it would result in a bronze star, the lowest of the army's medals for bravery. Col. Nelson or his proxy decided—no doubt correctly—that it was not worthy of that honor.

Cliff Hackett's next entry, for Christmas Day 1944, says the following:

> The 82nd Airborne returned us to what was left of Baker Company at Rouge Minière, Belgium, Christmas morning. There, rations were enjoyed as Christmas dinner and the company rested and received the small amount of equipment that was available.

— Not Me! —

I have no specific memory of Rouge Minière nor even, come to that, of any particular sequence of events for the next three weeks as the Ardennes campaign and the 28th's participation in it played themselves out. But I do have clear memories of a number of events and developments.

For example, shortly after we returned to the Company, a large contingent of replacements was received. Rouge Minière was behind the lines in a reserve position perhaps thirty kilometers west of Salmchâteau, where we had waded across the river, and we were there or in similar positions nearby for about a week.

It was also time for the company to reorganize, and to incorporate the fifty-six new men into the various squads and platoons. Now for the first time it became noticeable that some of the new arrivals were retreads from other kinds of units who would not have been deemed fit for the infantry in earlier stages of the war. Many of them were in their thirties and I even remember one luckless refugee from an anti-aircraft unit (these were being disbanded wholesale because of the diminishing threat from the Luftwaffe) who was balding, tubby and over forty! He would suffer much in the next few weeks.

With the reorganization came the need to name new non-commissioned officers to replace the many who had been killed or wounded in the previous two weeks. It came totally as a bolt from the blue that I learned I was to be promoted to sergeant and to be an assistant squad leader. And then within only days after that—I don't remember why—I was again promoted to Staff Sergeant and squad leader, while Gus became assistant. Apart from the events of December 23rd (which so far as I knew were not observed by any of my immediate superiors) I can't really remember or point to anything I had done which would have led to my having been singled out from the others for the elevation. In obedience to the GI maxim, I never volunteered for anything (not me!), nor had I ever been conscious of any officer's having taken particular note of my existence, let alone my abilities. But it nonetheless happened, and I can only surmise that one of the senior non-coms—perhaps it was Slick, he and I got on well together—sensed that I might not make too much of a botch of it. It was known to all by this time that I was a stickler for being sure of our location at all times. I somehow would get possession of a copy of the current map, ordinarily issued only to the officers, and would keep it, well folded, inside my shirt with my dry socks. The maps were large-scale, contoured and in Belgium, at least, quite accurate. Possibly my map mania may have been noted as a plus factor.

As I recovered from my surprise I also found myself wondering whether I really wanted to be a sergeant. I was accustomed to being not far from the bottom in almost every pecking order in my lifetime, and being required now to tell other people what to do—no, ordering them—would not come naturally to one who had lived a lifetime of devout diffidence. On the other hand, during the five or six weeks of my front line experience, I had developed a quite clear sense of what steps were necessary to enhance my squad's chances of survival and also accomplish its designated objective. And finally, when the chips were down as they had been when we were behind the enemy lines, it had happened without my thinking about it that I knew exactly what had to be done and that those with me were prepared to defer to my judgment. And so before very long (indeed, it may have been a very short time) I decided I should give it a try.

The blessed interval of reorganization and respite came to an end on January 5, 1945, when the company received orders to mount an attack on the small Belgian town of Spineux.

According to the National Archives' official records (which as we have already seen need not always be taken at face value), the 28th Division remained in reserve or "holding positions" in Belgium throughout the first two weeks of the new year. This is somewhat at odds with the fact that our attack on Spineux took place on January 7. In the interest of enabling the reader to reach his own conclusion as to where the truth lies, I quote Cliff's full entry on the subject:

> After receiving rations and communications, battered Baker Company moved out and arrived at the outskirts of their objective, "SPINAUX" [sic]. The company attacked the town at 1500 hours on the heels of an artillery barrage. The Germans were taken by surprise while they were eating their supper—a bit of irony as they had caught us the same way. The attack gained 120 prisoners and so well was the attack planned and executed, only one man was injured. Lt. Saad Khalil was in charge and the entire success of the mission was greatly due to his leadership.

It sounds very much as though these events actually took place, doesn't it? Evidently a river of blood must run before rear echelon historians will acknowledge that a unit has been in combat. In point of fact, blood did flow, and some of it was mine!

My memory of this venture is like a faulty VCR tape: there are parts that are crystal clear and others that are garbled or blank. Again, I've had the benefit not only of Cliff Hackett's account but of the collective recollections of Charlie Haug and those at our two reunions. These agree that the operation culminated in a coordinated, all-out charge across an open field with bayonets drawn, on the heels of a friendly artillery barrage, resulting in the capture of about 200 German officers and soldiers.

My own recollections, however, center on the approaches to the town the night before rather than upon its ultimate capture the next afternoon. Our line of march was through a dense, snowy, Hürtgen-style, woods which was intermittently defended by Germans. There had been casualties on both sides during the afternoon including some caused by our own green replacements who, trigger-happy, fired mistakenly on our own guys obscured by underbrush ahead. Early on I reacted to fatal errors of this sort with outrage, but since I did not myself see this one happen (indeed, I didn't hear about it until the next day), I was able by now to treat them almost as hearsay about which I could do nothing, and I put it out of my mind.

That night the line of march of my small group took us along a path through the inky forest when we were suddenly surprised by small arms fire very near at hand. We of course immediately embraced mother earth as the firing, which included both rifles and a machine gun, continued. From the noise and the blinding white muzzle blasts there seemed to be a couple of dozen Krauts directly ahead of us. We, on the other hand, were only a handful and were, of course, fully exposed because there had been no opportunity to dig in. We held our fire because they had altogether the better of the situation.

In a lull in the firing, one of the Germans—he could not have been more than 20 yards away—began yelling "Kamerad! Kamerad!" It was totally clear that this was a ruse to get us to give away our locations. He had the machine gun and we didn't. After the briefest of pauses, there was a tremendous detonation at the top of my head, my steel helmet flew off to one side and I felt a biting wound like a bad bee sting on my right clavicle. Involuntarily I cried, "Jesus! I'm hit!"

I was totally disoriented. Gus Gustafson who was next to me took charge, rolled me on my back, retrieved my helmet and called loudly for the medics. It seemed as though the end was near. We were pinned down in a snowy Belgian forest and I was badly wounded. I needed medical attention immediately, and it was impossibly far away.

But then, miraculously and totally illogically, we were saved! For no apparent reason, the Germans fled the scene followed by heavy fire from our little band. And even more miraculously in light of the enormously concussive blow to my head, I began to realize that I was not badly injured. True, there was considerable blood which I could smell and taste if not see, but it appeared to be coming exclusively from around my shoulder, not my head which appeared to be intact. My shirt and jacket seemed to have been torn, however, and I could not quite figure out why. I suddenly felt extremely cold and started to shiver uncontrollably.

After that I remember nothing until the arrival of daylight the next morning when I began to reconstruct what had happened. A rifle or machine gun bullet had penetrated my steel helmet at a point in the center of my forehead at just below the hairline, but instead of then piercing the inner helmet liner (a lightweight plastic mold of the steel) as well as my head, it diverged upward plowing a furrow about half an inch wide and four or five inches long in both the curved steel and the plastic liner, finally exiting harmlessly at the back. When I held the steel helmet and liner up to the light and looked underneath, I could see daylight the entire length of the furrow! That the bullet followed a path between the resistant steel and the fragile plastic instead of piercing both the latter and my skull seems as much a miracle today as it did at the time. Both the sleeves and back of my field jacket and shirts were also shredded, bloody and totally beyond repair.

The reason that I don't recall the attack on Spineux which took place that next day was because someone in authority realized how shaken I was by the events of that night and decided to let me have a day's breather to rest and scrounge for replacement clothing.

For a few days after this episode I continued to wear the helmet, and was not shy in showing it to those interested, of whom there were many. Then all of a sudden with a shudder of revulsion it came home to me how close an escape I had had, and I couldn't wait to get rid of it. As for my shoulder, it was long my belief that a sliver of metal from either the bullet or the helmet had knifed through the five or six layers of clothing (how did it miss my ear?) and pierced my skin, leaving a half-inch scab and eventually a small permanent scar. In Minnesota, however, Charlie

Haug and one or two others were firmly of the view that the wound and the rips in my shirt were caused by other machine gun bullets. I cannot be sure which version is correct. In any event, if I had sought treatment at the hands of the medics, I would have been entitled to a Purple Heart (and later to five points towards the total which would entitle me to be returned to the States for discharge), but I did not think I should stoop to over-dignify what had come to seem quite inconsequential, though my buddies urged me to do so.

There is a footnote to the Spineux episode which I feel compelled to mention. It relates to an article which appeared in the Army's daily ETO newspaper, the *Stars and Stripes,* a few days after the event. The article's headline was, "Colonel Throws Book Away, Leads Men on Bayonet Charge." I quote its full text:

> Spineux, Belgium, Jan. 10—Col. Gustin M. Nelson, of Philadelphia, led a bayonet charge by a battalion of the 28th Div., across 250 yards of open ground to capture this town and more than 200 Germans, including a battalion commander and staff.
>
> "It wasn't the way the book said it should be done," Col. Nelson said, "but we had to have that town by night. When the men were reluctant to leave the shelter of the woods to cross that 250 yards, I knew they'd say if the old man can do it so can we. So with Lt. Col. William M. Allen of Bowling Green, Ky., I walked out where the men could see me."
>
> "They hit the town just as the artillery barrage stopped and we caught most of the Jerries in their holes," Col. Nelson remarked.
>
> Two privates of Co. A told the story a little differently. James A. Spence, of Pulaski, Va., and Harold Walter, of Cullman, Ala., described him as a "gutty old bastard" and said they never had to look far for the "old man" during tough going.
>
> Officers on Col. Nelson's staff also added that he wasn't happy when he was away from the fighting. They told of Nelson's taking a four-man patrol into Trois Ponts to clear Germans out of a house. The patrol had started out with a full platoon and a lieutenant, but when fire pinned the rest down the colonel took four men and wiped out a machine-gun nest.
>
> Col. Nelson's Regiment was hit by the initial German attack

Dec. 16 and held its line for two days before moving back. The men had been in the line three weeks when they made the attack.

"They're cold, hungry, tired—they'd been eating cold food and sleeping in the snow all the time," the colonel said, "but when I asked them to 'get up and get' they acted like they were fresh from a rest stop."

The article was greeted by the men of Company B with outrage and disgust. Few of us even knew who Col. Nelson was and fewer still had ever seen him anywhere, let alone in the front line. The last two paragraphs were the only ones with any connection to reality, and the third last paragraph was deemed by all to be as much pure bullshit as the rest of the article. It was our collective recollection in Minnesota that (as correctly stated in Cliff Hackett's entry) the attack was planned by Lt. Saad Khalil, a B Company officer who was both respected and liked, and that the actual bayonet attack on Spineux was led by two men, Sgts. Tom O'Malley and Bill Kleeman of B Company's third platoon. Neither they nor anyone else at our Minnesota reunions could recall seeing either of the two colonels anywhere near any point of danger. Perhaps they were somewhere in the background, but their leadership played no role whatever in the success of the mission. Nelson's stature in the eyes of the men was virtually nil to start with (if he had any it would have been more on the order of a pompous old windbag), and if any was left after Spineux, it was effectively destroyed by appearance of the article.

A belated footnote to the Spineux-Nelson incident came to light when I phoned Bill Kleemen in Illinois to verify from his own lips that he had seen no trace of the colonel at the time of the attack. Not only did he confirm that to be the fact, but he added that somewhat later towards in the closing days of the war Captain Farrar, by that time the company's CO, had invited Bill to accept a battlefield commission as a second lieutenant. Bill told Farrar that he would think about it and asked him what he had to do to qualify. The only formality, said Farrar, was to stand up in front of a company formation to allow Col. Nelson to pin his new gold bars on his shoulders. That made his decision easy, Bill said. "I'd be damned if I'd pay the old bastard that much respect!"

Bill concluded our conversation by adding that Nelson had managed to parlay this perjured account of his exploit into a Silver Star for bravery. Even fifty years after the event this revelation turned my stomach![17]

During this mopping-up period the weather had improved and we even saw the sun from time to time. We were attached to an armored division or they to us as we marched one day from nowhere to someplace else. The tankers enjoyed what to us was the wondrous cornucopia of 10-in-1 rations, which were packed in a large cardboard boxes the size of a soft drink cases and contained No. 10 cans of peaches and pears, delicacies as remote as the spices of Arabia to us eaters of C- and K-rations. As we trudged endlessly behind the smoky behemoths it occurred to some genius in our midst that it would be only fair if the tankers, who were so much safer and more comfortable within their carapaces and who were foolish enough to store the 10-in-1's on the outside of their tanks, should share some of this bounty with their less fortunate infantry brethren.

And so it came to pass that during one of the standard ten-minute-per-hour breaks in the march a full case of their rations made its way into our possession, and a few of us literally gorged for those ten minutes. I

---

[17] Some years back, I had the pleasure through mutual friends of meeting Andy Rooney of CBS "60 Minutes" fame, and more recently of reading his book, *My War,* in which he describes his experiences as an ETO combat correspondent for the *Stars and Stripes.* I found his accounts both interesting and impressive because they make clear that he and his colleagues often voluntarily put themselves at extreme risk to obtain and assure the accuracy of the front line stories they wrote. Because the Spineux story seemed so at odds with this concept, I wrote to Andy enclosing what I had written about Spineux, telling him that while those of us in the front lines were always glad to read the paper, none of us "believed a whole lot of what we read, especially so if the story related to something we actually knew something about," like Spineux. Andy was able to remember (as I had not) that the author of the *S&S* piece was his colleague Russ Jones, later a Pulitzer prize-winner, and he suggested that Jones might well have written accurately about Spineux, because those of us on the ground could only have seen a small part of the action, while Jones would have had access to a fuller picture. I remained firmly unconvinced, but to avoid any possible injustice to either Jones *or* Col. Nelson I wrote Andy once again in the final editing process, asking if there was any way he might now document his support for Jones' version of the events. He evidently had rethought the matter, because he replied very briefly as follows:

"To tell you the truth, Russ Jones' report is written in a hot air style of journalism that I dislike and mistrust but I know nothing at all about the incident. Id [sic] go with what youve [sic] got and if you think Russ Jones was wrong, say so."

I do!

arrogated unto myself a large No. 10 can of peaches and ate the whole thing, juice and all which finished me and peaches for the rest of the war and for many years to come. It also raised hell with my digestion, exacerbating my already chronic diarrhea. But it was a voluptuous moment which I'll never forget!

It was later during this same march when it was almost fully dark that I had my one and only close experience with a hostile German aircraft. With the skies clearer, we had seen sorties of our own tactical airplanes, fighters and small bombers on missions in support of our offensive ground operations farther east, but the skies had mercifully been devoid of anything even faintly threatening to us, and so it was a total surprise that night when our column was bombed by a German plane. The incident was over almost as quickly as it began. I was almost half asleep as the column slogged along when suddenly I heard a low-flying aircraft approaching from the front, and quickly—very quickly indeed—arriving right on top of us. Two bombs fell, one ahead of me and one behind, but both harmlessly, and then the plane was gone. It was dark enough that I was astonished that the pilot had seen us underneath him, but what was even more remarkable was the sound it made: it was a whooshing, swooshing noise totally unlike the sound of any plane I had ever heard. While we all remarked on its peculiarity at the time, it was not until much later that the news of the Luftwaffe's startling new jet aircraft became known and we were able to piece together that what had bombed us was in all probability a Messerschmitt 262, a low-wing, two engine craft which was enormously faster than any Allied plane. It was another of Hitler's technological gambles which came on the scene too few and too late to do him much good.

I have recently been put in possession of a copy of the mimeographed order promulgated by the Headquarters of the 112th Regiment on 16 February 1945 which officially proclaimed that the many soldiers whose names were listed were awarded the Combat Infantryman's Badge. About sixty names including mine (with my corrected serial number) are shown under the heading of Company B and as to all of them, the award is stated to have become effective on 1 December 1944, shortly after our arrival at Lutzkampen. Men from many other units in the regiment are also shown as receiving the award, but on later dates, some as late as February first. Plainly, the regimental clerk who was responsible for this paperwork was doing some catching up at a time when (in Alsace, as will be seen) our activities were somewhat less strenuous.

Until receiving this paper, it had been my impression that it had not been until well into January 1945 that those of us who had joined the 28th in the Hürtgen Forest and were still around—I would guess that of those 150 there were perhaps twenty percent of us left—were declared entitled to wear the CIB. Now I am not so sure; it may indeed have been in early December, as the order would appear to indicate. At this late date it is unimportant, but it certainly was at the time because the badge really meant something to us dogfaces.

It took the form of a light blue (the infantry's color) rectangle about three inches long and a third of an inch high with an embossed likeness of a Kentucky long rifle within and surrounded by a silver laurel wreath.[18] The criteria for award of the CIB were minimal: one had only to be at the front on duty status long enough for one's unit's official records to have recorded the fact to be entitled to receive it. As a result, it was subject to abuse by rear echelon officers who would cook up an excuse to come forward on a "mission" of some sort which would be officially noted, and a month later, after the paperwork had been completed, the award would be duly announced. All the same, apart from insignia of rank, the badge was the single and only one any front line GI would wear, and every one of us was extremely proud of it. At the front it distinguished those who had "been around" from those who were newly arrived. And in the rear areas it served to set the infantry soldier apart from the hordes of ComZ troops, of whom it is said that there were nineteen for every man in the front lines.

There was deep, bitter and abiding hatred in the heart of every combat soldier for what in a later war would come to be known as REMF's (with the RE standing for rear echelon). It was excruciatingly unfair, so we believed, that all those men, officers and enlisted men alike, should enjoy the comfort and warmth of the rear areas while we were exposed to the discomfort, danger and terror of the front lines. We could conceive of no reason why they should be blessed with what would prove in many cases to be the gift of life itself, while we should be condemned to men-

---

[18] The CIB remains to this day one of the most esteemed and coveted decorations in the Army. It is conspicuously present, for example, well above the other ribbons on the left breast of such officers as Norman Schwarzkopf and Colin Powell in their recent photographs.

tal and physical tortures as awful as any designed by Torquemada.

Well, the Combat Infantry Badge went some very small way towards evening the balance between us and them, but the injustice is one which still burns hot within me, and I shall probably have occasion to refer to it again before I have finished with these pages.

I have described the problem presented by the Army's failure to afford its replacement soldiers an opportunity to zero in the rifles newly issued to them as they joined their front line units. Two of the combat episodes I have described illustrate the point. The first was my baptism of fire on December 16, when we confronted the German infantry which had advanced through Lutzkampen ahead of their tank force. They had taken cover behind a hedgerow, and in spite of concern as to our accuracy and as to the risk that our fire would give away our location, we had fired on them at a distance of 200 yards or so. My aim was apparently good enough to have hit at least one, but if I had *known* that my rifle was accurate, I don't believe I would have experienced the misgivings which I remember so well at the outset of this encounter. The second occasion was the one in which my helmet was knocked off. In that instance, we were much closer to the Krauts, and because it was totally dark, it wouldn't have made a particle of difference whether or not our rifles had been zeroed in, since we wouldn't have been able to see the gunsights to aim through them. What would have made a big difference in that situation would have been to have a weapon that could have poured out a torrent of lead automatically, rather than as single shots from an eight cartridge clip.

As the days went by, I found myself pondering how to rectify this situation, and then suddenly the occasion to do so presented itself. One of the platoon's sergeants was being sent to the rear with trenchfoot, and he happily donated to me his Thompson submachine gun. As a machine pistol, it was not a weapon of general issue, but was one of which there were a few in the company. The officers and non-coms were allowed a certain latitude in their choice of weapons, and the Tommygun was held in high regard by its proprietors.

But it too—like most weapons—represented a compromise. It used .45 caliber ammunition, the same as the standard issue automatic pistol, which packed nowhere nearly the wallop of .30 caliber rifle ammunition. (While its projectile was smaller in diameter, the rifle cartridge carried a much heavier powder charge; it had a muzzle velocity of 2,800 feet per second compared with only 910 feet per second for the Thompson). Hence, the Thompson was virtually worthless for any distance beyond, say, 25 yards. A second disadvantage the importance of which I was to better appreciate later was that it was "blow-back" operated. When one pulled the trigger, the bolt was released and traveled forward towards the breech of the barrel, where a fixed firing pin in the front of the bolt would make contact with the percussion cap in the base of the cartridge, causing it to detonate. This meant there was an appreciable interval—perhaps half a second—between the pulling of the trigger and the firing of the round. Thus it was very important to anticipate the need to use the weapon.

What the Thompson could do, however, was to pour out the "torrent of lead" referred to earlier. It fired at a rate of 700 rounds per minute, which was comparable to its German counterparts, though not to their machine guns. It carried a 30-round clip of ammunition. To me, this advantage in fire power was well worth the compromise. Experience had demonstrated that by far the greatest risks to my continuing health from small arms were those which were near at hand, against which the Tommygun offered maximum protection. Accomplishment of the Army's grand strategies might be enhanced, it's true, if I were able to pick off enemy soldiers a half mile away, but this now seemed unimportant and in any event was impossible because our rifles had still not truly been zeroed in. So I made the switch, and was never sorry for it.

By the time the Ardennes battle was over, the sight of wounded, dying and dead soldiers had become commonplace. It had what at first seemed an unusual effect on me, though I later heard others comment that it affected them similarly.

The initial reaction was one of fascination: you stared at the corpse, noting its invariably awkward position, its gray pallor and sometimes its sickly sweet stench. But after a time, you no longer felt the need to do this; you would be aware of the object but had no interest in any detail. And then still later, there would be a conscious effort not to notice, although you never could really keep yourself from doing so. By the time this stage was reached, it was inescapable that among the dead you had been exposed to would be people you had known and had counted as friends. A psychological side effect of the process was that you started to shrink away from the making of friends.

It was not a case of being rude, or even distant. The process was more subconscious than a matter of calculation. It was simply that in the effort to minimize one's exposure to emotional, as well as physical harm, it seemed better to keep all relationships as impersonal as possible, and thus to be able to treat the loss of an acquaintance as not very much different than that of someone in another platoon, or even of an enemy soldier. There would be an occasion later when I would lose a buddy who was indeed a close friend, but in that case the friendship was formed back in the repple-depples and before the combat-formed defense mechanism had arisen.

As predicted, my account of the Ardennes campaign has been fragmentary, episodic and probably not even chronological. It also, I fear, falls far short of conveying any sense of the tactical (as opposed to strategic) significance of the events in which I was involved. But I don't think I could do that even if I had taken careful notes and illustrated them with photographs. It is not given the worm to observe, let alone comprehend, what even the lowly robin is up to.

On the other hand, the reader may say with some justice that the events I have described do not appear to have had any significant impact on the course of the battle. There are several responses to that comment. First, the vast majority of the succession of incidents in which I was involved probably did not have any such impact. Second, no individual infantry man can ever have such an effect unless he is in the exact right place at the exact right time, and happens into the bargain to be utterly heedless of his own personal safety (Congressional Medal of Honor winners Audie Murphy, WWII, and Sergeant York, WWI, come to mind) and I was not. Not me!

Third, there were times when the activities of my squad, platoon or company *were* significant. Lutzkampen and Spineux would certainly be two examples. There were no doubt other like occasions which—for whatever reason—I simply fail to remember.[19] Moreover, our mere pres-

---

[19] I have been surprised as I have been recording my combat experiences at the way my memory has worked. At one extreme are events and circumstances which I always have and always will remember clearly—for example the attack at Trois Epis, to be recounted later. On the other hand there are vast gaps of days, some of which I have no doubt were deeply traumatic, which are a complete blank and as to which no amount of prompting or refreshment seems able to ignite the slightest memory. It's as though I'd made these memories "go away." In the middle, however, is a large category of occurrences of

continued...

ence meant that there was a force on the battlefield to be reckoned with, and that was of itself a factor which influenced the tide of events.

Finally, it should be added before closing my chapter on the Ardennes, that the 112th Infantry Regiment played a very significant role indeed in defeating the German initiative. Its activities and those my own Company B (helped greatly by that antitank gun) at the start of the Offensive at Lutzkampen and elsewhere along the line on December 16, 1944 would certainly qualify in this regard.

As my fellow survivor George Knaphus has observed, "If there hadn't been a Lutzkampen, there would never have been a Bastogne!" In other words, if the German timetable had not been thrown off schedule for two days by our defense at Lutzkampen, the 101st Airborne would never have arrived in time to defend Bastogne.

The Regiment's efforts in and around the town of St. Vith would be another example. While St. Vith ultimately fell to the Germans for a short time, the delay resulting from this defense permitted the 82nd Airborne and other Allied units to come into the line to the north and ultimately to choke off the German advance. The 112th's role in this effort resulted in its being awarded a Presidential Unit Citation (it specifically emphasized my own First Battalion's doings on 23 December), and considerable publicity at home, which I later learned was pridefully noted by my father.

My letters home during this period were notoriously uncommunicative, for the reasons explained in one dated December 30, 1944:

> If this letter doesn't say much, it's because your son is very much confused by the whole thing, and doesn't know what to write. The main message is, as usual, that I'm always thinking of you, when I have time, that is, and praying that this [the end of

---

...continued
which I was unaware at the outset but which come magically back to life either after being described by others or, more usually, by having myself focused on a particular time or place and finding that recollection blooms and sometimes even opens the doors to other rooms which now themselves become clear. And then of course there is another category which is all mixed up: I seem to remember clearly but very confusedly, as for example Rogery and the events of December 23, 1944. I find myself wondering how much might come back to me if I were to undergo, which I am not about to do, deep psycho-analysis.

the Ardennes offensive] means the end of the whole damned affair.

And in another letter dated January 13, 1945, the following:

I'm now licensed to tell "combat experiences" two weeks old, but I doubt whether you'd find them very amusing. I just hope that what few letters I have been able to write have been reaching you fast enough to keep your anxiety within endurable limits.

Of course when that letter was written, it would still be three weeks until I would learn that I'd been reported MIA!

One thing I did mention was the horrific effect the war had on the civilian population of Belgium. Those in the path of the German onslaught, having finally after four years been liberated from occupation and able at last to pick up some semblance of normal living were once more cast out of their homes in the dead of winter to stream pitifully towards the west with whatever primitive conveyances they could lay their hands on: baby carriages, farm carts, bicycles and gas-less automobiles towed by oxen. Worse, they were often such an impediment to military movements that there was no choice but to force them into the ditch, making even this meager transportation useless. It simply could not be helped.

Triumph and Tragedy, the last volume of Winston Churchill's monumental six volume treatise on World War II, puts my experience in the Ardennes Offensive in a somewhat different perspective. Churchill's discussion of it aggregates a scant twenty-two pages of the six thousand comprising the total work. The space which I have devoted to it here no doubt exceeds Churchill's proportionately. But you may be sure that its psychological and spiritual impact on me was very heavy indeed and that I emerged from it a very different individual than I was when I went into it.

While Baker Company's active participation in the Ardennes campaign had drawn to a close by the middle of January, the efforts of the Allied Armies, principally the American First and Third, did not finally restore the front line to its position of December 16th until about January 28, 1945. Indeed, it was almost the middle of January before the Germans were fully dislodged from around Bastogne, although the siege encirclement had been lifted just after Christmas. The Bastogne battle in and of itself resulted in over 15,000 American casualties while the overall figure for the entire campaign has been estimated at 76,000. These are large figures, but the conclusion reached by virtually all commentators is that notwithstanding early criticisms of Eisenhower and Bradley for their decision to hold the Luxembourg frontier so thinly, the Ardennes battle in the last analysis was a colossal German defeat. It represented virtually the last time that the Wehrmacht was capable of offensive action because by the time it was over, the bottom of the barrel had been reached in relation to tanks, planes and the manpower and gasoline to operate them. The war would drag on for four more months until the western Allies and Russians would meet in the middle of Germany, but it now once again became believable that total victory was just a matter of time.

Such, at any rate, is the perspective offered by hindsight. It was no doubt also the view of Allied strategists at the time. But for those of us in the "Bloody Bucket" the future which was foreseeable was much closer at hand. Ordinarily it was only a day or two away, or, if one was anticipating a three-day pass to the rear, say, it might extend as long as a week. But it never was as long as four months! And for those of us with this limited vision, the perspective was very different.

The National Archives' Suitland, Maryland, Reference Branch contains a variety of hit or miss (mostly the latter) documents pertaining to the 28th Division's activities during World War II. One document, entitled "After Action Report" for the division for the month of December 1944, shows that it lost 206 officers and 4,557 enlisted men (of which 3,509 were listed as MIA's). The same document goes on to say:

> In the middle of January, CT 112 [combat team, consisting of the 112th Regiment, plus other reinforcing units] rejoined the division after being released from attachment to the XVIII Corps in the First Army Sector. It was found to be in excellent condition though 700 under strength. They had received reinforcements during their absence in sufficient quantities to be kept at reasonable strength and morale was high. Because of this fact, the rehabilitation of the 112th Infantry offered no unusual problems, and it will not be mentioned again in this report.

This text appears over the one word signature "Cota," whom we have already identified. He is almost certainly not the author of the report, who no doubt was an underling staffer. While it might be possible to agree with this wizard that a unit 23 percent under its usual manpower was "at reasonable strength," one cannot help but wonder how he concluded we were in "excellent condition," and that our "morale was high." Use of such asinine phrases says a lot about the writer and almost nothing about his subject.

The fact of the matter was that like those of the division who had survived Hürtgen, we who had joined it after that battle could now also be fairly stated to be "demoralized." I don't mean that we were moping to the chaplain (standard GI advice to those who complained too long and loud was, "Why don't you go see the padre and get your shit ticket punched?") or that we were refusing to perform our duties. But what had been brought home to me with stark and inescapable clarity was that the war was far from over, that the Germans remained a wickedly dangerous foe, and that for every day which I survived, the likelihood of my being healthy when the war was finally over was inexorably diminished. Indeed, when I pondered as I often did the many narrow escapes I had already experienced and the seeming certainty that the war would not be over until the Russians and Americans shook hands in the middle of Germany, I became convinced that I would become a casualty, most likely a dead one.

I wanted passionately to survive. I railed against the monstrous unfairness of all those who had combined to put me where I was. They of course included Hitler, and while I did not for a moment doubt the justice of the Allied cause, I was in no way inclined to make fine distinctions between the politicians who were and who were not responsible for my plight.

Yes, they included Hitler, but they also included Roosevelt and Churchill and the legions of their subordinates—my superiors—who were part of the system which decreed that the way to solve political problems was to put guns in the hands of men who had no responsibility for creation of the problems and require them to kill each other.

It was Roosevelt and Churchill, after all, who had been responsible early in America's participation in the war for the decision that the only terms on which it would be ended would be unconditional surrender by the Axis powers. Was it not self-evident that such a policy made it unavoidable that the Germans would have to fight to the bitter end? Why hadn't it been made clear instead that if the Germans were to oust Hitler and unequivocally renounce his policies of territorial aggrandizement, racial intolerance and despotism, the Allies would be prepared to negotiate terms?

To have failed to do so seemed to be nothing more than an ego-trip for these leaders, to whom the phrase "unconditional surrender" without question had a wonderful macho ring. But while it spared them the need to cavil over terms, it was on my back that it was being done!

The subject tormented me at the time and has continued to concern me as I have revisited it in the writing of this book. As a result I have devoted some attention to a review of the historical record in an attempt to learn whether my perception of it in 1945 was an accurate one. The results of these researches have been incorporated in Appendix 2 to which the reader's attention is directed if he shares my concerns. Suffice it to say here that the evidence is ample that if the policy had been only slightly softer, an armistice could readily have been concluded at least by 1944 year end; that no fewer than 200,000 in American casualties would thereby have been avoided in 1945; and that most important of all, a very different post-war picture might very well have emerged. Viewed from a somewhat different angle, the policy was born of the fatally flawed views of the two western leaders, especially Roosevelt, that their forces of leadership and personality could effectively control Stalin's appetites, and that it was therefor unnecessary to take any steps prior to the end of the war to assure the establishment of an economically viable and independent Germany. Seen both from this distance but plainly visible then, this is utter nonsense!

It would have made very little difference to us in January of 1945 if we had known that we really were right in our clear perception that the continuation of the war was senseless and unnecessary. The anguish which resulted from the perceived injustice could not have been any greater. What did matter as we reorganized and attempted to assimilate the many new bodies assigned to Baker Company was that *our* war was not over and that there was little prospect of its being so within the limits of our vision. We were physically and spiritually depleted. There was not a one of us who was not nursing one or more ailments that would have taken us to a doctor or a hospital in civilian life but which now had simply to be suffered in silence. The specter of injury or death had not only not retreated but loomed ever larger.

— Not Me! —

How we felt could be read in our faces. The readiness to laugh was gone, replaced by a sullenness that is inescapable in the photos and newsreels of the time. We had become "seasoned veterans," a phrase in common use by the journalists of the day, but it didn't mean quite the same thing to them as it did to us.

— Not Me! —

nce 'Missing,' Hadden Is Safe

Pfc. Alexander Hadden, 20, reported "missing" on January 6 by the War Department, was same on January 25, date of a letter received today by his parents, Mr. and Mrs. John A. Hadden, 2787 Fairmount Blvd., Cleveland Heights. Also, he has been promoted to sergeant.

Sergeant Hadden is a member of the 112th Infantry, cited and decorated by Major General Courtney Hodges for holding the line and destroying a German column at St. Vith in the early days of the Rundstedt offensive. Sergeant Hadden wrote in his letter that he was quatered in a wine cellar, where the regiment was still in action in the Belgium salient.

Sergeant Hadden attended Milton Academy in Boston, Mass., and was attending Yale University at the time of his induction. He has a brother, Pfc. John A. Jr.

PFC. HADDEN

Clipping from the *Cleveland News*, January 1945.

— Not Me! —

Photo of author taken in Belgium, Winter 1945, and sent to Suzanne and René Bucaille in February 1945 and returned to the author in Carentan, France, August 1990.

Alsace

The Colmar Pocket

January 17-February 19, 1945

SPINEUX was our last participation in any combat activities in the Ardennes. The 28th Division did, however, receive replacements during the month of January consisting of no fewer than 99 officers and 4,059 enlisted men. Large as they are, these numbers still fall short by 107 officers and almost 500 men of bringing the division back to full strength when stacked up against our December losses.

It provides yet a further perspective to observe that the vast majority of the 3,509 soldiers reported missing in December must—unlike me—clearly have remained as such. Many of these would have eventually been confirmed to be POW's, but that would not have been known for many weeks.

During the three day period from January 17 to 19, 1945, the entire division executed a motor convoy movement from Belgium and northeastern France to Alsace, the country's eastern-most province, 200 miles to the south.

Alsace for centuries had been a bitter bone of contention between France and Germany. It was a German province after the Franco-Prussian War won by the Germans in 1871 and remained such until the end of World War I in 1918, when it was restored to France by the Treaty of Versailles. Then again in 1940, when Hitler's legions overran France, it went back to Germany and its young men were drafted into the German Army.

In the fall of 1944, as the Allied armies were pursuing the Wehrmacht towards its homeland, the principal thrusts were in the north towards the industrial Ruhr, and by Patton's Third Army through Lorraine and northern Alsace towards the Saar Basin. As we have seen, the effect had been to bypass and ignore the Ardennes between them. Very much the same thing was true of the central portion of Alsace to the south.

The eastern boundary of Alsace is the Rhine River, which has created an extraordinarily fertile fluvial plain lying between the Vosges Mountains to the west and Germany's Black Forest to the east. The plain averages about 30 kilometers in width, and the two mountain ranges face and are remarkably similar mirror images of one another. The valley floor in this area is about 700 feet above sea level, while the summits of the easternmost range of the Vosges rise to 2,500 feet and above. The mountains are analogous in form and appearance to the Green Mountains of Vermont, typically with rounded and forested crests.

While the alluvial plain is devoted to a variety of agricultural crops like wheat and corn, the dominant crop of Alsace is that of its vineyards, for it is in the foothills of the Vosges that are grown the famous varietal grapes such as Gewurztraminer, Riesling and Sylvaner. I knew nothing of this in 1945, but I was about to learn some basics.

In Alsace, American forces had reached the Rhine both north and south of the small city of Colmar, but they had found it convenient not to disturb the substantial German forces which had fortified themselves both in that city and, with much artillery, amongst the wooded crests of the mountains to the west. The resultant circular salient extended north, west and south of Colmar with a diameter of perhaps thirty kilometers. It was no doubt inevitable that the map mavens and headline writers would call the area the "Colmar Pocket."

The problem of the Colmar pocket was complicated by yet another of Hitler's personally directed initiatives. As the Ardennes offensive had been unfolding, it had become apparent to the Germans that a principal defense against it would be the diversion of substantial elements of Patton's Third Army from the southern front to attack the German flank at Bastogne and elsewhere. This, Hitler reasoned, would unavoidably weaken Patton's forces which were pushing towards the Rhine, which in turn suggested that a diversionary attack towards the French city of Strasbourg and beyond towards the Colmar pocket to the south would require the Americans to shift forces back from the Ardennes and thus once again enable the German forces there to make progress.

The resultant offensive was called Operation NORDWIND. It was launched on New Year's Eve with a force of several divisions and caused a considerable flap in the Allied high command when, without informing Gen. Charles de Gaulle, the French commander, Eisenhower issued orders to American Gen. Devers that he should withdraw from Strasbourg to maintain the integrity of the American line. De Gaulle flew into a rage because of the dire consequences to French morale and citizens if this should happen. As it turned out NORDWIND fell short of reaching Strasbourg, so the command crisis was averted, but in the meantime nothing had been done by the Allies to reduce the Colmar pocket. To the contrary, to take some of the Allied focus off Nordwind, the Germans within the pocket had begun counterattacks which had actually enlarged it.

To rectify this situation, the 28th Division, which had borne the brunt of the strategic neglect in the Ardennes was now to do much the same in Alsace.

I remember the afternoon of January 19th with great clarity. As an exalted non-com, I was now entitled to occupy an upholstered seat with springs in the cab of a 2½ ton truck, and I accordingly had a view of the countryside as the convoy groaned down the steep and narrow mountain roads towards the Alsatian plain. The town of Kaysersberg, our convoy's destination, registered indelibly. At the entrance to it stood a tall medieval clocktower astride the village street and the convoy passed beneath it with barely enough room for one vehicle at a time. The streets were cobbled and the gabled, half-timbered houses leaned out over the street towards each other. I had seen pictures of such quaint and charming towns and wanted badly to absorb more of this one. It was not to be, however; at least not for another forty-five years, by which time the main road had been detoured around the town, leaving the village street through the clock tower to the tourists and villagers.

The convoy proceeded inexorably through to the far side of the town, where it stopped and we were ordered to alight. It was now late afternoon and the light was fast fading as our company turned to a side road where signs pointed to the town of Sigolsheim, five kilometers away. Sigolsheim would be my home for the next two weeks.

Both Kaysersberg and Sigolsheim were typical of the wine-growing towns of which there are several dozens in the Alsatian foothills. Since the grapes grow best where there is assured drainage, the towns tend to be either at the toe of the foothills, like Sigolsheim, or 100 or 200 feet higher, as at Kaysersberg. They are typically only three to five kilometers distant from each other, and they are totally dedicated to the growing, fermenting and vinification of grapes and to the distillation of fruit brandies ("eaux-de-vie") as something of a by-product.

Under cover of darkness we marched into Sigolsheim, where we relieved another American unit. The 28th was now attached to the French First Army, which had come into being at the time of the Normandy invasion and was composed of the former Free French forces organized by Gen. Charles de Gaulle in England and elsewhere during the occupation, and which had been armed and supplied by the Allies.

I do not doubt that Sigolsheim had been as attractive a village as Kaysersberg before the war. Now, however, it had been almost totally leveled. It was a town of perhaps fifty houses in the center of which there remained as the only ruin more than one story high a church tower pockmarked with artillery and small arms fire. Some of those in Minnesota recalled that there were several priests living in the crypt of the church, but I don't remember seeing or hearing of them. In any case, the town appeared to be totally deserted.

As I was not to learn until 1990, it had changed hands three different times during December 1944 and January 1945, first when it was liberated by the French, later when it was retaken by the Germans about January first and still later in mid-January when it was retaken by the American troops whom we were now relieving. It is no wonder that it was largely rubble when we arrived.

Cliff Hackett's chronology describes our experiences of the next two weeks as follows:

> We arrived in this shell torn village with its ruined vineyards on January 19, 1945. Heavy snows, cold weather, intense artillery and mortar fire along with hostile combat patrols made the next twelve days very miserable.

I don't doubt the essential accuracy of Cliff's characterization, but I don't so much remember the misery as I do a number of specific happenings.

On first arriving, my squad was housed in the basement of a large house the upper floors of which had been razed by earlier bombardments. I described it as follows in a letter dated January 25th:

> War is a beautiful thing! We are installed in the wine cellar of

what was formerly the home of a rich vineyard owner. The walls are lined with 100 gallon kegs of the most wonderful ambrosia I can remember having sampled since Aunt Betty's Rhine wine became family property. [My elderly aunt had died shortly before I left the States and the contents of her large cellar had been dispersed among my parents' generation.] Consolations are few and far between, but right now I could take on the whole German army single-handed!

My whole squad, now virtually at its full complement, was housed in a single large cellar. It was about 30 by 40 feet in area with the ceiling fully 15 feet high. The "kegs" (more exactly casks, "tonneaux" in French) were themselves 10 feet in diameter and must have held, if full, much more than 100 gallons.

It will have been noted that I was not a stranger to alcoholic beverages, but in spite of the worldly reference to my aunt's cellar (which, if the full truth were known, had largely spoiled), I knew virtually nothing about wine. We had never drunk it at home, and while the joys and evils of champagne as a party drink had been experienced, the notion that still wines were ordinarily to be enjoyed as an accompaniment to food was alien to me.

We were all quite tentative at first in tasting the stuff. But it was clean and dry—words which would not have come to my lips in 1945—and slid down easily, and after a day or two of experimentation in which it became clear that the stuff was not contaminated, it did so in generous quantity. Indeed, in short order it supplanted water in uses other than as a beverage.

There was plenty of water in Sigolsheim, too much in fact. Floor level in our cellar was well below grade. About five feet of the headroom of its heavy masonry was above the ground, with ten feet or so below the ground, and the result was—the temperature hovering around freezing as it did—that there were from two to three feet of water in its lowest levels. We were using heavy trestle tables, no doubt used for wine tasting or "dégustation" by tourists in peacetime, as sleeping places, and every few hours it would become necessary for bailing parties to man a bucket brigade to assure habitability for another interval.

But the watery oversupply had an unpleasant aroma, and few of us wanted to use it for any hygienic purpose whatever. Sure, we could have put halogen tablets in our steel canteens, but that was like drinking battery acid. It thus wasn't long before it was discovered that a little Riesling on one's toothbrush made a marvelous dentifrice. A few of us even experimented with using it to wash hands and face. Things were a little sticky when it dried, but the wine's alcoholic content actually did lift grime away!

It did not necessarily follow that we all went around stoned all day long, though no doubt a few of us did. As Cliff's note makes clear, there was serious business being transacted, both by the Germans and by us. Ours was the manning of listening posts to our front, which faced to the southeast towards Colmar, about 8 kilometers distant. Sigolsheim's situation was flat; it sat at the very edge of the plain with its back to a low ridge which overlooked the town and tapered down to the plain about a kilometer to the northeast.

Just why this site was picked by the brass as an appropriate one for a forward outpost never became clear to me. We knew that the Germans were installed in large numbers not only in Colmar and in other towns and positions to our east and south, but also in the foothills and mountains to the southwest. These latter vantage points enabled them, as we soon learned, to place artillery with pinpoint accuracy on any movements which we attempted during the day, and significant casualties resulted. Thus we became nocturnal animals, much as at Lutzkampen, burrowing during the day time and emerging mostly at night.

The outpost that was my squad's responsibility lay directly to the east, a few hundred yards to our front. It consisted of a shallow bunker three or four feet deep and ten feet wide with dirt piled up along its edges and logs and dirt laid on top for protection against artillery. A slit between the logs and the ground afforded vision to the southeast but not to the south. This would shortly prove to be a mistake. There was room for a three-man observation team, and that was how we customarily manned it. The drill was for three of us to leave the town at dusk and take up our posts in the bunker, where we would maintain watch through the night.

Two of the men maintained watch, while the third curled up in the covered portion of the bunker to sleep, though the situation was anything but restful. The Krauts employed so-called harassing fire, meaning that artillery and mortar shells would fall at odd intervals both in and around the position and along our line of march to and from it. Not only was this dangerous, but it created a troublesome communications problem. The difficulty was that our connection to the platoon CP in town was maintained by a so-called voice-powered phone, which meant that the energy generated by the spoken word would be converted into an electrical impulse which would be transmitted over a wire laid on the ground between us and it. This wire would be cut by the artillery two and three times a night, whereupon one of us would have to schlep back towards town running the wire between his fingers until he found the break, which could then be spliced. This happened so many times that eventually splicing was no longer possible and the whole thing had to be re-laid. The need to patrol the wire was irritating at best but it ended up being infuriating because we all recognized that it eventually would mean that someone would get hurt. It was also a disturbance of one's normal entitlement to ordinary peace and quiet![20]

That normal entitlement to peace and quiet was also much curbed by the constant awareness that German patrols were in the vicinity. There was a farm road through the vineyard to our left running back towards town. The view along the road was unencumbered, but there were vines to its north as well as directly in front of us and to the south. As the minutes ticked by and one stared at the murk, it was almost impossible not to conjure up human forms among the grapevines which moved in the wind against the snowy background.

I don't myself recall actually being disturbed by any German patrols, but of the fact of their presence there can be no question.

As we wound up our stay in Sigolsheim an event took place which shook me up badly. My closest friend in the infantry was a lad named Emerson Hazlett. Em was from Kansas, had attended the University of Kansas at Lawrence, and was a fellow alumnus of the ASTP. We both had come over on the *Mariposa* and had progressed together through the repple-depples. He had even become a squad leader and Staff Sergeant at the same time I had. The thing which drew us together most, however, was that we shared the same need to discover the ridiculous in the people and events around us. Since we did not lack for candidates, we had much

---

[20] It had to have been in Sigolsheim that I first got to know George Knaphus, then Baker's Communications Sergeant and now a professor of botany at Iowa State University. George was and is a buoyant man of great warmth and personality, and the phone wire was naturally a matter of vital concern to both of us. Yet it was not until my re-acquaintance with him at Baker's 1992 reunion that my memories of him were rekindled.

to discuss.

On the night in question, Em and a couple of his men had the duty in the observation post, while my group remained in the luxury of the cellar. The night seemed unremarkable. There was the usual intermittent artillery, and for a time the usual routine of a phone report from the outpost every half-hour was fulfilled by calls stating that there was nothing to report. Then, however, the line went dead. Since this was more usual than not, no one thought anything of it for a time. The time lengthened, however, and eventually we became concerned. A patrol was finally sent to investigate, and in due course it reported back that all three men in the outpost were gone!

We nursed hope for a time that they might have gone off to pursue a Kraut patrol or had otherwise left their post for sufficient reason and would turn up soon, but after a couple of hours the conclusion became inescapable that they had been taken prisoner.

Even then, I couldn't believe it. It seemed impossible that such a thing could happen to Emerson. He and I had often discussed the things one could do to limit the risks of combat and I knew he saw things exactly as I did in this regard. The only thing I could imagine which might have brought about his capture was an approach by a German patrol from a blind side of the outpost to the south. When I was on duty I often stuck my head out the back of the bunker to check in this direction; the approach would have to have been across a small stream and through the grapevines. It had not seemed likely, but it was at least possible. And so I consoled myself that something of the sort must have happened to Emerson and his men. But I didn't know then and didn't find out until our 1992 reunion in Minnesota when Emerson related that there really was not much to explain. He had been the one who was sleeping when the Krauts snuck up through the vineyards to the south and got the drop on his two men. "It was all over before I knew it was happening," he says. [See Appendix 3.]

Why did it make such a difference to me? Well, I suppose it's because if it had happened to him, it could so easily have happened to me, too. I don't know whether it was this or the disappearance of a good friend that bothered me the most. Together, they were a real blow and it was many days before my depression began to abate. I kept telling myself that the worst that could have happened to him was that he was a POW, and that helped a bit.

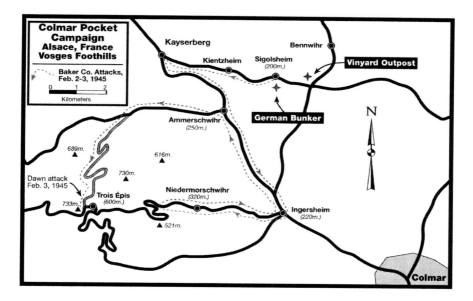

Confirmation that Emerson had indeed been taken prisoner did not come for several months. I finally got a letter from him when I was in Berlin the following July. The letter also included the information that he had lost thirty pounds (off a frame that was not a rugged one to start with), but he was on his way home and otherwise in good health. I breathed a sigh of relief!

The flooding problem in our cellar persisted, and after several days of rain, a portion of it became uninhabitable, with the result that a number of us were forced to find quarters elsewhere. We moved up the street to another cellar. The owner of this establishment was clearly not as prosperous as the proprietor of the first one because it was considerably smaller and not dug quite so deeply below street grade. That, of course, was its virtue; it was comparatively dry, though our only roof was the floor of the first story, and the rain leaked through. This room, too, was lined with wine casks. Their dimensions were smaller than in our first abode, but the contents were just as drinkable.

One of the most distressing experiences of the entire war befell me here. By some miracle, I had come into possession of two fresh hen's eggs. I think they were part of a larger find that had been shared out with the others, because I remember that these two eggs were clearly mine and mine alone. A veritable river of saliva surged into my mouth as I began my preparations. There was a small fireplace—jury-rigged, I'm sure—in our cellar, in which I kindled a fire. I'd somehow scrounged some butter or fat in which to fry them. I put it in the bottom of my mess kit, put it on the fire, and with infinite care cracked first one egg and then the second into it. God, they were gorgeous! They quivered, glistening in the pan as the butter curled at their edges. The aroma was overpowering; I hadn't smelled anything so delicious for months!

And then I became aware of that familiar whooshing sound of an approaching shell. I dove for cover because I knew it was going to be close, and it was! It detonated somewhere in the upper wreckage of the house with an awful crash which rattled and shook the entire structure. None of us in the cellar was even scratched, but as I picked myself up cursing at the despicable Kraut artillerist who had the gall to interrupt what was virtually a religious ceremony, I cast my eye at the pan on the stove. Judas, what a disappointment! My two beautiful eggs were covered with hundreds of bits of dirt and plaster which had been knocked from the ceiling by the concussion. The eggs were inedible and had to be thrown out! It was like losing a member of the family!

Towards the end of our stay at Sigolsheim our platoon was ordered to send out a daylight patrol to take German prisoners. We did not know it at the time but our division was shortly to undertake offensive operations to close out the Colmar pocket, and the purpose of the patrol was clearly to find out from prisoners details of enemy positions and strengths, etc.

Cliff Hackett's chronology states that the patrol was under the command of 2nd Lt. Harold Schilling (I barely remember him) and consisted of ten of us. He says, "The patrol killed nine Germans and wounded six others without losing a man, but no prisoners were taken." Those numbers are not within my memory, but the patrol itself surely is.

Its focus was on a large bunker occupied by the Germans in the open vineyards about a half mile to the south of Sigolsheim. The bunker consisted of a large mound of earth ten or twelve feet high and stretching about thirty feet along the south bank of the same stream which farther east ran next to the outpost from which Emerson Hazlett had been taken prisoner. Several of us were to approach the bunker from the north or front, while another group led by Gus Gustafson was to come in from the west. We actually did what we had all seen depicted in Hollywood treatments of World War I, that is, synchronize our watches so as to assure as much as possible that we'd arrive at the same time.

The plan was for both groups to utilize the stream bed as cover and thus to escape observation by enemy artillery. The stream was really not much more than a small brook, with banks no higher than four or five feet, but it must have served its purpose because I don't recall any artillery, at least not as we were approaching. Gus and two or three others were to attempt to get behind the bunker to my right before discovery of our presence, get the drop on its occupants and force their surrender.

It almost worked that way. My group had crossed the stream and arrived directly in front of the bunker about fifteen feet from it when suddenly Gus loomed up thirty feet away on my right at the west end of the bunker aiming his BAR towards its rear and shouting "Kommen zie aus!" or the equivalent in pidgin German.

At the same instant, a helmeted figure rose up behind the bunker directly in front of me with a rifle aimed right at my head. I had put my tommy gun to my shoulder when I'd seen Gus draw near, and I instantly pulled the trigger. The time interval between that action and the bolt's reaching the cartridge seemed endless. The man I was aiming at elected not to fire—or perhaps his weapon malfunctioned, I'll never know. In any case he started to duck down behind the earthwork just as my weapon fired a burst. I had aimed slightly below the line of snow which lay on top of the bunker to be sure I got him and to counteract the natural tendency of the Thompson to pull up when fired.

As this was happening, all hell was breaking loose at the right end of the bunker. The Germans had plainly elected to fight rather than surrender because Gus and his cohorts were blazing away at them with everything they had. My guys had joined in to lob grenades over the top.

Now, however, the artillery did chime in with a vengeance. It started to rain down both on us and the bunker occupants without distinction, and we immediately hightailed it out of there back into town, where the artillery pursued us and kept at it to punish us for our temerity.

One aspect of that episode deserves a further comment. It was invariable that prior to any pre-planned patrol such as this one I would be almost overcome with anxiety and dread. In prior instances, the dread of anticipation had always been followed by terror in the midst of the event. But somehow, by the time I got to Alsace, I had undergone some sort of metamorphosis. The apprehension in advance was every bit as bad, but for some reason the fear fell away when the action started, and I even found a sense of outrage boiling up inside me that seemed to roar, "Pour it on!", and that was exactly what I felt when I let fly with my tommy gun. It was a considerable satisfaction to get the later casualty report because I was confident that one of them was mine, and as before, I felt no remorse whatsoever.

I don't really understand why my fear was overcome by a thirst for blood, but it may have been in part due to Gus Gustafson. I never saw a more fearless guy in my life nor one to whom leadership in combat came with such ease and grace. He was a dark-haired slender guy with a quiet manner and a ready smile, but he was a very private person and I never felt I got to know him very well. Aggressiveness seemed alien to his character in most situations; for example, I don't remember his ever volunteering for any hazardous missions. But, boy, when he got such an assignment, he ran it to perfection. It would be an overstatement to say that he relished combat action, but he did derive a very evident satisfaction in doing dirty jobs well. Maybe a very little of this spirit rubbed off on me.

On January 31, 1944, the 28th Division carried out the execution by firing squad of Private Eddie Slovik, who had been a member of G Company of the Division's 109th Infantry Regiment. This occurred at Ste. Marie-aux-Mines, France, a few miles north of our location at Sigolsheim. Slovik had been court-martialed for desertion, based on evidence that he had twice abandoned his duty posts in combat engagements of the Division prior to Hürtgen. The execution was ordered by Gen. Eisenhower after careful personal review of the trial record. It was the only instance in 40,000 desertion cases and 2,800 trials in which the death penalty would be carried out. Indeed, it would be the first time in eighty years that such a penalty would not automatically be commuted to life imprisonment. According to David Eisenhower's book *Eisenhower at War* (Random House, 1986), his grandfather was concerned about the large number of desertion and self-inflicted wound cases and particularly so in the case of the 28th Division in which many such cases had arisen. It is not surprising, given this historical context, that the decision should turn out to be a controversial one. The book reports that in a survey conducted among commanding generals in the European Theater slightly more than half felt that the penalty was not essential to the accomplishment of their missions, while a minority thought the penalty "proper."

Obviously its purpose was to serve as a deterrent, which makes it odd that it was not publicized outside of the 28th Division. Within the division, however, it was required to be made known to one and all, which ordinarily would be done by the commanding officer of each unit reading the decision to his men at a formation called for the purpose.

I have no recollection of any news of the Slovik execution being communicated to us in Sigolsheim. There was, of course, no way that a formation could have been convened for the purpose, but copies of the order may well have been circulated. That I don't recall it is scarcely surprising because it would have been meaningless as a deterrent or otherwise to me or to any of those of us who had now been in combat for three months. In that period we had all been presented with dozens of opportunities when the company was on the move to slip away unnoticed and to join the estimated 10,000 deserters (the equivalent of a full division) who were known to be hiding out in Paris. The forces that held me to my unit were many and complex, but fear of death at the hands of a firing squad was not one of those which had had any part in keeping me from straying.

Cliff Hackett's chronology relates the following about our departure from Sigolsheim:

> Baker left Sigolsheim on the 2nd of February and went through Kientzheim and Kaysersberg to Ammerschwihr where the 1st Battalion assembled to attack the town of Ingersheim. Baker spearheaded the attack through the endless vineyards and were constantly hampered by sniper and accurate mortar fire. By the time we reached Ingersheim, thirty men had been killed or wounded. The town was reached about 1730 hours and taken with practically no opposition. The Germans had pulled out leaving only a handful of men as rear guard. The town was secured that night.

The events of that day are, I think, among those which I have almost deliberately repressed. It was one of those seemingly rare occasions on which my unit, in this instance my platoon, had been designated as the company reserve and hence followed behind the other two platoons as they advanced through the flat vineyards towards Ingersheim. I remember marching and countermarching—we must have covered 20 kilometers that day to cover the route Cliff describes—and I also remember mortar and machine gun tracer fire coming from the dominating Vosges foothills to our right as our column proceeded southeast towards the town. This fire was, however, directed at our leading elements rather than us, and because it didn't involve me, I shut my mind against it; I simply didn't want to know about it and especially about the casualties. But the next two days, February 2nd and 3rd, were indeed memorable.

It started out with more marching and countermarching. We headed west from Ingersheim back to capture the small resort town of Trois Epis atop one of the Vosge mountains at 2,000 feet of altitude. Ingersheim is a near suburb of Colmar, and the direct route from it to Trois Epis was thus the main road from Colmar. It led through Niedermorschwihr and then wound up the mountain with many hairpin turns which were directly under the eyes of the Germans in Trois Epis. Company A of our First Battalion was leading the march, and it got in trouble with mortar and artillery fire. As a result, we were ordered to march back down the mountain and to go up the back road to our objective. This approach was from the north by way of Ammerschwihr, which added another few kilometers to our travel.

This route is today a blacktop highway, but in 1945 it was a forest trail, which the Germans had obstructed by felling trees across our way. It was steep and it was dark, and it was a very long night indeed. In a departure from the usual practice, we were told well in advance what the plan was: Trois Epis was thought to be well fortified by SS troops and we were to attack at dawn with a bayonet charge into the center of the town.

It was commonplace to bitch about never knowing what was going on but for once I wished that I'd been kept in the dark. Bayonet charges were nothing I wanted to hear anything about, and the climb up the mountain was thus torture not only physically but mentally. We finally reached the top about midnight and were fired upon when we arrived, so we dug in as best we could and waited fearfully until daylight.

When the first rays of light appeared, we found we were in a pine forest on top of a rounded hill, with some buildings visible below about a hundred yards away through trees and clearing mist. By the time the order to fix bayonets was given, I was more frightened than I have ever been before or since and shaking almost uncontrollably. But again it disappeared instantly when the cry "Charge!" rang out and we all ran down through the woods and into the town square, screaming like bloody banshees.

It was over almost before it started. The Germans were on the run, and while there was some firing at us in the course of the attack, it was not very effective and only one of our company was killed, while twenty Germans were captured.

Almost as memorable as the attack was what happened next. When the dust had settled, the Catholic Fathers and Sisters of the Abbey above the town greeted us warmly, offered us bread and milk and invited us to a special mass in our honor and in recognition of their liberation. We all went into the Eglise de Notre Dame, a tiny, jewel-like church in the center of town to partake for a few moments of the peace and sanctuary of the singing and the service. It was like entering a different and lovely world, even though firing could be heard still from the outskirts of the town.

I have learned only recently that the one American who was killed caught a sniper's bullet as he stood guard at the church doorway while the rest of us were inside!

I was quite astonished on my return to Alsace in August 1990 to discover how few residents of Sigolsheim and Trois Epis could be found who had been around in 1945. The town had been spared heavy bombardment and when our attack was over, its enthusiastic civilian inhabitants were many. I did eventually find two old-timers with whom I could share experiences. One was a lady in Trois Epis whose name was Mme. de Mangeat, who both now and then was involved in the operation of a restaurant named Mon Repos, which was where I found her. She remembered the day vividly and with great nostalgia. She said:

> What a glorious day! We knew you were coming and the Germans of the SS knew you were coming. There was a 'Route Forestière' which forks to the left into the woods off the road from Ammerschwihr about one kilometer below town—that's how you came up. I was here with my husband and little daughter, age one-and-a-half. There had been much bombing and artillery, and we hid in a cave nearby, and it was just at the cave entrance that we saw our first Americans. Oh, how happy we were! ... Thank you for coming to free us!

In Sigolsheim we had a long and wonderful luncheon with a man named Bernard Dietrich, a native of the town who had been with the

French First Army forces who first liberated the town in December 1944, and who had also made the same long climb up to Trois Epis as I had on the night of February 2, 1945 and had participated in *its* liberation the next day. He had even visited with Mme. de Mangeat that very morning and had allowed her small daughter to sit on his knee, whereupon she went "pi-pi." The daughter, now in her mid-fifties, has been forbidden to sit on Bernard's knee ever since!

Bernard's wartime reminiscences were fascinating, as were the comments of his wife Martha; their experiences during the German occupation explain a great deal why many Alsatians even today detest the Germans. Those interested are invited to peruse the entry in my travel journal for Monday, August 27, 1990.

Only the shortest of time was allowed for the savoring of the joys of liberation, and before midday we were hustled to our feet again for a hike down the mountain to take yet another town. As Cliff's account points out, we had now gone without sleep for forty-eight hours, and had not even had a resupply of K rations!

This now caught up with me. My letters home through the winter had mentioned pharyngitis—an exotic name for a chronic cold and sore throat—but it now flared up and was accompanied by a fever. By the time we got to the bottom of the mountain I could scarcely put one foot in front of the other, and I was ticketed for a trip to the hospital.

I was packed aboard an ambulance with three other men, each of us on a stretcher, two on the top and two on the bottom. The trip took a couple of hours; the hospital was in the town of St. Dié, Alsace, about forty kilometers to the west. One of the patients was a case of battle fatigue. I had been exposed to other men who had sort of "come apart at the seams" and lost emotional control in one way or another. I had seen men whose wounds were with little doubt self-inflicted (e.g., shot in the foot from above), but I had never been in extended contact with a lad like this one.

He was a beardless teenager, soft of countenance and slight of build. He was strapped in the stretcher over mine—I'm not sure whether it was to protect him from the rigors of the rough road or to restrain him from injuring himself. But he kept rolling back and forth in uncontrollable restlessness, all the while chanting to himself in a whining, sing-song voice a repetitive refrain that went something like this: "I can't take it anymore. I can't stand it. I can't stand the sight of blood. I don't know why; I never could. Even when I was a little boy, it made me sick when I cut my finger. Please help me. I've never been able to stand pain. When I had to go to the dentist I would cry before he even touched me. Oh, I'm so ashamed! I can't stand it any more. I want my mother. Oh, please, please, someone help me," and on and on.

My initial reactions were a mixture of curiosity, sympathy and then amazement, but very quickly, it became embarrassing and painful to listen to him. Finally he sobbed himself to sleep and I was left wondering what to make of it. His emotion seemed altogether genuine, and there was no question that he was disabled from functioning as a soldier in his present condition, but I still had and have the lingering suspicion that his monologue was more calculated than spontaneous. Well, I never saw him again and will never know.

At St. Dié, I was installed in an upper bunk in a ward with perhaps twenty others who, like me, were sick and needed some rest. It was pure bliss to be warm, dry, clean and safe (I am not sure which of those represented the greater luxury) and to be able to sleep as long as I wanted.

I had been there only a day or so when I and others from Baker Company had a visit from our company commander, Captain Russell Farrar. My prior contacts with him had been few and I have no particular recollections of any of them, but he was a wonderful man and was revered by everyone in the company. The very fact that he would leave the company to travel forty kilometers to look in on his sick and wounded men tells much about him. He was one of the infinitely small number of officers who genuinely cared about their men and strove constantly to do the very best job for them, while at the same time managing to get the military job done. There is an inherent tension in any combat command responsibility, since one knows that it will be necessary to order men to do things which will cause injury or death to some of them. Thus it is a rare man who can retain both the affection of his men and the respect of his superior officers. Captain Farrar was such a guy.

In any case, it was evening and I was dozing in my upper bunk, not really wanting to be disturbed, when I became aware of his presence, checking on and talking softly with other men of the company. Eventually he came to my bunk and stood quietly looking at me. For whatever reason—maybe it was because I still felt feverish, or maybe because he might want to talk about coming back to the company—I didn't feel like mustering the energy to talk to him, and I continued to feign slumber. He stood there for a few moments and then raised his hand to my forehead to brush the hair away from my eyes. He remained for another moment and then moved away.

I have always been sorry that the conventions surrounding the relationships between officers and enlisted men never afforded the opportunity to get to know Capt. Farrar better, nor, unfortunately, even the occasion to say thank you. I have recently learned that he died of a heart attack in 1990 after a career as a bank executive in Long Beach, California.

I was in the hospital for almost two weeks, doing absolutely nothing, I am sure, to accelerate my release from it. It was during this period that the mix-up regarding my serial number came to light, and I also corresponded with my dentist and parents concerning being listed as MIA. One passage from a letter dated February 7th is of interest:

> I have an idea that it is going to be a little hard to settle down after the war to college, or whatever I may decide to do. The past six months have been unique—something has always been happening. I've been going somewhere, or meeting new people—new countries, etc., and I don't know how I'll like to sit down with no shifts of scenery for six months at a time.

Mussolini is said to have remarked that "War is to men what childbirth is to women." Another formulation of the thought is that of Robert E. Lee: "It is well that war is so terrible—we should [otherwise] grow too fond of it." Well, what the hell, I was only a twenty-year-old kid, and had not developed a talent for epigram.

I mentioned that the murder, mayhem and misery of the Ardennes had been disposed of by Winston Churchill in only twenty pages of his history of World War II. His treatment of the Colmar pocket in its entirety is as follows:

> The first task was to clear the enemy from the Colmar pocket. This was completed at the beginning of February [1945] by the First French Army helped by four American divisions.

I guess I should be glad that he mentioned it at all.

Back Into Germany and to the Rhine

My Shooting War Ends and I Am Alive

15 February-6 April 1945

I finally returned to Baker Company on February 15th, remarking in a letter home when I arrived that "I got sick at the wrong time... for since I left to go to the hospital, the Company has been doing nothing but sitting around in the soldier's pastime of doing nothing."

For the next month or so, we moved and marched many, many miles. The first segment was a trip by truck to a town near Toul, France, where we stayed several days before embarking by forty-and-eight's back to Aachen, Germany, where the division was attached once again to the American First Army. The Allied push towards the Rhine was now well under way, but the 28th's mission, whether by design or accident, became one of "cleaning up pockets of resistance," in the journalistic phrase. It really involved subduing and rounding up German soldiers left behind by the advancing armored columns.

Unlike the days of active combat where because of censorship—both official and my own—my letters spoke of almost anything except what was really happening to me, this period is much better described by what I wrote, rather than what I remember, which is really not very much; in my mind it is mostly one big kaleidoscope.

From Aachen we started to march. We marched down roads, we marched across fields, we crossed rivers on bridges and at fords, and we marched through the Siegfried Line, which by this time housed only remnants of the German Army waiting to be taken prisoner. It was an astonishing work of engineering: camouflaged concrete emplacements with interlocking fields of fire, interconnected by a honeycomb of tunnels and guarded by formidable fields of dragon's teeth, the pyramidal hunks of reinforced concrete to prevent the approach of tanks.

We spent one night in a German pillbox for lack of better shelter and were appalled by the conditions we found inside. Dank and dripping to start with but with all manner of discarded small arms, ammunition and filth, including human waste deposited by men who obviously were afraid to go outside. What we did *not* find was much in the way of permanently emplaced armament, such as cannon and anti-tank weaponry. I learned a great deal later that during the winter of 1943-44 when Hitler had made Erwin Rommel responsible for fortifying the Channel coast of France in anticipation of the coming invasion, Rommel had concluded that the only way to get the job done quickly was to cannibalize the Siegfried Line for armaments.

As the weather slowly improved, we kept hiking ever eastwards towards the Rhine, most of the time now not bothering to dig in at night, but still living outdoors.

On March 7, in a miraculous coup that no doubt shortened the war, First Army troops succeeded in crossing the Rhine over an intact railroad bridge at Remagen, about 60 kilometers east of our location at Schleiden.

Two days later I wrote as follows:

> For the first time in our career we are billeted with a German family. I don't quite know what I expected, for much to my surprise they seem to be just as human as anyone else, and their hospitality, though not quite as 'all out' as the French and Belgian[s]... is quite overwhelming, considering everything. To be sure there are those who are Nazis and those that are not, but on the whole they don't seem too sorry to see us. In fact, when we first came marching into this town the reception we got was nothing short of what we got in Alsace, for practically the entire male population of the towns in this part of the Reich consists of drafted Polish farm hands who have waited six years for the day. They immediately buddied up with the Polish boys in the Company and are getting along famously.

I've forgotten the name of the town where that happened, but white flags or bed sheets were draped from every house and I clearly recall enjoying—as the NCO in command in the house where my squad was billeted—the master bedroom with feather bed. I was a little nervous about whether these people could be trusted, but we rigged a guard schedule and nothing, but nothing, then kept me out of that bed! When I finally awoke the next morning, wonder of wonders, the buxom 22-year-old who seemed to be the hausfrau had cleaned and polished my beat-up old combat boots until they glowed and had then arrayed them in careful line beneath the bed!

The next day, March 10, I wrote:

> I shouldn't pass on rumors, but for once they seem to be unanimously optimistic. The end of the war is predicted any day now, and while it may come any day, I still refuse to think about it until it actually happens. I remember I didn't think the Jerries had enough punch left to pull their counter-offensive, and I still believe they may have a couple of trumps tucked away somewhere. I know that the German people are fed up with the war and would throw in the sponge immediately if given half a chance, but all of the prisoners we have taken lately have told the same story—that is, because they fear reprisals against their families by the Gestapo[21]—they have to put on some sort of a mock battle, at least; and often the 'mock' battles are just as costly and as much of a delay to our advance as the real thing—and in any case, it's just as nerve-wracking.

We had heard previously that Eisenhower's headquarters at SHAEF had announced what became the "No Fraternization Policy." In light of the uncertainties concerning the reception which American troops would be accorded in Germany, it was probably inevitable that the Army bureaucracy should decree that we should be kept apart from the civilian

---

[21] It is also the fact that in the latter stages of the war, ruthless "punishment battalions" lurked directly behind the front prepared to apprehend and summarily execute German soldiers found to have shirked their duties. This was another "Hitler program" designed to prevent a recurrence of what he felt to be the traitorous actions on the Western Front in 1918. It is reliably reported that more than 20,000 Wehrmacht soldiers perished before firing squads as a result.

population as much as possible, but it didn't seem right as applied to our particular situation, as I wrote on March 11:

> Yesterday afternoon the military government boys arrived with their heads just buzzing with ideas, the most prominent of which was that it was very naughty for soldiers to live with Germans; basically it is probably a very good idea, but they thought of it just a little too late... We had been living with the civilians of [town name censored] for two days, and strange as it seems, we were getting along famously together. Last night the 'démenagement' took place—civilians moved in with their neighbors, and soldiers moved into the houses thus vacated. Our delightful 22-year-old hostess was in the middle of the preparation of a tremendous birthday cake for one of my boys [notice the proprietary turn of phrase] and, sad to relate, I guess she had to eat it all herself. When the other half of my squad moved out of the [the house next door] the old lady [there] cried just as loudly as any Belgian I ever saw. The result was, as you can see, pretty much of a mess, and I'm sure I can't imagine what the Germans think of us now. The 'Good Neighbor' policy was working pretty well... I'd bet that... as a policy it's every bit as good as Non-fraternization, and twice as natural.

That I was wise beyond my years would soon be demonstrated.

I continued to have thoughts about the futility of the "unconditional surrender" policy. On March 12, I wrote as follows:

> A thing that strikes me a little strange about [my father's] letters... is the unqualified optimism which characterizes them. In all probability, this is just a reflection of the way the news is presented in the papers and on the radio, in which case I think that they are doing the nation a great deal of harm. As far as I know, the war may very easily end any day, but more 'impossible' coups have been pulled off by the German Army—but this time, it must be remembered, it will be impossible for all hostilities to cease until every square foot of German territory has been occupied. The German people—all of them—have admitted surrender, but for the Nazis who control them it is a fight to the fin-

ish—and I've seen enough prisoners to know that the average German soldier, regardless of his personal opinions, will obey them until the situation becomes so hopeless that he is at the point of being annihilated. He will then surrender, but in the meantime, his artillery and mines will be causing as many casualties on our side, almost, as though both sides firmly believed in ultimate victory. It seems to me that Russian and American will have to shake hands in the middle of Germany before the thing can end. A revolution is practically impossible, and the Nazis will never admit defeat for to do so means death.

It is obvious that I was continuing to experience intimations of mortality, but these moody ruminations were about to be interrupted by two events, the first of which was the three-day pass back to Belgium of which I have already written. It was then that I participated in the peculiar dinner party at Eupen with Christine and her family and the young Belgian who tried so hard to make time with her. But in spite of his attentions, Christine and I had once again spent a good part of the three days alone together and had much rejoiced in the intimacy of each other's company. She had sewn on my sergeant's stripes and escorted me to a photographer's studio in Verviers where the portrait was taken of which was eventually returned to me by Suzanne Bucaille in Carentan in 1990.

On my return to Baker on March 20, 1945, I wrote a long letter which spoke only of the pleasures of speaking French for three days with my old friends—unidentified—from Verviers, and how full the shops now were with powdered eggs and dried vegetables. I also mentioned that I had posed for some photographs. But of what was really important, not a word! My parents must have wondered why my letter was so wordy yet so uninformative. They could not of course have begun to imagine my relationship with Christine and I didn't begin to see how I could have explained it to them.

The March 20 letter was written from the town of Andernach, on the west bank of the Rhine River just north of Coblenz, to which Baker had moved during my absence. The jeep trip back from Belgium was a revelation, because unlike my earlier approach to the Rhine which had been on foot, I now got to see in rapid panorama the vastness of war's devastation of the German countryside. It was not so much the damage to towns and human habitations, although there was plenty of that, as it was the enormous quantities of armor, artillery and other matériel which had been smashed, burned and strewn alongside the road for its entire length. The ride also revealed to me for the first time the extent to which the German Army had been dependent on horse-drawn transport. The way was littered with the bloated corpses of these poor creatures, most of whom remained in the traces of the ruined equipment they were pulling, in odoriferous proximity to the road. I felt a lot more sympathy for them than for their deceased masters, whose misshapen remains were also much in evidence.

On my arrival at Andernach, I found Baker billeted in houses adjacent to a cement factory whose labor force consisted entirely of Ukrainians brought in as forced laborers. They were housed in barracks in a barbed-wire enclosed compound, the gates of which had now been torn away. There must have been a hundred of them, mostly women, but with a smattering of teenaged boys who would have been much younger when first brought there. Almost all the Russians were short, round and sturdy, and none exhibited any of the emaciation which the world would soon come to associate with the concept of "slave labor." I never found out why these laborers had fared so much better.

There was a young lad of about sixteen who had clearly established himself as the guy in charge. It was amazing to see the deference paid to him by all the women, some of whom were grandmothers. But his sway over them was exerted not so much by force as by their affection for him. He made it clear that he loved them all, which feelings, I judged, were expressed not merely through the smiles and caresses which he bestowed on them freely.

It was discovered that the Ukrainians and the Americans shared a common desire to party. In the mysterious ways of armies and also, apparently, prisoners in labor camps, copious quantities of alcohol were somehow uncovered, as were musical instruments—harmonicas and guitars by us and balalaikas and concertinas by the Russians. The weather was still cool so we assembled in the young boss's hut where dancing and revelry went on until all hours of the night. No one had felt it necessary to post any guards. I wrote on March 25:

> ...[A]lso in town is what was formerly a prison camp for the Russian workers whom the Germans brought from the captured

Ukraine to man a couple of factories in town. I spent the evening there last night, and we were entertained with Russian songs and dances by some of the girls, who are, without exception, built like gorillas. After they had gone through their repertoire, the Americans responded with such folk pieces as 'Beat Me, Daddy, Eight to the Bar.'

The leaden hand of the self-censor had again fallen heavily on that letter. There were two reasons which will become clear as I describe the night more fully.

The dancing had started out with the Ukrainians enthusiastically demonstrating their native steps, all ruggedly athletic. They included wondrous variations of the bear dance danced singly and in twos and fours from a deep knee-bend to the accompaniment of ever-faster music. We Americans responded with jitterbugging, nowhere nearly as adeptly as the Russians. During these demonstrations and undeterred by the muscular physiques of the Russian ladies, a process of pairing off was taking place between them and the GI's. As exhaustion overtook those who had given performances, the musicians seemed to sense a change of mood. The tempo slowed, and soon the center of the room was filled with swaying couples.

If the mood was romantic, the appearance was comic: the Russian women averaged five feet in height and their waists were probably a good 35 inches, while the GI's were mostly thin and a foot taller. It didn't seem to matter; everyone who seemed interested had attracted a partner.

The dancers and revelers slowly drifted away and at last the music fell silent, to be replaced by (to use a phrase much relished by an old French friend of mine) "les murmures d'amour" and the rhythmic creaking of the double-decked wooden bunks in the Russian dormitories. One can only wonder how many Ukrainian-Americans were conceived that night and whether they have any inkling of the identities of their fathers.

There was yet another detail of that celebratory night which I deemed not suitable for civilian eyes. I had stashed my Tommygun in what appeared to be a discreet location outside the Russian barracks and when I came to retrieve it after the party it was gone! The discovery sobered me up in half a second. It was a court martial offense to lose your weapon under circumstances like these, and I was very disturbed. How could such a thing have happened? I got help to look for it, but to no avail, and later in the day, with great trepidation, I presented the situation to Slick, and with him went to speak to Captain Farrar. After five seconds reflection, he looked me in the eye and said to Slick, "Give him a rifle, Slick." What a wonderful man!

The second circumstance that once and for all lifted the perpetual knot of anxiety that resides in a combat soldier's breast came from the blue. I described it thus in a letter of March 21:

> Since writing you yesterday a very startling thing has occurred. About the last thing that I expected and it happened so suddenly that I am not quite sure what to think about it. I still don't know all the details, but even so, I am pretty sure you will be glad to hear about it. Nobody has told me when, but unless a sudden change of plans occurs, I am to be sent to Officers Candidate School in or near Paris. The training period... is ninety days, after which time, all having progressed smoothly, I will be commissioned as 2nd Lieutenant, and if the war is still not over will then be assigned to an infantry division as platoon leader. My acceptance of the proposal is largely based on the supposition that the war in the ETO will be over by that time, which is admittedly a dangerous one, but if I were asked to guess when the war might end I think that might be just about the time I would say, so I am willing to take my chances as far as that is concerned.
>
> There are a number of other considerations though, chief among which is the possibility that officers will be retained in service a lot longer than enlisted men, but if I can be assured of coming through this thing with a whole skin, I think will be able to stand another six months, or whatever time I may have to serve...
>
> The whole thing happened so quickly that I did not have time to consider these things. I was merely asked by my platoon sergeant whether or not I wanted to go, so I tentatively said 'Yes.' Five minutes after that the names (one from each platoon) had been [put in] a hat and mine was the one that was pulled, and within five minutes after that—fifteen minutes after I had first been asked—my name had been sent into the battalion and there

was nothing more I could have done about it even if I had wanted to...

...which I clearly didn't, because in a later paragraph I referred to the "call of those shiny little gold bars" as being "overwhelming," and to the fact that I could not let my elder brother, who had been commissioned a few months earlier, "outshine me."

Four days later I wrote again, saying that there had meanwhile been no further mention of OCS and that I had more or less forgotten about it but that I had received instruction that day to report to the battalion surgeon for a physical exam. I added in veiled terms that it now appeared that the 28th would probably henceforth be assigned occupation duties and that that was tending to make me think again about accepting, but I concluded that "the decision was almost made for me" and that there was no use "crying over spilt milk." Of course, the real truth was to be found in my remark about a "whole skin." I was not about to expose myself to the slightest additional risk of having, in the words of the Cockney song, "me bollix shot awye." Not me! And even if I had known, as was later to prove to be the fact, that I would be in the Army for almost a year after Baker had gone home and its men had been discharged, I don't believe it would have affected my decision, especially so in light of the astonishing and wholly unanticipated adventures which were later to befall me.

I apparently did not write again for almost two weeks. During this period, Cliff's chronology has the company crossing the Rhine and passing through half a dozen other towns which he names, including Bonn, before proceeding to the town of Leutesdorf, which he says was my departure point for OCS. His description is no doubt entirely accurate, but for some reason the only memory I retain after Andernach is of a trip by truck convoy on the eastern side of the Rhine which followed the route of one of Hitler's autobahns.

Some of the autobahn bridges had been destroyed by amazingly accurate bombing. This required numerous tortuous descents by the trucks down muddy one lane tracks to the streams below where our engineers had rigged Bailey (trestle) bridges to cross the spring torrents at the bottom, after which the trucks would groan back up to the seamless ribbon of concrete at the top. One could not fail to be awed by the scope and immense sweep of this engineering marvel: hilltops truncated and huge steel and concrete bridges leaping even the smallest rivulet in order to maintain the high continuity of the highway. There was nothing like it at the time at home, not even the Pennsylvania Turnpike which then represented the state of the art but which had originally been built not as a highway but as a railroad.

Cliff Hackett and the author, Germany, March 1945.

Ken Janne and the author, Germany, March 1945.

Cliff Hackett and Gus Gustafson, Germany, March 1945.

Combat

A Summing Up

MY last letter from the company was written on April 5, 1945, just over a month before the official end of the war in Europe on May 7. I said:

> I must say that I feel very badly about leaving B Company. We have as good a bunch of men and officers as will ever be found in one company in the Army. I have made a lot of friends whom it will not be easy to say good-bye to. It may not be the safest place in the world, but there is a certain tacit understanding between the men that is hard to describe. They are all proud to be a member of "The Queen of Battles" [the infantry's classic title], and though each wishes to hell that he might go back to the States or get a job in the rear echelons, he derives great satisfaction from the knowledge that he doesn't have to kow-tow to anyone—from generals on down—he is doing the toughest job there is and doing it well. Whatever may be said to the detriment of the infantry, it has an esprit de corps of such pride and fierceness that is unequaled in any other type of outfit.

I don't think I could say it any better today, but I feel compelled to add that as warm as my feelings were (and are) for Baker Company and for my friends in it, they extend no farther.

The simple fact of the matter is that above the company level the quality of the 28th Division's leadership was atrocious. In the five months of my combat career, I never saw my battalion commander, Lt. Col. Allen (I know his name only because it appears in the *Stars and Stripes* article quoted earlier), or Col. Nelson, the regimental commanding officer, let alone Gen. Cota, the division commander. These men were absentee landlords in the worst sense.

It is said that with the exception of a single visit to the headquarters of one of his three regiments, Cota remained at his remote division headquarters throughout the slaughter of Hürtgen, never bothering to find out first hand the terrible conditions confronting his men or to adjust the impossible attacks he required of them to those conditions. Indeed, so overmanned was he by the responsibilities of his command during the height of the battle that when one of his regimental commanders who had been badly wounded was carried into his safe rear echelon command post, Cota fainted dead away.[22]

I, of course, knew nothing of that until a very recent time, but I can attest to the strong belief amongst my enlisted colleagues, arising from their unavoidable awareness that there was a total vacuum of any apparent leadership or "command presence" above the company level, that the men in those higher echelons were assholes who should have been cashiered or court-martialed for their cavalier disregard of the welfare of their men. Mercifully dim in my memory are the details of unnumbered instances in which orders were issued and then countermanded, or were issued in ignorance of where their recipients were located and proved to be physically incapable of being carried out, or resulted in artillery fire falling on our own troops. This was not mere chicken shit, the enhancement of one's own status by the intentional demeaning of subordinates, that was so rife in the States, but it was the product of the same mind: "I don't care what happens to anyone else (or what anyone else thinks) so long as the safety to which I am entitled by virtue of my exalted rank is not disturbed." Craven cowardice is another name for it: the commander would issue orders on the basis of ignorance or misinformation because of his unwillingness to expose himself to the danger entailed in learning the true facts. It was unforgivable.

At the company level, however, things were very different. Captain Farrar was deeply respected by all the men in the company, and although I favorably remember only one other company officer, Lt. Saad Khalil, platoon leader of our mortar and machine gun platoon, there can be no

---

[22] As mentioned earlier, Cota's collapse may well have been in part the result of the hot breath of First Army Commanding General Hodges, who had something of a martinet's reputation for relieving division commanders first and asking questions later.

doubt that Farrar's example permeated the company's command hierarchy from top to bottom, especially among its non-commissioned officers. There were two reasons.

First of course was Farrar's personality. He was unfailingly courteous and cheerful and always ready with a kind or encouraging word. There was almost never a day when he would not be seen at least once by every man in the company, and we all had the sense that our concerns were his concerns. Yet there was nothing soft about him. Although he would listen to argument, no one doubted when he issued an order that full and prompt compliance was the only possible response. We all adored him and strove to be worthy of his esteem.

The second reason arose from the nature of our activities at the front line. There were very few secrets there. If you were a coward there could be no hiding it, and you either shaped up or exposed yourself to the scorn of those around you. There were many who were quite prepared to pay that price, but most of us, including most assuredly me, found ourselves behaving in ways which were very different indeed from those which were instinctive. We did *not* run at the first sign of danger, and we *did* lead the patrol into enemy lines. Self respect made us all demand it of ourselves.

This is not to say that we were superior as individuals to those in the rear echelons. It was simply that nowhere above company level was this same dynamic present. General Cota and Col. Nelson in the safety of their command posts were virtually never required to choose between courage and cowardice. The worst that could happen to them would be the occasional artillery round, and everyone was expected to take cover from those. They were no whit different from the "chateau generals" of World War I who made it a point never to visit the front lest it cloud their judgment. They were accordingly reviled by the front line troops. But on the line we had to make this choice every hour of every day. Simply to *stay* there represented such a choice.

It is thus probably not surprising that the fierce sense of camaraderie and esprit de corps should have arisen among us, or that we should find it continuing to burn bright at our two reunions. During our first few minutes in Minnesota it was as though there was an electric current coursing through us. It made no difference that we weren't all friends or necessarily even remembered everyone there. There was an invisible bond of brotherhood and we all felt it.

How then is one to judge the performance of men like Cota and Nelson, given that many of us, if removed from the fishbowl of the front lines and placed in the haven of their command posts, might also have played it safe? This is not, in my judgment, a hard decision to make. There were any number of examples of generals, and I'm sure colonels as well, who well understood that there were two indispensable elements to effective leadership: first, *genuine* concern for the well-being of their men, and second, frequent presence among them, both to convey that sense of concern by sharing their dangers, and equally importantly, to gain an accurate and firsthand understanding of the military situation.

Two such names spring readily to mind: General George S. Patton, Jr., commander of the Third U.S. Army, and General James M. Gavin, commander of the 82nd Airborne Division. Patton's name is, of course, a household word and Gavin's somewhat less so, but the critical point about both of them is that long before the war ended they were both known to and respected by every dogface.

Patton's reputation was mixed. Very few of us in the First Army would have elected to transfer to the Third because Patton was relentless in the pressure he put on his troops. But at the same time it was well known that the men in his units were in awe of him and that he did genuinely care for their well-being.

Though he did not become as well known as Patton, Jim Gavin in the opinion of many of us was an even finer example of what a general should be. He became commanding general of the 82nd when he was in his middle thirties, and took it from the beaches of Sicily and Normandy to an essential role in arresting the thrust of the German columns in the Ardennes and eventually to the meeting with the Russians on the banks of the Elbe River in Germany. He jumped with his men, was frequently in a foxhole next to them, and was in every way a shining example for them. His book *On to Berlin*, published in 1978, is a vivid account of what he did and how he did it without for an instant being self-serving or immodest.[23] He was idolized by his men as I came to know personally in

---

[23] The contrast between Gavin and a man like Cota can be no more vividly illustrated than by a passage from Gavin's book in which he describes the horrors which the 82nd Division uncovered when in February 1945 they finally recaptured the Hürtgen area and the Kall River valley where the 28th had been decimated. He describes the hundreds of corpses still left unburied three months later and the outrage they aroused in him concerning the failure of

continued...

my brief exposure to them when we scrambled out of the Salm River in Belgium on Christmas Eve, 1944 and passed through the 82nd's lines.

Yet another example, though not one which served as any inspiration to those on our side of the line, was German Field Marshal Erwin Rommel, against whom strong criticism was laid by Wehrmacht senior staffers that he was *too* much in the front lines and often shaped strategy by the seat of his pants rather than on broader logistic factors. But an illuminating current biography of Rommel entitled *Knight's Cross* by David Frasier (Frasier Publications Ltd., 1993), himself a distinguished British general and author, leaves no doubt either of the startling results he achieved or of the strong, two-way bond of respect and affection that flowed between him and his men.

Patton and Gavin were both products of West Point, but it is not as though leadership of men in battle was a secret available only to cadets at the Military Academy. Indeed, it had been historical commonplace since Alexander the Great and Wellington at Waterloo.

Nor was it any secret to Gen. Cota, who was himself a West Pointer, Class of 1917. A review of his earlier service in the war is most enlightening in this connection. Prior to being promoted to major general and becoming commander of the 28th in July 1944, he had served as assistant commanding general of the 29th Division and had landed at Omaha Beach in Normandy in the first hour of D-Day. In a biography of Cota entitled *Division Commander* by Robert A. Miller (Reprint Company, Spartanburg, South Carolina, 1989), his activities in Normandy are described in detail. He was the first officer of general rank ashore, where the scene was one of total disorganization and confusion. Men from different units had been separated from their officers and were seemingly demoralized. Cota is said to have taken charge of this situation, to have personally opened and led a way up the bluff from the beach, and in effect to have saved the day in his area. In subsequent days he remained in the thick of the action as he carried out specific trouble-shooting missions on behalf of his division commander both on the beach itself and at inland locations, and there were apparently two occasions when he re-

---
...continued

    leadership that could have produced such a result, adding that he tried without success to obtain some accounting from higher headquarters for the causes of the debacle.

mained at the front to lead detachments of troops on particular missions when he could quite easily have remained in the rear in relative safety. He was wounded once and decorated three times for these deeds, receiving the Distinguished Service Cross and the Silver Star with Oak Leaf Cluster.

What then happened to Cota when he assumed command of the 28th? A partial answer may lie in the explanation offered by his biographer concerning the differences between the roles of division and assistant division commander. Miller observes that in his new position he now would have sole responsibility for the performance of every element of his command, a much heavier burden than that of assistant, who was much more likely to be assigned to "task forces, independent commands [and]... special missions."

But the real answer no doubt lies in the evaporation of the battlefield dynamic. On the invasion beachhead there is really no possibility of a general officer's escaping who and what he is. His presence is notorious and he has no choice but to conform to his ideal of himself. If he doesn't he will be forever disgraced. But when he becomes commanding general of a division with a large headquarters surrounding him, the flame that had animated him on the beaches apparently grew dim. He was an officer who knew how to lead and had led conspicuously well, but he disappeared into his command post and was never seen again by his men. It is an illuminating sidelight that at a crucial moment in the Hürtgen struggle, Cota elected to delegate to *his* assistant commanding general, Brig. Gen. George Davis (said to have been universally detested by everyone on the division staff) forward on the essential mission of learning what was *really* going on at the front, and that Davis failed to do so.

What then should these men have done to carry out their responsibilities as leaders of the division? It does *not* mean—as we have seen—that they should do as Col. Nelson claimed to have done and charge down the hill to Spineux with fixed bayonet. No one expected or would have respected such grandstanding. Nor does it mean any form of the false or superficial solicitude that we occasionally saw in the States, where for example the brass would appear in retinue and pretend interest for a moment in the quality of the company's mess.[24] There was not a GI

---

[24] There was a wonderful cartoon that appeared in *The Stars and Stripes* that illustrates the point. It showed a general and his aide inspecting a chow line
continued...

in the Army who would not instantaneously pierce such transparent hypocrisy. What *was* required was that these officers should feel and therefore manifest a genuine interest in the well being of their subordinates. If their concern was real, there were dozens of ways that the men would quickly become aware of it. Visits by the general to the front line foxholes in Lutzkampen or elsewhere along the line, for example, would have exposed him to no real danger, would have been an absolute revelation to the men and would have produced a startling and lasting morale impact among them. The same would be true if we were to have seen his face as we came off line in relief and be told that we had done a good job or that Montgomery had congratulated us for the good work at St. Vith. And Ike, for further example, was known to distribute written messages of encouragement to the troops in addition to being seen among them, and there wasn't a soldier who wasn't aware of it. What a difference it would have made to us if we had known our leaders were dedicated to help and stand up for us! Alas, the message we instead received was that they didn't know who we were and didn't give a damn.

It seems somewhat improbable, in retrospect, that the vacuum of leadership at the top failed to affect those of us at the bottom any more grievously than it did. We were, of course, bitterly cynical about our divisional leadership (for some reason the scorn reached no higher[25]). But we learned to expect and to endure stoically (that is, with profuse bitching but obediently) the endless orders that treated our existence and well-being with the same indifference as a gardener feels for ants. Not only did we overcome this huge emotional hurdle, but we also managed, collectively that is, to surmount most physical obstacles, and in the end, to get the job done.

Perhaps it is not amiss then, as I finish my account of combat, to try

---

…continued
where the men were gagging, clutching their throats and throwing the food to the floor. The aide was saying to the general, "A little good-natured grousing, sir, is a sign of good morale."

[25] Ike and Bradley, despite their remote distance, were held in high regard by us GIs. We didn't know quite what to think about the commanding general of First Army, Lt. Gen. Courtney Hodges, who seemed to us sort of faceless. There is reason to believe that he may have had some responsibility for the debacle of Hürtgen, because he was known to put heavy pressure on his division commanders and to be ready on the instant to relieve them if their progress was inadequate.

to say a little more concisely just who it was we were and why we were able to do what we did. We were in fact a crazy mixture. We were, of course, predominately young. Virtually all of us save perhaps a few of the non-coms were in our late teens or early twenties. We were from all parts of the country; any concentration of Pennsylvanians had long since vanished by the time Hürtgen was over. And we were equally mixed from a nationality point of view, though of course there were no blacks. There were Indians, noted for taciturnity but also for caution and courage; they would often function as scouts and point men. We were diverse religiously, with many Catholics and not a few Jews. Lieutenant Saad Khalil was even of Middle Eastern extraction, though I know no more as to his origins. We were from all conceivable backgrounds, including many like Slick and Bill Kleeman from rural or farming origins. There were also the inevitable representatives from Brooklyn and the Bronx to round out our almost stereotypical Hollywood cast.

There was, however, a significant variation from the melting pot profile when we ASTPer's arrived. At least half of the 150 of us who joined Baker on November 11, 1944 must have been undergraduates from our nation's colleges, but apart from that educational difference, there was as much variation between us as there was among the rest of the men.

Our arrival did, I think, bring about a change in the atmosphere of the company. For a time there was without question a sense of elitism among the new arrivals, an "us-and-them" kind of feeling. And I have no doubt that the sentiment ran in both directions, with resultant tensions. But if some of us may at the start have held the view (and I probably did) that intelligence was in direct ratio to education, it did not take us long to learn we were wrong. We discovered for starters that our ablest and most influential non-coms were *not* college men. And we also found out that men who could not compose a grammatical sentence if their lives depended on it were gifted with abundant common sense.

This, too, worked in both directions. As Bill Kleeman observed in Minnesota, our arrival gave the company "a whole new character." What really happened as we got to know each other, as we did most rapidly in the goldfish bowl of the front line, was that we all came to realize that education counted for little as regards the talents that really mattered: reliability and the ability to absorb survival skills, and this in turn led quickly to the development of mutual respect on the part of those who possessed them, regardless of backgrounds.

Our company and its platoons were thus able to develop a fabric of cohesion and a sense of direction which I don't think many of us were aware of at the time, certainly not me. We weren't particularly well disciplined, certainly not so in the conventional spit and polish sense. None of us ever saluted our officers but on the other hand neither did we ever call them by their first names. Somehow from all these disparate sources there came together a group of men who developed the resolve, without expressly acknowledging it to each other, to depend on each other and to get the job done, and we did.

I have become aware as I have tried to analyze how this all came about that my thoughts have focused heavily on those of us who managed to survive. No doubt we are to some extent living proof of our own success, but there were so many others, a large majority of us in fact, who did not return and have remained unmentioned. There must, for example, have been well over a dozen men, both young and some in their thirties, who joined my squad as replacements, were there for a time, and then disappeared. Some of them no doubt were every bit as capable as any of the rest of us, but in some cases they were with us so briefly that I hardly had time to learn what they looked like. I can see a few faces, awed, painfully naive and totally unprepared for what was in store for them. We tried our best to give them a cram course that would equip them to cope, but in so many instances it was virtually hopeless, there just wasn't enough time, or they couldn't be made to understand, or they were just unlucky, and a healthy youngster would end up a shapeless bag of gristle because he hadn't dug his hole deep enough, or didn't take cover quickly enough. It was especially dispiriting in the later months when the replacements were culls from the Air Corps and anti-aircraft units,[26] or who had been inducted only weeks before and who hadn't even had the meager advantage of infantry training. At times it seemed like heartless butchery. Yet all those kids were there, they did what they were told and didn't cut and run, and thus they too were part of the fabric who helped to get the job done. They all deserve to be remembered.

I could so easily have been one of them. Those of us who managed

---

[26] The drastic and unanticipated need for rifle company replacements resulted in non-combat units throughout the ETO being directed to comb their ranks for surplus manpower, and in spite of strong efforts from above, their commanders could not resist designating misfits and screw-ups to answer such calls.

to endure, wriggle through and survive, didn't do so because of any great talent, intelligence or superabundance of courage or leadership ability. Far from it. The single most important factor was that of pure blind chance. How else can you explain that I was not erased in the artillery tornado at Lutzkampen or in the other instances where I was a millimeter from death?

A second factor, almost as important, was the instinct for self-preservation, in many respects the antithesis of courage and leadership. Fallstaff's quip about "fighting and running away" is smack on the mark. We all ran away on occasion: I was not the first to run but certainly not the last. Not me!

There was, I think, a certain denominator common to all of us who played a role at any level in the curious activity called "combat." With scant exceptions, none of us was there because we had chosen to be, and very few of us were much good at doing what we were doing. There were, of course, variations among us. Very few of our rear echelon commanders had elected warfare as a profession. Most were made-over civilians masquerading as warriors rather than career military men. Among them there were more than a few who discovered once they were in the service that they reveled in the drama of war and the trappings of rank and authority as they awarded medals to each other. It was of the very essence of the incompetence of these people that they stay as far as possible from any risk to themselves. Although it may be accurate to say that they too were there and may have made a minimal contribution towards getting the job done, I shall never, as I have perhaps made over-abundantly clear, find it in my heart to forgive them.

As I have been trying to describe my combat experiences, I have found myself groping to understand, and now to put on paper, just what it is within the American soldier that has made him—not just in "my" war but throughout our country's history—such a formidable fighting force. In the Civil War illiterate farm lads on both sides of the line threw themselves at each other with such selfless abandon that they were able to produce a victory only after hundreds of thousands of them had gone to their deaths. The story has been little different an any of our later conflicts, not omitting Vietnam.

In both World Wars we were confronted with an enemy whose national psyche was steeped by rigorous traditions of discipline and obedience and whose military record was one of merciless efficiency. Hitler shaped his troops to this vision, and they believed fiercely not only in it but in him and in themselves, and yet they were beaten to the point of annihilation by the Russians in the East and by the British and the Americans in the West. Was it only superiority of materiel that made the difference, or was there more?

I don't know the answer to this question, but I do know that within the core of most of us in Baker Company on the Western front there was a solid determination to get the job done whatever it might take. I am put in mind of Bill Kleeman's explanation in Minnesota of his baptism of fire in the hedgerows of Normandy: When the order came down to attack across the open field towards the opposite hedgerow manned by the Germans, he said, "It was pretty rough on this ol' farm boy" to get up courage to rise and charge, but he somehow found the will to do so, and he did it not only then, but repeatedly thereafter and even following recovery from wounds, as when he helped to organize and led the attack on Spineux. Like Bill, none of us was very good at this when we started, but those of us that survived got better at it, and a few of us even got quite good indeed in spite of our low disciplinary level, in spite of the humiliation of our Stateside training, in spite of the disorganization of our replacement-fed units and in spite of the low quality of our distant leadership.

I took away with me from the 28th Division only the most meager of physical mementos, one of which was the small scar on my right clavicle which was reminder of the woodland firefight we got into near Spineux. The other was the lingering case of trenchfoot which had deadened the feeling in my toes and which did not finally disappear until fifteen or twenty years later. As I have said, I was everlastingly lucky to have been able to walk away at all.

Harder both to define and describe are the emotional and psychological consequences or scars which were visited upon me by combat. There is one in particular that surely flowed from my experience as a squad leader. When I was a simple GI concerned mostly with my own well being, I never encountered any difficulty in sleeping. I did undergo the various declensions of dread, fear and terror, just as I did as a sergeant, but they rarely kept me from slumber whenever the opportunity appeared. But when I was promoted, the picture changed. It was as though my physical being, previously limited to the dimensions of my flesh and bones, had suddenly been extended to include the foxholes of the other eleven men for whom I was now responsible. So long as there was risk to them, and so long as I did not know to a certainty that none of them was in danger, I could no longer sleep soundly or deeply. I would wake up at the slightest sound or disturbance alert to fathom its meaning. In Sigolsheim, for instance, the only times I felt this burden lifted from me was when one of the other squads was on duty at the outpost and all of my men were safely in the cellar. I don't doubt that the fever that took me to the hospital in St. Dié was precipitated or complicated by fatigue, as well as by the other ailments which chronically plagued me.

Even today—to the chagrin of my beloved spouse who sometimes likes to read in bed—I find it almost impossible to go to sleep unless her light is out and I know she is ready for sleep. If I try, I will be roused by the slightest sound and it is not long before somnolence vanishes altogether.

There is yet another facet of my psyche which was permanently altered by combat, though it may not be accurate to ascribe it solely to that cause. The many emotional crosscurrents which I have described seemed to lead inexorably to the need—as essential to simple sanity and survival—to limit my attention only to those concerns which were strictly within my ability to control or influence. To say it another way, I found no profit in speculating on what might happen tomorrow, or even two hours from now, unless and until I knew for certain the exact circumstances in which I would be required to act. You may say, "Yes, but your letters and accounts are full of examples of how you hated those near and far who you felt were responsible for your predicament; obviously that bothered you." Sure it did, and perhaps to bitch about it was to counteract it in some small way, but I recognized that I couldn't really do anything about it and never let it really get to me. In the same way, that which was over and past, however grotesque or awful or even how recent, was quickly put out of my mind, which no doubt helps to account for the large gaps in my memory.

These reactions soon tended to develop into the habit of hunkering down into my tiny immediate universe—the cocoon phenomenon earlier described, but it now was transformed from a problem to something of a solution—and living altogether within it, often at the intensified level of sensory awareness that I've also mentioned. I am well satisfied that this orientation served me extremely well in combat, but it is much less appropriate to the solution of problems in civilian life, particularly as the same mechanism was later reinforced by civilian experiences. I leave that, however, for others to judge because there's not a whole lot I can now do about it even if I were disposed to.

I have only very belatedly realized—almost fifty years later, in fact and only after having reread the preceding portion of my account—that I have failed for all that long time both to understand, and thus to accurately describe, the true significance of what I have semi-facetiously characterized as the "celebratory" night in Andernach. Indeed, I have laid stress on two events, my pass to Belgium and my being selected to go to OCS, as being those which finally lifted from my psyche the specter of death in combat. It's true that they were influential, but it has finally dawned on me that neither one of them was the operative event.

The true fact of the matter is that there wasn't a single "event" that did the job; it was the complex combination of circumstances coalescing at Andernach that really became V-E Day for those of us in Baker Company, and indeed for all of us who participated in that night of revelry. Consider: we were all now many miles behind the "front" if indeed there could still be said to be one anywhere. The kettle-drum counterpoint of artillery had finally fallen silent. The occupation of Germany had effectively already begun. The Ukrainian forced laborers had been liberated, and the likelihood of any of us in Baker being exposed to any further hard fighting had diminished virtually to the vanishing point. If any of us had been asked that night whether the war was over for us, the certainty of its continuance was so deeply ingrained that I think we would have questioned the asker's sanity, and with the inherent and well-justified cynicism of the GI, we would have hotly denied it. We would have answered instead that we were simply enjoying a welcome party, but viewed from the long perspective, the facts are really too clear to admit of much doubt, never mind how long it took me to realize it. It was not only a celebration, it was really a festival of life that took place that night. Each one of us had at last been handed back the rest of his life to begin to savor and enjoy, and we obviously fell to it with a will.

If any reader should question whether I may perhaps be attempting to elevate a drunken and licentious revel into a transcendental epiphany, let him consider the meaning of the negligently stashed Tommy-gun— something that would have been inconceivable a few short days previously—and Capt. Farrar's quickly absolving me of responsibility for it. We both knew the war was over for us, though neither of us was quite ready to admit it or to abandon its formalities. Had it been otherwise, I would have remembered forever the trip from Germany back to Fontainebleau, for that would have represented my personal salvation. But I remember nothing of it because there was no reason to, I had already been saved.

In winding up the account of my combat experience with Baker Company, I have attempted to express a number of impressions or reflections concerning that experience the purpose of which has been to try in some small way to distill for others what combat "was really like." What I have written, I fear, will serve to inform the reader about combat just about as adequately as I was informed by the rotogravure pictures in the World War I books in our library at home: they convey at an intellectual level an understanding of what *happens* and what it *looks* like, but they cannot begin to recreate the sheer unmitigated horror of it. They cannot convey the many aspects of physical discomfort: cold, hunger, filth, illness, fatigue and all gradations of pain (from an itch to intense agony) and especially are they incapable of conjuring up any of the emotional spectrum that is fear. Starting with nervousness, one ratchets his way though foreboding, anxiety, dread, fright, horror, terror and panic, each of which has its own small catalog of special attributes. There is yet a larger dimension, too, which has to do with the sense of moral outrage against all of those who are responsible for the perpetration of such monstrous injustice.

There were many times when a voice inside me would scream silently: "There is nothing, nothing, nothing that can possibly justify men inflicting such anguish and injustice on others." That there never was an answer to this outcry simply confirmed its correctness.

None of this spectrum of emotion can be experienced vicariously.

I have lately read a book entitled *The Forgotten Soldier*, an autobiographical account by Guy Sajer, a Frenchman who was conscripted into the German Army and who spent over two years on the Russian front. He was exposed to an assortment of horrors (including such things as famine and cannibalism) which make my five months in combat seem like a trip to the beach. His account adds to the literature of war what for me is a new dimension in the effort to try to recreate for others a real sense of what a combat soldier goes through. I should like to quote one brief passage from his book which comes close to putting this message across:

Too many people learn about war with no inconvenience to themselves. They read about Verdun or Stalingrad without comprehension, sitting in a comfortable armchair, with their feet beside the fire, preparing to go about their business the next day, as usual. One should really read such accounts under compulsion, in discomfort, considering oneself fortunate not to be describing the events in a letter home, writing from a hole in the mud. One should read about war in the worst circumstances, when everything is going badly, remembering that the torments of peace are trivial, and not worth any white hairs. Nothing is really serious in the tranquillity of peace; only an idiot could be really disturbed by a question of salary. One should read about war standing up, late at night, when one is tired, as I am writing about it now, at dawn, while my asthma attack wears off. And even now, in my sleepless exhaustion, how gentle and easy peace seems!

Those who read about Verdun or Stalingrad and expound theories later to friends, over a cup of coffee, haven't understood anything. Those who can, read such accounts with a silent smile, smile as they walk, and feel lucky to be alive. (*The Forgotten Soldier* by Guy Sajer, Brassey's (U.S.) Edition, 1990, McLean, Virginia, page 23)

I smile, and am glad to be alive!

Captain Russell Farrar, Germany, June 1945.

Officer Candidate School, Fontainebleau, France

April 6-June 11, 1945

I left Germany for France on April 6, 1945, but have no recollection whatever as to how I got to Fontainebleau. It would have to have been by truck or train, and I would have to have passed through Paris, but it's all a total blank.

The Fontainebleau OCS came into existence because of the terrible and unexpected attrition in the ranks of infantry platoon leaders experienced in Europe. The casualty rate for these officers was higher than for any other job in the Army, including even squad leaders, which I believe was the next highest. Indeed, by early 1945 there was a severe manpower shortage at all levels in the infantry, but the problem with platoon leaders was particularly severe, and the OCS course designed to remedy it had even been reduced from the standard Stateside twelve weeks ("ninety-day wonders") to eight weeks at Fontainbleau in order to accelerate the flow.

When I arrived there were seventeen 240-man classes already in training, and a new class was begun each Monday, so I had to wait a week for the eighteenth to start. Writing on April 9, I said:

> Today and tomorrow are to be spent collecting equipment—it will seem strange to own a lot of it when for the last six months my only possessions have been the clothes on my back. It also seems strange to be living in quarters designed to be lived in. Strange but good. What's bad is reveille and doing everything by the numbers.

The quarters may have been designed to be lived in but they weren't all that ritzy, at least not the way they were furnished for us. Because of the Château de Fontainebleau, the most famous palace of French kings and of Napoleon outside of Paris, the town was a tourist mecca, and it abounded with hotels of various sizes and classifications. It was for this reason and because the city was surrounded by the Forest of Fontainebleau which afforded excellent training grounds, that it had been chosen as the site for the school. My class was installed in a large hotel located at the eastern edge of town. The building was about five stories high and of the Belle Epoque school of architecture peculiar to France which features mansard roofs sprouting filigree iron work. Formal gardens, now untended, surrounded it. About twelve of us were crammed into each normal-sized hotel room, sleeping on double-decker pine bunks with straw mattresses.

My fellow officer candidates were an interesting bunch. As I wrote on April 11:

> Most of the men here are not from the infantry, the majority of them having come from ComZ and the Air Corps. Most of them have, however, given up perfectly safe jobs in the rear echelons to volunteer for the infantry, a highly commendable thing to do, though perhaps it doesn't speak very well for their sanity.

I also surmised that because the training would deal with the theory underlying the actuality that I had already personally experienced for the last five months, it would be easy sledding for me, and it was.

We were divided into two 24-man sections, and each group of forty-eight was headed by a "Tactical Officer," in our case a man named Wilcox. He had not experienced combat, and he therefore left me quite alone, except in occasional instances when he would ask me on the basis of my experience to verify some fact or observation he was making to the group. I was its only member who had come from a combat unit. But he was an excellent officer, very painstaking and proud of his men, and we responded in kind, trying to do the best we could for him.

Though we spent a fair amount of time in a classroom setting learning about such subjects as the manual for courts martial, the tables of organization and equipment for any infantry division, etc., most of our hours were out of doors in the Forest, and we got to know it well. It was a spectacular preserve, 170 square kilometers in area. It had been a hunting ground for the nobility since the Middle Ages and its trees, typically enormous oaks and beeches, now just leafing out, had been protected for hundreds of years. In the nineteenth century, its intersecting broad paths and craggy rock formations had also become attractions for city-dwellers and alpinists. In 1945, there were two primary activities in the Forest: charcoal burning and military training.

The charcoal burners performed a humble but very necessary function that spring. Gasoline supplies for legitimate civilian use were nonexistent. During the German occupation a charcoal-burning device had come into general use to provide fuel for motor transport. A cumbersome device similar to a potbellied stove would be installed on a car's rear bumper which would be loaded with wood charcoal, which when ignited would emit a combustible gas which could be used in the engine. Over distances of a few miles, vehicles so equipped might possibly go as fast as twenty-five miles per hour, and GI truck drivers who were stuck behind such French civilian traffic would curse and honk until they got by.

At any rate, the large beehive-shaped ovens of the charcoal burners were scattered throughout the forest next to their crude huts, which brought very much to life for me the famous precept of French liberty, "Chez soi, le charbonnier est roi." (In his own house, the charcoal burner is king.)

Since the Revolution, the Forest had also been used as a training ground by the French Army. Accordingly, there were all manner of firing ranges ("champs de tir"), including small arms and artillery ranges, and we spent long hours learning how to assemble, disassemble and fire all of the many weapons used by the infantry. Much of this was, of course, second nature to me, but the training relating to machine guns and mortars, for example, was new territory.

The same was very much the case with artillery. While I was usually way ahead of the game in regard to matters of practice, as opposed to theory, it came as an enormous surprise to me to learn—and to actually observe with my own eyes—that it was possible to follow the flight of an artillery shell from its firing howitzer, provided you knew where the cannon was and when it was going to be fired. However, it was never possible under combat conditions to duplicate these circumstances, so I guess even this revelation turned out in the last analysis to be of theoretical value only.

The hours were long and the work was hard, but we were treated very civilly—a vast difference from Camp Rucker—and we were entitled in the evening to go on four-hour passes into Fontainebleau if we weren't too exhausted to enjoy them. They would be spent drinking beer at sidewalk cafés in town or going swimming in the Seine, which meandered tranquilly in its pastoral bed about a mile east of our billet. It was wonderful to distance oneself from military authority and routine for even a short time.

My letters from OCS were full of speculation as to what the future would hold for us lieutenants-to-be. It was clear that the war was winding down, but it remained my belief that Nazis would never quietly fold their tents and surrender. There was similar speculation in the news (*The Stars and Stripes*, the daily Army newspaper, was the only one we saw, though I did get an out-of-date airmail edition of *Time* magazine) that hard-core Nazis would hole up in the Alps in Bavaria or Austria and try to continue hostilities from there. Though this turned out to be wrong, it seemed altogether plausible at the time.[27]

During this period, too, the Army announced its "point system" for determining when soldiers were to be entitled to be rotated home, but by its terms it applied only to enlisted men and the rules that would apply to officers hadn't been announced.

In addition, of course, the island-hopping style of the war in the Pacific was moving fitfully along. Okinawa had been invaded and was the scene of vicious resistance, foot for foot, by the Japanese, at the cost of many American casualties. The atom bomb had not yet emerged from secrecy, and there was every expectation that similar bloody combat and casualties would be inescapable in the invasion of the Japanese home islands. Thus there was a real prospect that some of us might be sent to the Pacific or to the dreaded CBI (China, Burma, India) theater. All of this made us very leery, and the cessation of hostilities in Europe did not thus loom as an event to be much celebrated.

Life was, however, not without its entertainments. One of them took

---

[27] Indeed, the "National Redoubt" hypothesis was so plausible that it became the basis for SHAEF strategy in the closing weeks of the war, leading Generals Eisenhower and Bradley, over the opposition of Montgomery, to divert offensive forces away from Berlin towards the south, thus permitting the Russians to capture the German capital. There has been much argument since as to how the development of the Cold War might have been altered if the Western Allies and not the Russians had taken Berlin.

place on April 28, when, as I wrote two days later:

> The first class graduated two days ago, and the town is suddenly flooded with new shavetails. I hope and pray that if and when the great day comes, I will not be as conspicuous in my pride as they are! I know I will be, but it certainly makes me laugh. They go walking down the street, saluting awkwardly, and trying to look like they have been doing it all their lives! Serious as a minister in his pulpit. They certainly get an infernal razzing from the Officer Candidates.

In this same letter I referred to the fact that the convention to organize the United Nations had just started in San Francisco. I asked my parents what the opinion in the States was about Harry Truman, who had become president on the death of Roosevelt on April 12th, but then I said:

> My own thought is that it matters little [who is the President]—the thing to watch is what happens in San Francisco—we may find out then whether our suffering has been for nothing but the sport of politicians and international crooks. It seems from here that it certainly will be a miracle if anything good comes from it.

How right I was! Even now, fifty years later, an effectively functioning world government remains elusive.

In spite of my reluctance to celebrate enthusiastically the arrival of V-E Day on May 7, I found a galling irony in the fact that the death of Roosevelt was observed by the school with a day off (unheard of!), while V-E Day was not! It made little sense to me (I came from a Republican family, but my political leanings in those days were distinctly liberal) that the death of a president, however respected, should be exalted above the happening of an event which would spare many of us from death in combat.

On May 6, I wrote:

> The coming week is one of three crucial ones—on Saturday the first 'Board' meeting of officers will be held to consider the cases of men whose dismissal has been recommended by the

Tactical Officers (one per forty-eight men). As preliminary to each board, we are to make out a rating for each man in our section (twenty-four), grading each according to standards set up by the school. In several ways this is good, in some bad, for it provides a very underhanded way for the redressal of grievances, but in general, the good outweighs the bad.

As it happened, the "Boards" were quite ruthless in their winnowing. By the time the third one had been held, our 48-man group had been reduced by half, but I remember only one moment of concern or difficulty in my own case, and that one, in a way, was self-inflicted. I had almost never been faced with the necessity of doing any public speaking, and lo and behold, my name appeared on the duty roster as being required to lead my group in a discussion of current affairs. I was thunderstruck! I read *Time* and the *Stars and Stripes* until I had memorized them, and I was still very concerned that I might make an ass of myself in public. The day and hour drew inexorably closer and at last were at hand. To my total surprise, it went swimmingly! I was a little nervous at first but soon got the hang of it, and the hour was over before I knew it. As was customary, the discussion was followed by a critique in which the men of the group were encouraged to express "constructive criticism" of their colleague's performance, and the comments were uniformly laudatory, except for one man who said I should have addressed them as "you men" instead of "you guys." I responded that I understood that would be appropriate if I became an officer and was addressing enlisted men, but that was not the situation now.

The Tac officer told me privately later that the discussion was the best-led one he'd had the pleasure of listening to, so I was, in current jargon, "psyched"!

On June 2, I wrote:

Today a great event happened, second only to the day the colonel pins the bars on (Monday, June 11). We went down to the Officers' Sales Store and went through the delightful process of buying our clothes. Surprisingly enough, I look almost like an officer. It certainly was a thrill to put them on for the first time! (You may remember, yourself, Pa [my dad had been a sergeant and then an officer in World War I]).

— Not Me! —

In the last week of school, I was finally able to wangle a one day pass to Paris where my brother John (better known as Nick) and I, who had long been trying to arrange a meeting, were at last able to spend the better part of a day with each other. He was a patient in a military hospital in the city with, of all things, an intractable case of athlete's foot, but he was able to go out on passes, and so we took a taxi, at the then outrageous price of $16.00, for a tour of the Bois de Boulogne, which was followed by dinner at a Red Cross club at the Hotel Crillon on the Place de la Concorde. I apparently wrote no letter recording the detail of this long-anticipated event but I certainly do recall the wondrous sensation of being together with my brother in the miraculously undamaged and beautiful city of Paris, and being young, not unattractive and *safe!*

At last graduation came, and my gold bars were pinned on. The ceremony was a blur, as really is also the case with most of the eight-week school itself. I don't recall making a single friend, and the only classmate I even remember was a fellow named Harrah. He, as will be seen, became memorable only several weeks later and then only because his name was next to mine in the alphabet.

OCS was a strange and unnatural interlude, and even though being commissioned did indeed mean that I had to stay in the Army almost a year longer than I otherwise would have, the events and experiences of that year more than justified the extra time, so I was later glad to have gone, and in June 1945 to get out of, OCS!

Back Into Germany
The Potsdam Conference

June 12-August 2, 1945

WELL, the war was over, and what was the Army going to do with all these new Second Lieutenants? It took a while to find out.

The first thing that happened was that I was put in charge of a package of fifteen enlisted men who for one reason or another had become detached from their units and now were being returned from France to Germany. This we did in what was my final trip by forty-and-eight. While it wasn't exactly the Orient Express, it was a damn sight better than my previous trips. The weather was agreeable, and there were only the sixteen of us in a car said to accommodate forty. It was just as well, because each of the men had a large duffel bag and I had all the changes of uniform which an officer was expected to possess. (It was a novel sensation indeed in my new life to be able to arise in the morning and actually have a choice of several different styles of uniform to put on.) We also had a kitchen on the train and were fed hot meals.

Our destination was Marburg, Germany, a small city about fifty miles north of Frankfurt. At Marburg, I and the rest of my OCS class (all of whom had shepherded like groups of soldiers back to Germany in the same train) were installed in a Casual Officers Center (it meant not that we were blasé but that we were not yet assigned to a particular unit) located in a tent city on top of an open hillside overlooking the bucolic German countryside. The experience bore no resemblance to my last tent city. In a letter written June 20, I said of it:

> I find that an officer's life is so much more comfortable than an enlisted man's that comparisons are foolish. The food is su-

perb—I have really eaten like a king. Steak, French-fried potatoes, green salads, pie, ice cream, decent living quarters, and one is treated as though he were more than 175 pounds [my then weight!] of ectoplasm. And as yet the responsibilities are not such that I find them overwhelming. I don't know why [referring to my momentary indecision about OCS] I was so reluctant to lend the Army the benefit of my amazing talent for so long. Lord knows how they have got along without me this long!

This state of affairs continued for about ten days, during which speculation ran rife as to what our futures held. The three possibilities were: (1) Assignment to an infantry division (in my case, it would probably mean the 28th, which was spread over central Germany in occupation duty), which would be stripped of all men with over 85 points, who would be discharged, while the balance of the outfit would be retrained in the U.S. for reshipment to the Pacific. (2) Shipment to the States in an officers' pool. Or (3) Shipment in such a pool directly to the Pacific. Understandably none of these held much attraction for any of us.

The point system in my case had produced a number of about 50: one point for every month of service, one for every month overseas, one for each battle star (each major campaign was enshrined with a name, such as Battle of the Ardennes, Battle of the Rhine and the Battle of Central Europe, and I was entitled to all three of these). Although decorations were awarded five points, the Combat Infantry Badge was not so dignified; and I rued my decision not to take the steps necessary for the Purple Heart. It had also become clear that the point system *would* apply to officers, so I was a long way from going home! After laying out these possibilities in a letter of June 27, I expressed the following surprising thought:

> I have pretty much resigned myself to a trip to the other side of the world—something that two months ago, I was willing to commit murder to prevent. The sharpness of the memories of the past winter seems to be rapidly fading, and I am not ungrateful for it, though in the interests of my future well-being, it would be better if I did not forget too quickly. Laissez-faire is a dangerous policy.

Three days later, the entire picture changed dramatically. One hundred of us second lieutenants, all from Fountainebleau's Class No. 18, were ordered to fly to Berlin on July 1st to participate in some kind of ill-defined ceremonies with the Russians. My letter of June 30 described the little I then knew:

> As far as I can gather the purpose is to participate in a victory parade with the Russians, to promote 'international good will,' if such a thing can be actively promoted. How long we are to be gone is a matter of speculation, ten days or two weeks, I would imagine. We are to be on detached service.

We were all agog with excitement! This was so different from anything we had expected, and though the indications were that the visit to Berlin would be only momentary, that was a lot better than anything else that seemed to loom.

I don't know if any of us did, but we should have smelled a rat, because the explanation was clearly specious. Who ever heard of one hundred lieutenants—without any troops—being sent to march in a parade?

But this was a very unusual rat indeed, as I learned the moment I got to Berlin. I wrote on July 2 with the dateline "Berlin District Headquarters, Germany":

> We flew up here yesterday from Halle, which is the last American Headquarters in Germany (the most eastern, that is). It is interesting beyond description to be with the Russians. They are, of course, on all sides.

I was most impressed with the Russians, praising their "efficiency" and dependability on the basis of my large twenty-four hour experience and marveling at the colorfulness of their uniforms, but I clearly now knew what was up because I also said:

> ...The plague of censorship has set in again, though this time with good reason, so all I can tell you is that I am now at the Berlin District Headquarters, and expect to be here for approximately a month. The nature of my duties is classified as 'Top Secret' information, so you will just have to be patient. When I

am able to tell you, I have the feeling you will probably have to read the letter several times before you believe what has happened.

Events were occurring with incredible swiftness, and some background must be provided. As noted, hostilities in Germany had been officially declared terminated on May 7, 1945. During the following month extraordinary efforts were afoot between the three occupying powers to formalize arrangements for the occupation. There had been no meeting between the heads of state since February at Yalta in the Crimea, when Roosevelt, Churchill and Stalin had agreed on the general arrangements for the occupation including the geographical outline of each zone, and including also the understanding that though the city of Berlin would be 100 kilometers deep within the Soviet Zone of Occupation, it too would be occupied by military units from each (as well as a contingent of French forces).

At a meeting in Moscow in early May, Harry Hopkins, who had been Roosevelt's closest confidante and who was now acting for Truman, had concluded an agreement calling for a Summit Meeting (they were called "Big Three" meetings then) in the vicinity of Berlin in mid-July to work out the details of occupation, the government of Germany and the myriad of other matters which required urgent attention.

Before the meeting could be held, it was necessary for the Allies to reach detailed agreements as to the number of occupation troops to be sent to Berlin by the British and Americans and concerning the air, highway and rail routes to be employed by them to supply both troops and civilian populations in the city.

Incredibly, these subjects were not addressed in any detail until June 29, when Lt. Gen. Lucius Clay, who was designated as Eisenhower's representative for the purpose, met with Soviet Marshal Zhukov in Berlin and agreed, among other things, that American and British occupation troops should commence moving into Berlin on July 1 and that the entire movement would be completed two days later. (See *Lucius D. Clay, An American Life*, by Jean Edward Smith, Henry Holt, New York, 1990, page 270.)

Pursuant to these arrangements, orders were immediately issued that the American 2nd Armored Division, a veteran outfit which had been re-equipped and trained for the purpose, should move over the single autobahn (superhighway) and single rail line designated as the access from the American Zone of occupation through the Russian Zone into Berlin to take up occupation duties.

Thus on the very day that the 2nd Armored was loading its tanks onto rail cars and moving its wheeled vehicles onto the autobahn to make this journey, we piled into C-47's (the transport workhorse of the war and the then backbone of the domestic airline industry as the Douglas DC-3) and rode in bucket seats from Halle over the 200 kilometers distance to the western edge of Berlin, there to land at Gatow Airdrome. We did not know it at the time (indeed, I became aware of it only in research to assure the accuracy of the dates I here record), but we one hundred new Second Lieutenants effectively became the first American occupation troops to arrive in the city.

Viewed in the context of over forty years of the ensuing cold war, this seems more than a little foolhardy, but matters at the time were on a much different plane, and, as indicated by my letter of July 2, we were prepared to be impressed by and to admire the Russians and to cooperate with them. From what we could observe, their attitude towards us seemed very much the same.

But what we were to learn on arrival was that we were not to serve, strictly speaking, as part of the occupation forces. Instead, we had been shipped up as a group to help run a conference which was to be held between President Truman, Prime Minister Churchill and Generalissimo Stalin, later to become known as the Potsdam Conference. It seemed impossible to believe that we were to participate in such a momentous and significant event. I hadn't the slightest idea what to expect, but the reality far outdistanced any possible expectations I may have had!

Though the world was to know it as the Potsdam Conference, it was not actually held in Potsdam, but in a luxurious residential suburb between Berlin and Potsdam known as Babelsberg. Babelsberg lay just to the west of a small inland lake named the Griebnitzsee which separated it from the western edge of the American Zone of Berlin. The Griebnitzsee was about 3 kilometers long and not much more than 100 meters wide, and thus looked more like a wide, placid river than a lake. A forest preserve blanketed its eastern shore, while on the Babelsberg bank, which sloped in wide lawns down to the water, stood imposing private residences of varying architectures of the sort found in the most prosperous suburbs of any large American city. Lot sizes of about an acre seemed to be the average, and they too were pleasantly landscaped with large shade trees.

Since the Russians had insisted that the conference be held in their zone of occupation and had been the ones to designate Babelsberg, they were in charge of the overall security arrangements for the compound, but within it, separate areas were designated for the American and British delegations, and these were to be staffed by officers and men of each nationality.

The American compound consisted of perhaps fifty houses, some of which were on the lake shore, and others, less imposing, on other residential streets to the west. It also extended a distance to the southwest into Potsdam proper, where it incorporated Germany's largest movie studio complex known as UFA, which was to serve as the administrative headquarters for the American portion of the conference.

In keeping with its evident bourgeois luxury, the residential area of Babelsberg had been home to many socially and politically prominent Germans during the war, not the least of which were Josef Goebbels, the Nazi Propaganda Minister (whose house was now to be occupied by Winston Churchill), and Admiral Karl Dönitz, the German naval commander in chief. The identity of these highly-placed residents must not have been known to Allied intelligence, because apart from a few craters and minimal small arms bullet scars, the town had been spared most of the devastating bombing so evident nearby in Berlin.

Soon after our arrival we were all assembled in the 600-seat theater which was an adjunct of the UFA studio, where we were briefed on what was about to happen, and at the end of which we were each given our assignments. A vast assortment of jobs was available and we were asked for a show of hands by those who had experience in running such things as, say, an officers mess, or a post laundry. I remember being embarrassed as others held up their hands, but since there seemed to be none involving combat infantry operations, I had to sit mute, and when the volunteers had all been assigned to the jobs they desired, the rest of us were appointed in alphabetical order to the list of jobs in the personnel officer's hand.

Each of the houses to be occupied by the American dignitaries was to be taken in charge by one or two of us. As the list was read off and names assigned, I waited to see what might turn up as the letter "H" came near. Finally the major said "Hadden" and I responded in the conventional Army way by giving my first name. He than said "Harrah," who also answered back. The major said laconically, "You two are in charge of President Truman's house."

There was an audible murmur from those assembled. Had we thought about it, most of us would have assumed that the traveling party from Washington would include all staff necessary for the Babelsberg White House and that there would be no place in it for any of us Army nonentities. In any case, none of us suspected that such an assignment might be in the cards, but there it was and we were it! Astonishment does not begin to say what I felt!

Harrah and I were immediately taken to a large stucco house on the lake shore. It included open landscaped lots both north and south of the house, had an open porch overlooking the lake and stood three imposing stories high. It was the sort of abode which would have been built at the turn of the century by an industrialist with plenty of money and lots of servants, and according to information provided by the Russians (which turned out to be deliberately misleading), had been the home of the head of the UFA studio. We were instructed that our duties would be to assure the security of the building, to prepare a written inventory of its contents and to report to our superiors any deficiencies or other conditions seeming to us to require correction or repair.

We fell to our tasks with a will, looking on our assignment as a wondrous adventure and a priceless experience. I described the house thusly to my parents in a letter dated August 3:

> The downstairs was very well furnished, somewhat on the style of [a downtown men's] club—big leather chairs and dark colored drapes, etc. A little on the depressing side. On all the other floors, it looked to me as though the Russians had carted away all the decent furniture and supplanted it with horrible Grand Rapids or its German equivalent. Maybe they figured the President came from Missouri and he wouldn't know any better, but somehow, I don't give the Russians credit for that much subtlety. It was pretty gruesome, believe me. Of glassware and silver there was only a token left, enough to fill what glass-fronted sideboards there were. I really thought that the houses occupied by some of the lesser dignitaries were much more tasteful. General [George C.] Marshall and Gen. ["Hap"] Arnold lived together in

a house about three doors down from the White House and it was just like home.

I should have added but didn't that there was only one bathroom on each floor, including the second floor where the master bedroom and four or five guest rooms were situated.

It is not surprising that these arrangements were found less than ideal by the presidential party, which included Secretary of State Byrnes, Admiral Leahy, Chairman of the Joint Chiefs of Staff, and six or seven other dignitaries. According to David McCullough's recent biography *Truman*, the President was not pleased, but resolved to make the best of it. (McCullough also discloses that the official Soviet line regarding the prior ownership of the house was a total fabrication; many years later, Truman received a letter from the son of the former owner stating that for many years the house had been the family homestead of his father, Gustav Miller-Grote, a well-established Berlin book publisher. Russian soldiers who had captured Babelsberg and the house in May, had raped the daughters before their parents' eyes, destroyed china and glassware, and removed a library of old books as a means of filling nearby shell holes. Later, Soviet authorities had replaced the antique furniture with cheaper stuff from other houses nearby. It was no doubt a blessing that neither Truman nor any of the rest of us knew anything of this in 1945.)

There was some other information about my sojourn at the Babelsberg White House which was also omitted from this letter, and that was because, like the incident of the stolen Tommygun in Andernach, it did not reflect especially well on the writer.

When Harrah and I took over the house, we moved into a small maid's room on the third floor. While the beds may have lacked something in "tastefulness," they were in no way deficient so far as comfort was concerned. Indeed, they were traditional European feather beds, with eiderdown quilts and mattresses which were wondrously comfortable, in very marked contrast to the bare ground and straw pallet to which I had lately been accustomed.

After the first day or so, having been left completely on our own, we had completed all that had been asked of us and had turned in our reports, so there was really nothing more for us to do. Accordingly, the urge to arise in the morning markedly diminished. We had an alarm clock, but we saw no reason to set it. This was a mistake.

— Not Me! —

We were unceremoniously awakened the next morning by an austere presence in the bedroom doorway. It turned out to be a 'bird' (full) colonel who was the leader of the White House advance party from Washington on a preliminary inspection tour to assure that everything was in order. The fact that we had not yet arisen at ten-thirty in the morning seemed to him inappropriate, and in a manner which was kindly but stern, he let us know that our conduct was unacceptable and would be monitored carefully. We of course apologized profusely and promised to do better, while I managed to get in a word or two about combat and the infantry. He was a trim and handsome man with a stiff military bearing, but this brought a nod and a faint smile to his face, and he left saying he would check on us the next morning.

We redoubled our efforts during the day, finding small things to be done and a report to write which we addressed to him to demonstrate our thoroughness and reliability, and finally went to bed, carefully setting the alarm for 7:00 a.m.

Alas, the next morning was an absolute carbon copy of the day before! The alarm failed to go off, and there we were in bed at 10:30 a.m., as the sunshine coming through our bedroom window glinted off his silver eagles. He shook his head ruefully and said, "I'm sorry, but I think I'll have to recommend that you men be reassigned." We were speechless, acknowledging by our silence the correctness and inevitability of his decision. The names of Hadden and Harrah went back into the officers' pool, thus ending our White House service.

There really was no reason why I could not have described these events in my letter of August 3, but did I do so? Not me! Not only did I not explain what had really happened, but I felt constrained to reshape the story to present a more congenial (to me) picture. I said:

> I [was] ousted from [my first] job on account of disagreements with my boss, a crotchety old West Pointer. It was good our association ended when it did; we would have come to blows if it had lasted much longer.

Yecch! Not only did I mis-describe the colonel—I would have loved to work for him!—but I actually shifted the blame from myself to him, trying to make him seem truculent and myself patient and forbearing, when it was we that were at fault and he that was forgiving, because he simply requested that we be reassigned without entering any adverse comment in our records. Bless him!

His decision proved a fateful one for me, because it naturally resulted in my being pointed in a totally new direction and given a very different job. What might have followed at the close of the conference had I remained at the Little White House can only be speculated at, but my name did not linger long in the officers' pool. I was immediately reassigned to the Provost Marshal's office of Berlin District Headquarters, the commanding officer of which—the Provost Marshal—was Lt. Col. James P. Smith, Jr., a pixie-ish, gray-haired man from Ipswich, Massachusetts, who was about forty-five. He had been a stock broker in civilian life, and as it turned out, numbered my cousin John Sheldon's father Percy among his friends, which did me no harm. Smith was desperate for help and effusively glad to see me.

The Provost Marshal is the officer on the staff of an army headquarters who is responsible for the establishment and execution of policy by the military police and coordination with other branches. "Headquarters Berlin District" was the name which had just been assigned by SHAEF to the American portion of what had previously been known as the First Allied Airborne Army, which among other less famous exploits had been responsible for the unsuccessful airborne drop, "Market Garden," on Holland the previous September. The FAA furnished a convenient cadre of staff officers to take over the administration of Berlin.

Headquarters Berlin District had moved into a complex of office and manufacturing buildings which had previously been the seat of Telefunken, the largest radio and electronics firm in Germany. The complex was located a mile or so east of Babelsberg in the southwestern Berlin suburb of Zehlendorf, a mainly residential and only lightly damaged area within the American Zone.

Where Col. Smith needed the help, however, was not inside Berlin but in Babelsberg, where large numbers of Washington and foreign dignitaries and support units of all sorts would shortly be descending for stays estimated to be from ten days to a month. It was our responsibility to design and place in effect all appropriate security arrangements for this horde, and we had to do it quickly, for the Conference preliminaries were scheduled to start within ten days of our arrival.

I don't begin to remember all the detail that was involved in this undertaking, but I was immediately given the title of "Assistant Provost

Marshal, U.S. Berlin District" (I hadn't the slightest idea what that meant or even how to spell it—some time later Col. Smith gently pointed out that "marshal" was spelled with only one "l"), and installed in a small second floor office building with two secretaries, one WAC and one German, at the UFA studio. The WAC secretary, an American girl, was really Col. Smith's. He had a larger office next door to mine, but he was rarely in the office, having manifold responsibilities both in Berlin and on the ground in the Conference Compound.

The paperwork fell largely to me and my English-speaking German secretary. There was a ton of it. This was absolutely my first exposure ever to an office environment and procedures, and had the circumstances been even slightly different, I would no doubt have found them novel and even perplexing, but there was no time whatever for such reflection.

We had first to draft bulletins to the various units which would be within the Compound, or which would have to have access to it, to inform them of the location of the military police checkpoints where they could enter and leave the Compound, their hours of operation and concerning the various credentials which would be necessary for their vehicles and personnel to be permitted to enter and leave. The 713th Military Police Battalion was the unit assigned to the Compound and these procedures had to be coordinated and cleared with them. And then we had to get the rosters of all the units which would be within the Compound so that individual and vehicle passes could be issued to each for presentation at the checkpoints. These, in turn, had to be provided with copies of the rosters against which the passes could be checked on presentation. Since at the height of the conference there were no fewer than 5,000 troops who needed to be thus vetted, the project was a large one. On July 16, the day before it was scheduled to open, I wrote, still unable to say what I was doing or where I was (other than Berlin):

> The great flurry of activity is over with, thank God. For the last two weeks I have worked from nine in the morning until twelve or one o'clock at night, without so much consolation as a Sunday off. It started slowly at first, and built up to a crescendo of confusion yesterday and the day before, but now all is peaceful, and all we have to do is see that the machinery that we so laboriously put into motion keeps running smoothly.

I was the one who had to sign all the passes. My signature disintegrated rapidly over the two week period. It started out "Alexander H. Hadden," then went to "A. H. Hadden" with the initials separated and periods after each. Finally it became a single indecipherable scrawl which it remains to this day. Since my full name was typed underneath the signature blank, I always wondered why an alert MP didn't turn in some of the later arrivals for trying to gain entry with forged passes.

When the work of setting up procedures for the Conference finished, I was at last able to get into Berlin. It was a revelation: I wrote on July 16:

> In the American Zone it is not quite so badly damaged as in the portion the Russians have... The heart of the city itself—Unter den Linden and what used to be the fashionable shopping district, and many square miles of built-up area around, an area of about the size of Manhattan Island I should say, is completely flat—not a building left standing. You may gasp when I say Manhattan as a comparison, but so did I when I saw [it]. It really is a terribly depressing place. The only people around are a few ragged scarecrows wandering around over the rubble looking for anything that may have some small worth. The weather is warm and the whole thing gives off an aroma that makes me all too mindful of some of the dreary months we spent during the winter in places like it, living like rats in our holes in the ground and scurrying whenever we heard the familiar whooshing of the shells. I was glad to get out of the place, but also glad that I have seen it. Until you have seen something like this, and on the grand scale never before even approached in warfare, you don't realize that man has already in his hands the weapons that can raze the whole earth. Berlin was a short time ago a healthy, modern and busy city. Now it only stinks of decay and death.

Later in the same letter, after commenting on the lush life being led by those about me, with steak, rare old scotch whiskey and the like, I went on to say (still being unable to reveal that I was at the Potsdam conference, though by this time the general nature and the location of the conference had been in the news for almost two weeks):

...It's all very interesting, but also nauseating from a certain point of view, because it is from our sweat that present events are made possible, and the seriousness of the occasion is not what I think it should be. It's all very well to have a certain degree of comfort, but when it becomes necessary to make arrangements which can't fail to cost many millions of dollars, in the face of those who sweated out the winter in our foxholes, the contrast is ludicrous and I can't help but wonder which of the two parties is closing its eyes to reality. Frankly, I don't know.

A week later these pieties had vanished as I wrote another letter describing in detail too fulsome to repeat here a lucullan dinner party which I had attended (and which I have totally forgotten) and obviously enjoyed without a single pang of conscience.

When the Conference finally started, my responsibilities altered somewhat. I continued to have to man the office at UFA for part of the day, but I was also required to keep tabs on the activities of the military police within the Compound. Among other things, that meant that I had to be at Truman's house regularly, where an MP detachment mounted peripheral guard, supplementing the security arrangements provided by the Secret Service. I got to know one of the principal Secret Service men, a guy named Jim Rowley, and also to see how these men and the other staffers at the Little White House functioned. At one level, I was impressed, and at another, appalled.

When it came to their security duties, they were all business. They went about it quietly and efficiently and with an air of calm authority that was in marked contrast to the military way of barked orders and ostentatious execution of them. It wasn't long before their style seemed to preempt ours, and I for one regarded it as an improvement.

Their off-duty activities, however, were a revelation. Here was the problem: The three Allies had agreed prior to the occupation of Berlin that the existing German currency should be replaced by "occupation marks," a paper currency with small denominations represented by bills the size of a playing card, and larger ones, up to 100 marks, the size of a dollar bill. By a remarkably ill-conceived arrangement, plates for this currency, prepared by the Americans, were given to the Russians, who printed up enormous quantities of it for distribution to their troops. We were told that the Russian soldiers had never been paid during the war, and that the decision to pay them now for all their years of service was a calculated device to enable them to buy and take home to Russia whatever movable objects of value happened to strike their fancy. If this was indeed a deliberately adopted policy, it worked to perfection, for a black market sprang up overnight and began to flourish unbelievably. The Secret Service guys in the Truman White House jumped into this traffic enthusiastically and with both feet. And it wasn't limited just to them. Truman's military aide, Harry Vaughn, an old crony of his from Missouri who had been elevated to be a brigadier general, was also deeply involved.

It became known that the Russians were passionate to possess time pieces. They were completely undiscriminating; the flashier the better. The one item of value beyond reason was a Mickey Mouse watch; it commanded a $500 price at the Brandenburg Gate in downtown Berlin, which was the hub of the market. Other watches were priced accordingly. Similarly, a carton of American cigarettes, readily obtainable in the PX for $1.50, sold for $125 downtown. And you didn't really have to go there, because the nature of this commerce was known to everyone, Germans and British as well as Americans, and the "market" price or amounts close to it, were thus available throughout the Babelsberg Compound.

The reason the traffic was so widespread was that though we all referred to it as the "black market," it wasn't illegal. Apart from serial numbers, there was no way of distinguishing between the marks issued by the Russians and those printed by the Americans, and all of them, without distinction, were readily convertible into U.S. postal money orders to be sent home.

The Truman staffers had one enormous advantage over Army personnel. They had access to a diplomatic pouch which was flown daily to and from Washington, and urgent messages were sent westbound to wives and associates to buy up cheap watches and send them in the eastbound pouch. (Through Jim Rowley, I was able to get my letters home into the pouch, and for two weeks, my parents enjoyed almost overnight service). The Mickey Mouses (Mice?) flowed east in large quantities. If a man had a dozen, he could clear a cool $6,000, and there were those that did.

I was interested to read of General Lucius Clay's impression of this practice. He said:

[B]lack market... [trafficking] was damn prevalent among a lot of people. Some of Mr. Truman's personal staff sold wristwatches and whatnot in Berlin, and turned the military Occupation currency in for dollars. I don't want to be critical. I'm just trying to give you the atmosphere, because, really and truly, I don't believe they fully appreciated the fact that the United States government was paying for all that. (Smith, *Clay: An American Life*, page 304.)

I think Gen. Clay was being excessively kind. Yes, the practice was widespread, and yes, it was technically "legal," but he himself refers to it as "the black market," and it borders on naiveté to suppose that White House personnel could conduct such a blatant commerce for their personal enrichment without realizing that the U.S. government, whose post office was accepting all those Russian marks, was paying for it. As a 20-year-old second lieutenant and clearly no genius, I found this business to be both sordid, and at the White House level, disgusting. I should quickly add that I was no angel. I freely swapped packs of cigarettes for "walking around money," but I steered clear of the large-scale operations exemplified by the White House people.

As one might guess, the temptations represented by all of this available cash did cause some of our military guys to abandon all restraint. Our MP's apprehended a Conference mess sergeant who had backed his company truck up to a supply depot, filled it with food and supplies, and drove it to downtown Berlin, where he was conducting an informal auction, selling the goods to any comer who would offer the going price. The value of everything had flown through the roof and bore no relation to reality. Similarly, another non-com with some confederates drove a group of vehicles into the Russian Zone and was in the midst of selling them for $25,000 when he was arrested. These were strange days!

I had other, happier relations with the Little White House and its occupants. One evening fairly early in the Conference, President Truman invited Churchill and Stalin to a State dinner at his house. It was a warm summer evening and preparations were laid on the rear verandah overlooking the water for the serving of cocktails before dinner. Churchill arrived first, emerging from a tall and ungainly Humber automobile with a single security man whose only armament appeared to be a tightly furled umbrella. The car deposited him at the street end of the driveway and he walked to the front steps of the house, where he was greeted by the President. He was followed a few minutes later by Stalin, who arrived in a long gray limousine with all of the rear blinds drawn. It reminded me of nothing more than the clown-filled vehicle in the circus, because as soon as it had pulled into the driveway and stopped at the steps, the rear door opened and a series of small round men got out, closing up jump seats as they did so. There were many of them, and their function was evidently that of keeping their bodies between Stalin and anyone with whom he might come in contact. He finally emerged himself, resplendent in a high collar silver gray uniform with minimal decorations, making his way slowly up the stairway and into the house.

In my military police capacity I was entitled to remain on hand until the end of the dinner, which lasted about three hours. As after-dinner drinks were being served on the verandah, I was stationed below it and could hear some of the conversation taking place above. A round of toasts was drunk, including one that I remember in particular, which came from Churchill's lips. The general vein of the remarks had been for each of the three leaders to congratulate the others on the feats of his country's armed forces, and when it came Churchill's turn, he said in that wonderful rumbling voice of his that he wished to drink to the "magnificent accomplishments of the glorious Red Army!", and it seemed to me that these words rolled off his tongue with such an excess of stress that they could hardly have been other than sarcastic. If they were so intended, however, the moment was smoothed over by the interpreter, whose translation was even and unaccented.

I described the British and Russian leaders as follows in my letter of August 3:

> Stalin looks much older than he does in... pictures. His hair is a very beautiful shade of gray and matches his mustache exactly. He is... a short, dumpy, but vigorous old man. Churchill is the same, only less vigorous... He is very pale, and struck me as being fat to the point of unhealthiness. He still put on a good show, though. When the dinner was over, he walked down the steps, handed his cane to the driver of his car, and turned to the man who was accompanying him and said "I think I shall walk." Without further ado, he pranced out the gate, and walked right down the middle of the road in the direction of his house, which

must have been a good half mile away. Several cars had to slow down and follow behind him.

With the dinner over, I was selected together with another American officer who was an interpreter to take packages containing empty suitcases, gifts from Truman to Stalin and Churchill, from the American Compound into the Russian and British areas. We were put into a command car, a large four-wheeled vehicle with a convertible top, and driven by an American driver to Stalin's house, which was about a mile away. We were stopped at two separate barrier gates manned by sentries. At the first one, the interpreter, who was a White Russian and a major, leaned over to me and said, "Whatever you do, don't make any sudden movements or the Russian guards will shoot you dead." I needed no second warning. As we drove through the Russian Compound, the headlights illuminated in turn the elite Russian guards in brilliant white and blue uniforms (the colors of the NKVD), each of whom—no more than five yards apart from each other—brought his machine gun to the "present arms" position as our vehicle passed.

When we got to Stalin's house, the major suggested that I should be the one to unload the gifts while he remained in the vehicle. In light of his prior warning I did not rejoice at this suggestion. There were five guards on the porch each of whom had his machine pistol pointed right at my head, as I very slowly put the two packages for Stalin on the pavement by the car and very slowly got back in. A similar delivery to Churchill's house on the way home seemed like giving an apple to the teacher.

I also had a chance to visit the Cecilienhof Castle, which was where the Big Three meetings were held. I described it in my letter of August 3:

> The conference hall was a place to see. Contrary to printed reports, it was not Frederick the Great's palace, Sans Souci,... it was the summer castle built by the Kaiser called the Cecilienhof. Whether or not the Russians decorated it or whether it was already decorated when they took it over, I don't know, but it was a gem. The conference room was one of the most striking rooms I can remember having seen. It was almost cubic in shape, the ceiling being as high as the width of the room. Ceiling high windows comprised one entire end of the room, and the view from it

was superb. In the [enclosed] article from *Stars and Stripes*, the "placid lake" is mentioned. The conferences were usually held in the late afternoon or early evening, and the delegates witnessed some magnificent sunsets. The drapes, carpeting and the table cloth for the round conference table were all of a deep maroon to harmonize with the walnut paneled walls. The three chiefs sat around the table to form a triangle, and each of them had four smaller chairs between them for their foreign ministers, chiefs of staff, and anyone else who happened to be needed. There were three small anterooms adjoining, one assigned to each of the three nations. And the place was big enough so that one large wing was put aside for the delegates of [each]... country. On the second floor were apartments for the secretaries, aides, etc., who had to be present in the building at all times. At conference time every day, three convoys would pull up at three different entrances to the building, surrounded by Scotland Yard, NKVD, or the Secret Service, as the case might have been. Doors would open, and people would scurry through a phalanx of armed guards into the building. In my position of Asst. Provost Marshall [sic], I was several times put in charge of the MP's who rode with the Presidential convoy and I rode with the Secret Service men immediately behind the President's car, which was the one used by General Eisenhower during the war—a tremendous sixteen-cylinder Cadillac with three-inch thick windows and all of the features of a substantial Prohibition automobile. So I had a wonderful opportunity to see the whole show from up close.

My appetite for participation in the entertainment aspects of the Conference was also keen, and I also described a concert and a show staged by Bob Hope. From a letter dated 25 July:

Last night was one of the most interesting I can remember having spent in the last year. A concert was given by the Symphony Orchestra of the RAF at Sans Souci Palace, a tremendous place which was built by Frederick the Great about 1760 and which looks like Versailles gone wild. The grounds that surround the palace are what is really worth seeing. To get to the palace from the highway you must drive down a long, absolutely straight driveway at the end of which you can see the portico of the Palace. The driveway is hedged and is punctuated at intervals of every four hundred yards or so with pools and fountains of various sizes and shapes. The Russians had them all turned on last night in honor of the visiting dignitaries, and had spotlights playing on the whole works, making a very effective show. I have never seen such a tremendous expanse of formal garden anywhere in my life, and it wasn't crowded together as the majority of gardens are.

The concert itself was well worth the time; the orchestra has evidently just completed a tour of the United States, so you may have heard of it. They played a concert of Beethoven, Elgar and Tchaikovsky to a very chic audience, largely British and American, with a sprinkling of Russians. Intermission was a great surprise, for our British cousins went the whole way and served champagne, whisky, vodka, and several other concoctions of less fame calculated to please the taste of whatever nationalities might be present, even including international teetotalers. The atmosphere of the whole performance was something that I had been out of contact with for so long that I had forgotten it existed.

I mentioned the Bob Hope show in several letters, the first of which dealt with my tribulations as a military police functionary responsible for assuring order at the 600-seat UFA theater. The GI's, and officers too, for that matter, were starved for entertainment of this sort, and there was a near riot at the theater when the Special Services people, who were in charge of the arrangements, announced that Hope's plane had been late and that the show would therefore have to be rescheduled to the next night. But the show finally did come off. On 2 August, I wrote:

Bob Hope finally put in an appearance last night and was a sensation. He had a USO troupe with him including Jerry Colonna, but it was a one-man show. I never saw such a howling, hooting audience in my life. At the end of the show when it was obvious he was about to wind things up, the applause was deafening, and wouldn't stop. After making about five exits and entrances for bows, he finally came to the microphone and said "I want to thank the men of Special Services who made the arrangements for the show. It was really wonderful, but they forgot one thing. How the hell do they expect me to ever get out of here without a curtain?"

What this account omits is the totally raunchy content of Hope's material. If there was a clean joke during his hour-long performance, it must have been an oversight. For the GI's, it was the ultimate in relaxation, with no concern for proprieties of any sort and with the added spice of seeing their stiff-necked superiors unbending to revel in it as much as they!

At the end of the conference on August 2, I found myself greatly impressed with the courtesies extended by the conferees to those of us who had provided the manpower for it.

I wrote:

Everyone whom I have talked with who has had anything to do with the Presidential party has nothing but good to say about Truman. After the experiences of the last twelve years it is refreshing to have someone who regards himself as a human being and not as God. Before he left, the President went around and personally thanked everyone who had had anything to do with the running of his "Little White House." He shook the hands of the MP's and had a word for each of them. Two of my fellow shavetails were in charge of his house [I had not yet found a way to mention to my parents that I had originally been assigned that job], and he personally drafted and signed a letter of thanks and commendation for them which he directed be put in their AGO [personnel] files. He also had his picture taken with them, with the orderlies, and with the MP's. Really quite a democratic fellow. I must admit that I was surprised at the appreciation expressed by every one of the delegates. General Arnold and Gen. Marshall each gave some sort of personal remembrance to those who had been concerned with their mess, house, etc. It really means a lot to the GI's who have worked so hard. As a general rule, most brass seem to think that such things are a matter of course, and have forgotten how to say thank you.

One of these "thank you" sessions caused me a bit of embarrassment. I was standing at the front steps of the Little White House as Generals Marshall, Arnold and Omar Bradley were thanking and shaking hands with some of us. Early in the war Bradley had been the commanding general of the 28th Division and later had commanded the 12th Army Group when the 28th Division had been a part of it, and noticing the Bloody Bucket patch on my shoulder, he asked me what my unit had been. I told him Company B of the 112th Infantry Regiment. He responded, "A good outfit. Who was your regimental commander? Was it Col. Fuller?" At the moment, Col. Nelson's name did not spring to mind, but not wanting to appear stupid, I instantly agreed. It was only somewhat later that I learned that we were both trying to impress each other (and the others present), because Fuller had commanded a different regiment of the 28th. But at least Bradley was trying to be cordial.

As I have noted, censorship had been re-imposed on those of us at the conference from the very beginning on July 2. As indicated by the comment in my letter of that date, it seemed to be warranted; we all assumed that the security of the conferees fully justified keeping the fact of the conference secret. But while the holding and location of the sessions became publicly known almost immediately, censorship remained rigorously in effect, and those of us at the conference continued to be barred from saying what we were doing. I was puzzled as to why. I didn't figure it out until very recently, after I had an opportunity to review copies of the *New York Times* for the period.

According to the *Times*'s contemporaneous accounts, it had already been agreed as a part of the preplanning for the conference that there would be no publicity whatever with regard to the agenda or to the decisions reached until the end of the meetings, at which time a formal communiqué would be issued. The subject was again addressed at the opening session of the conference on July 17, at which time, in the interest of promoting frank and open dialogue, and over the mild objections of Churchill (see Churchill, page 650), it was reconfirmed. As was expected, this provoked a storm of protest from the Fourth Estate, including the filing of formal petitions with the authorities, etc. The policy remained firmly in effect, however, and notwithstanding the release of bits of information regarding the social scene (such for example as the holding by Truman of the state dinner on July 18), I suppose it can be argued that the confidentiality of the deliberations might conceivably have been jeopardized if all of us there had been free to write letters about what we were seeing and doing. In any case, censorship was not finally relaxed until the end of the meeting.

One startling happening during the conference was that the results of the first general election in the United Kingdom since before the war became known. The actual voting had taken place on July 7, but because of the delays involved in getting the servicemen's votes tabulated, the outcome was not announced to anyone, including the principals, until the 26th. Churchill, brimming with confidence concerning the likelihood of the Conservative Party's being reelected, had nonetheless brought Clement Attlee, leader of the Labour Party, to the Conference. Attlee was a mousy man, whose inconspicuous appearance seemed to fully justify Churchill's classic comment that he was "a modest man, with much to be modest about."

Nonetheless, when he and Churchill went home to England to await the election results, it was the Labourites who were swept into power by a landslide, and it was Attlee who returned, which was a surprise and disappointment to virtually everyone including Stalin, who had become convinced with some justice that he could "handle" Churchill.

Developments of monumental importance were taking place, however. As was only much later revealed, it was in Babelsberg that Truman received word from Los Alamos, New Mexico, that the atomic bomb had been successfully tested in the desert. The first coded message, received July 17th, revealed that the "baby boy" had been born. A fuller account, received the next day, disclosed that the detonation exceeded some of the most optimistic predictions, fully justifying Churchill's later characterization of it (*Triumph and Tragedy*, page 638) as assuring "a speedy end to the Second World War, and perhaps to much else besides."

Much discussion then took place between Truman and Churchill and their staffs as to what use should be made of this startling information in the course of the Conference. It would of course not do to fail to mention it to Stalin, ostensibly a trusted ally, only to order its use on Japan a few days later. Neither, however, were Truman and Churchill anxious, now that almost immediate victory was assured in the Pacific, to give him any encouragement to declare war on the Japanese, which Russia had not previously done, and thus assure itself of a seat at the peace conference with standing to make territorial demands, etc.

It was finally decided that following the close of a formal session at the Cicilienhof, Truman would make mention of it to Stalin in an apparently offhand way. He casually announced to the Russian leader that a novel bomb of "unusual destructive force" had been detonated, to which Stalin responded equally casually in a way suggesting that he did not truly understand the significance of what he had been told. It is the astonishing fact, however, that Stalin already knew a good deal about the atomic bomb through intelligence agents at Los Alamos, and that his low-key reaction was intended to protect these sources. (See Margaret Truman, *Harry S. Truman*, Pocket Books edition, page 301.)

It will surprise no one who was an active participant in the war, but may cause raised eyebrows amongst readers of less mature years, that there was never suggested by any of the American or British leaders assembled at Babelsberg that the bomb might not be used. Churchill's memoir makes this inescapably clear. Noting that the ultimate decision was Truman's, he says:

> ...I never doubted what it would be, nor have I ever doubted since that he was right. The historic fact remains, and must be judged in the after-time, that the decision whether or not to use the atomic bomb to compel the surrender of Japan was never even an issue. There was unanimous, automatic, unquestioned agreement around our table; nor did I ever hear the slightest suggestion we should do otherwise. (Churchill, *Triumph and Tragedy*, page 639.)

And so it happened. The directive to use the bomb on Japan went out from Babelsberg to the Armed Forces, as a result of which the first one was dropped on Hiroshima on August 6.

On my 1990 trip to Europe, I revisited Babelsberg and found the site dramatically and ironically altered from the scene I knew in 1945. For details as to its present state, I invite the reader's attention to the September 3, 1990, entry in my journal. It will suffice here to record only that in 1961 the front lawns of the Truman, Churchill and Stalin residences had all become a part of the front line of the Cold War when an unbroken extension of the Berlin Wall was built between each of the houses and the lake, which, with barbed wire and machine gun towers, was designed to prevent the escape of East Germans across the Griebnitzsee into West Berlin's American Zone.

As regards the other important issues considered at the Potsdam Conference, the historical record is clear that its true significance was to mark the starting point of the Cold War. While the discussions were characterized by a surface cordiality, the grim reality was that beneath the surface, Stalin was completely intransigent on almost all issues of substance. They were enormous and complex, including as they did his having already reneged on his promise at Yalta to hold democratic elections in Poland, his demands that the German-Polish-Russian borders should be moved many miles westward, how to resettle and feed the millions of Germans and Poles thus displaced, what economic policies should be followed by the occupation forces, etc., etc. The bargaining strengths of the parties had already been altered by the American withdrawal of forces from their line of furthest advance and by an unwillingness on Truman's part to insist that the hard decisions be made on the spot. Churchill was quite willing to press for a showdown, and if necessary, a public break with Stalin, but he of course never returned to the conference after the election. Thus the best that could be done was to refer all of these difficult issues to a council of foreign ministers which was to meet regularly in the future. Although a few of these were held, there never was any possibility of agreement.

The result was that the Eastern Europe border questions were settled in accordance with Stalin's wishes and Communist governments were installed there because of the presence of the Red Army, rather than by international treaty.

The Conference's final communiqué was released on August 2. Not unnaturally, it emphasized the areas with respect to which the conferees had been able to reach agreement, such as reparations from Germany to the Allies and how the latter would conduct the occupation and government of the country. But correspondents instantly focused on the areas on which accord was not reached, commenting in one instance at least that failure to settle territorial boundaries represented a "glaring omission" and that referral of such questions to foreign ministers was unpromising because they would have no power to reach any conclusions. (See Hanson Baldwin article, *New York Times* of August 2, 1945.)

A few days earlier, on July 26th, there had been a release of another sort which dealt not with the subjects under discussion at the conference, but with the surrender terms which the three powers at war with Japan—the U.S., Britain and China—were now willing to accept. Because it was not as yet at war with Japan, the Soviet Union was not a party to this document, which was somewhat misleadingly called the "Potsdam Declaration." Its terms, which had been communicated to the Japanese a few days earlier, were remarkably close to the policy which it had long seemed to me should have been the basis on which peace with Germany had been approached, but wasn't: that is, complete disarmament, elimination of the military dictatorship; establishment of democratic government, temporary occupation by the Allies, etc. The Declaration also contained, however, firm assurances of eventual sovereignty, and of the right to rebuild her industries and to have access to the world's raw materials. It also promised "complete and utter destruction" if the terms were not accepted, which of course they were on August 14 after the dropping of the A-bombs on August 6 and 9. The USSR meanwhile had declared war on Japan on August 8!

I summarize the results of the Conference simply to round out the context in which it wound down, and without intending to suggest that I had any particular awareness of them. To the contrary, my letters during the conference were full of speculation regarding my own immediate future, rather than the world's. Towards the end of it, it was becoming clear that my assignment as Assistant Provost Marshal, U.S. Berlin District, would in all probability continue. My letter of August 2 opened with the following:

> Well, it's all over but the shouting; everybody that is anybody left this morning. Now all that remains is the monumental task of getting all the soldiers, equipment and what have you back to Berlin. I expect that the next couple of days will reveal a lot about what will become of me. Colonel Smith hasn't said too much about whether or not I will remain in the Provost Marshal's [finally the correct spelling] in Berlin. I would like very much to, as I think I have said before. I asked him yesterday, and he was very evasive about it, but he sort of smirked complacently as if to say I shouldn't ask such stupid questions, so I think my chances are good. His manner would make one think so anyway.

And so it turned out. Two days later, I closed a letter with a postscript which said:

P.S. Office closed—moving to Berlin, R.I.P.

I have found it difficult to put myself back in the shoes of the 20-year-old lieutenant at Babelsberg and to try to see those events again through my youthful eyes. I am appalled at the repetitious references, from which for the most part I have spared the reader, to all the dining and wining which I felt compelled to lay before my hometown audience. It was by no means the first time in my wartime correspondence (nor yet the last) that I was at pains to project the image of a devil-may-care bon-vivant, but I shudder as I reread my letters to see how sophomoric they must have seemed to my parents, and only God knows what my teetotaling grandmother must have thought!

Well, perhaps there were some extenuating circumstances. Part of it, I'm sure, was the lingering effects of combat. Yes, I had celebrated my "salvation" at Andernach, but that was only three months ago, and it was a very long time indeed—years in some cases—before some of the traumatic after effects of the foxholes flickered finally out. I sometimes would wake up in the morning in Babelsberg after a good night's sleep (not including the two at the Little White House) marveling at where I was, scarcely able to believe it. But for every night like that there would be others when sleep was clouded with anxious dreams. Any loud noise would awaken me in a sweat. So perhaps I may be forgiven if a note of exaltation was allowed to creep occasionally into a letter. It was still hard to realize that I had survived and had a life of normal expectancy to lead.

But I am still chagrined at my total lack of interest in the significance of the events which were unrolling under my nose. I did make the comment in my July 16 letter regarding the egregious contrast between life in the infantry and the lush existence at Babelsberg, but that appears to have been mostly lip service, because I was ready a few days later to revel in the latter without apology. Also, I couldn't have learned anything about the concerns of the conference even if I had wanted to, because the Cecilienhof's doors during plenary sessions were sealed even to someone like me who had a plausible reason to be there.

The real reason for my indifference lies, I think, in the very deep-seated cynicism which had settled upon me by the time the war ended. Some sense of this emerges, I am sure, from letters I have quoted from. In short, I didn't think that anything that might be happening behind those doors would really represent a sensible management of the world's affairs.

In retrospect I marvel at the wondrous coincidence that landed me at the Potsdam Conference, and as a result on the permanent staff of the U.S. Berlin District. Of course, the multitude of evils which loomed before me at Marburg would have completely evaporated with the surrender of Japan, and none of the alternatives could possibly have been very dire (they most likely would have involved routine supervision of occupation troops in the American Zone of West Germany), but my experiences at the conference and those I was about to have in Berlin were unique and irreplaceable; and for once I think I was properly grateful, even though I may not have known whom to thank.

One whom I did thank, and most profusely, was Col. Smith. We really got to be good friends, notwithstanding the large age difference. A good number of my fellow lieutenants from OCS did manage to make the leap from Babelsberg to Berlin, but there were many who didn't, too, and they were sent back west for other duty, so it was only through the Colonel's good offices that the opportunity opened up for me in Berlin.

On August 5, I sent the following cable home:

AM ASSIGNED BERLIN DISTRICT PROVOST MARSHAL. WELL AND HAPPY. LOVE TO ALL.

I learned of the dropping of the A-bomb on Hiroshima the very next day. If I was indifferent to the results at the Cecilienhof, my reaction to this news was one of both astonishment and relief. My own future was of course already reasonably secure because of my assignment to Berlin. But I also recognized that any slight likelihood of a trip to Asia was now eliminated.

In Berlin in 1945, any American raising a question as to the propriety of the decision to drop the bomb would have been regarded as crazy. Even today I would agree with Churchill's pronouncement that while there may eventually be a different view in the "after-time," the decision was not only unquestionably correct but probably inescapable.

My one contemporaneous comment on the subject was in a letter dated August 13:

> ...I am grateful for the [A-bomb] because it certainly put the Japs on the skids in a hurry. I may now be able to cram [in] five

— Not Me! —

years of civilian life before the whole thing starts all over again.

I may have been wrong about the five years, but was I also about the inevitability of war?

Berlin

Paris

The Trip Home

August 1945-July 1946

Berlin: First Duties

Viewed as a clock face with the Brandenburg Gate as its center, the 1945 map of Berlin was divided roughly as follows: The sector from 12 o'clock to 4:30 was the Soviet Zone, that from 4:30 to 9:00 was the American Zone, from 9:00 to 11:00 was British, and a small sliver from 11:00 to 12:00 was French. Because of a non-symmetrical distribution of suburbs, the Soviet Zone had well in excess of fifty percent of the population, while American and British Zones, being blessed with a number of lakes and parks, tended to have the largest concentration of affluent suburbs.

While there was absolutely no part of the city which had entirely escaped damage, the heaviest toll had been visited upon the city center and the industrialized portions to the north and east; these were the directions from which the heaviest Russian attacks had come. Hence the southwestern suburbs, such as Dahlem and Zehlendorf, had come through largely unscathed, the cosmetic scars of small arms fire and broken windows being about the worst that had happened. It was in these areas that the American administrative machinery was installed.

There were two principal headquarters. One, known as the U.S. Group Control Council (later the Office of Military Government—United States, or OMGUS) was located in a former Luftwaffe headquarters complex in Dahlem. The buildings were imposing, some of them clad in white marble, and it was here that General Clay, whose steadfast support of the city's status as a western enclave over the years was to pay such rich dividends in 1989, had his headquarters. I did not set foot in this building until 1990, by which time the government functions of the occupiers had long since been turned over to Germans and the complex had become the headquarters for the 5,000 or so troops which remained as the U.S. garrison. I had a fascinating meeting there on September 4, 1990, with Maj. Gen. Haddock, the commander of those forces, to which entry in my Journal those interested are invited to turn.

In 1945, however, Headquarters, U.S. Berlin District was located in the Telefunken complex, an ugly set of buildings, two to three stories high, with an unadorned concrete exterior painted in a drab gray-green. A five- or six-story clock tower surmounted the main entrance. The whole complex covered about five acres, and it was here that I now took up my labors.

I had now been somewhat exposed to office life in Babelsberg, but I was a complete and total stranger to the functioning of an army headquarters, and this was a large one.

There were probably as many as 20,000 U.S. troops in Berlin at the time. These included the 2nd Armored Division, later replaced by the 82nd Airborne, and a wide variety of auxiliary and supporting units. All of the activities of these units were controlled by the army headquarters, which was organized, as it took me arduous trial and error experience to learn, along standard military lines, as follows:

G-1 - Personnel
G-2 - Intelligence
G-3 - Plans and Operations
G-4 - Supplies and Ordnance

The Provost Marshal's office, being concerned largely with the policing of Army personnel, came logically under the wing of G-1, headed by a bird colonel to whom my boss, Col. Smith, reported. The G-1 area of the office complex was near the main entrance in a wing extending to the right. There were probably fifty people, including officers and enlisted men, in G-1. The PM area at the outset consisted of three offices and a large work space about forty feet by thirty feet. Colonel Smith had one office, an adjacent one was occupied by a first lieutenant named Martin Gabel and myself (we both held the title of "Assistant Provost

Marshal"), and the third one housed two or three non-coms, who also used the work area. This latter space was used for a variety of functions, the most important of which was the planning and design of maps and traffic control devices for use within the U.S. sector of Berlin. In addition to the enlisted personnel, we had two or three civilian employees.

One of these, whose name was Otto, was a trained engineer. He was about 45 years old and was emaciated by malnutrition to a degree which was remarkable even for civilians in 1945 Berlin. But he exhibited all of those traits, both commendable and less so, for which the German character is justly known. He was diligent, bright, meticulous and respectful to the point of obsequiousness. But if you gave him a project to do and made sure that he understood it (not always easy with the language problem, but that decreased over time), you could be sure that it not only would be done, but done in a way that might well be an improvement over what you had in mind. It would be inaccurate to say we became friends—he was too deferential—but we liked each other and even found ways to share small jokes from time to time.

It is worth noting here that the non-fraternization policy officially announced by Gen. Eisenhower towards the end of 1944 was revoked in mid-July, 1945. It was high time. It was well-intended, but based on the erroneous assumption that Nazism had somehow altered the basic human make-up of every German.

There can be no doubt that the vast majority of Germans were strong supporters of the Nazi regime and believed in Hitler's propaganda proclaiming the "mission" of the "Master Race." But it is also clear that during the war the worst depravities of the Nazi regime—the concentration camps, gas chambers and genocide—were largely secret and if suspected were certainly not acknowledged by the man in the street. When they were revealed, most Germans—at least those who were not members of the Nazi party—reacted with repugnance, horror and disgust not only at their intrinsic horror but also at the enormous scope of the program, and a deep sense of shame and collective guilt descended on them. When that happened, it placed in an inescapable klieg light how total and deserved was Germany's defeat, and whatever merit there might once have been in the policy evaporated.

A final, practical observation about non-fraternization is that very few paid much attention to it even at the beginning. There were no doubt violations and attempts to enforce the policy through discipline, but I recall no such instances, and if there were any, they would necessarily have been overturned or commuted when the policy was revoked.

At the beginning, my job in Berlin focused on traffic direction and control. There were many aspects to being "Traffic Officer," which was another title I acquired. An officious civilian consultant whose name was Gross and who hailed from Chicago arrived on the scene at about the same time I did, and the two of us with a GI driver spent much time on the streets of Berlin learning the lay of the land and developing a plan for the routing of traffic.

For the most part it was American military traffic. This came into the city from Helmstedt, 110 kilometers to the west over the single autobahn reserved for American use across the Russian Zone of Occupation. It then had to be routed over a series of main arteries to the locations of the various, and regularly changing, military units stationed in the city.

When we arrived, the highways were a mess. There were many of them which were blocked by the bombing, and appropriate closures and detours had to be arranged. There were no up-to-date maps available. The autobahn and the streets within the city were a forest of Russian and American signs; the Russian ones were no longer relevant, and the American ones were often out of date and conflicting. So we set about to remedy the situation through the development of a traffic plan, the preparation of maps implementing the plan, reproduction and distribution of copies to all units, arranging newspaper and radio publicity, coordination of the whole affair with other police entities (German civilian, and military police for the other three occupying powers), and last but not least, removal of all the old confusing signs and replacement of them by standardized new ones. Much of the physical labor connected with these efforts was delegated to our crew of civilian employees, but it nonetheless took many weeks of work to get the job organized and completed, much of it tedious.

One of its more interesting aspects was the coordination of it with the German civil police. Their concern, of course, was law enforcement with respect to the civilian population, which was estimated at about 2,500,000 people. The German police were mostly new to the job, having been installed by the Russians after they had cashiered the majority of the old force. Police procedures were new to many of them, and even the few old timers found it hard to comprehend such novel concepts as requiring pedestrians to cross at crosswalks. Thus there was a process of mutual education which took place, no small part of which consisted of my learning some of the basics of traffic control from my more knowledgeable associates.

The total volume of vehicular traffic in Berlin was not large by stateside standards, but even so we had a real problem with accidents. Civilian vehicles were limited mostly to municipal officials, doctors and other emergency personnel, and while the military traffic was considerable, it seemed to give rise to injuries and deaths way out of proportion to its volume. The civilian population was weighted with elderly people many of whom were in desperate straits when it came to nourishment. They had no choice but to spend almost all daylight hours foraging for food and fuel. They would take baby carriages or other primitive conveyances to the Grunewald, a large forest preserve on the western edge of the American Zone, to gather wood which they would drag back home, and they were of course exhausted and inattentive, while the GI's behind the wheel were not inclined to be particularly considerate.

One way we attempted to address the problem was to inaugurate a quite stringent set of speed limits on the main drags which we then vigorously publicized over the Armed Forces radio station in Berlin. (I remember hearing one GI shriek that he would go crazy if he heard the announcement about the 30 mile per hour speed limit on Potsdamer and Schloss Strasses one more time!) Many arrests and disciplinary proceedings ensued which did not endear the MP's to their compatriots, but they did help cut down on accidents.

By a strange coincidence, I myself became an accident statistic in the first week of September. I described it as follows in a letter of September 9:

> Last Thursday I was involved in a slight automobile accident. We (myself and a driver) were driving along a double lane road with an island in the middle and were going along about 30 when a 2½ ton truck driven by a GI came out from our left between two of the islands without stopping. The driver of the jeep put the brakes on but it was a smooth road and we skidded into the truck, hitting it in the rear tires. The halt was abrupt, to say the least, and I continued right on forward towards the windshield, hitting it and breaking it all to hell. For its part, it managed to give me quite a cut in the forehead, and I commenced to drip

buckets of blood. The jeep was pretty well smashed up, but I climbed under my own power into the truck and it took me to a dispensary which luckily was a couple of blocks away.

I ended up with six stitches, a scar over my left eye and an unnecessary but enforced hospital stay of five days. The driver of the truck, you may believe, was petrified at having run into a Military Police vehicle, but the matter was processed before I got out of the hospital and I don't believe anything dire happened to him.

Unfortunately, the same could not be said of my jeep, but one of the great advantages of being associated with the military police was that jeeps and vehicles of all kinds kept coming into our possession with no one coming forward to claim ownership. This was the result of a rather casual attitude which had developed among soldiers at all levels during the war with regard to Army property. We were all accustomed to seeing it damaged, destroyed or misappropriated, and the strict record-keeping and accountability which were supposed to be the rule had become very haphazard. All the same, if a vehicle fell into the hands of the MP's it could not be recovered without proof of ownership, and it thus often happened that a jeep impounded for illegal parking, for example, would remain unclaimed because those who had parked it could not explain how they came to possess it nor produce evidence of title. No doubt as MP's we should have been above reproach and have turned all such vehicles in to Ordnance, and for the most part we did, but not until our own needs had been met (surely that was only reasonable!), and thus I enjoyed the luxury of my own jeep throughout my stay in Berlin.

It was also distinctly unkosher for an officer to be seen driving his own vehicle. In theory, every jeep or truck was supposed to be in the charge of an enlisted man whose job it was to drive and care for it, and officers were supposed to travel only as passengers, as I had been when I had been hurt. This rule, too, had gone by the boards and no one in Berlin paid it the slightest mind, which was a very substantial convenience both to my business and social life.

Our jurisdiction over vehicle ownership provided me with an exciting evening's entertainment one night when I was duty officer in the Provost Marshal office at Telefunken. An edict had come down from on high that all German civilian-style vehicles in Army custody should be registered with Ordnance, which theoretically was responsible for their maintenance. This ukase had been duly distributed and publicized, and after a decent interval directions were sent out to the MP units that vehicles found on the streets without the proper registration sticker were to be towed and impounded.

It turned out that most of the many cars brought in were the "property" of senior officers who stormed into the office enraged that the "idiot MP's" had dared to interfere. Naturally they all wanted to shoot the person responsible. It was only with a certain difficulty that I was able to persuade the more irascible of these dignitaries that it was not me. A copy of the printed directive over the signature of Floyd Parks, our Commanding General, finally proved convincing.

One of the more routine functions of the provost marshal office was the collecting and compiling of statistical information relating to disciplinary matters, such as arrests, courts martial, sentences to the stockade and the like. The Army regarded venereal disease as a "command responsibility," meaning that it was believed that the commanding officer of each unit should be able to educate his men through proper training programs as to the means of avoiding such disease and thus eliminate the problem. Hence the officer was himself subject to discipline if the incidence of disease in his unit rose above a very low level, something like one or two percent, as I recall. On one weekly report an all time world record was set: a unit known as the 827th Quartermaster Laundry Detachment, consisting of twelve men, reported twelve cases of venereal disease. The poor second lieutenant in command was no doubt guillotined!

Im Schonower Park
In a normal army headquarters, such as one in the States, unmarried officers would be housed in the Bachelor Officers Quarters, or "BOQ" on the post. I never had the misfortune of having to dwell in one of these spartan buildings. Each officer so housed would of course have his own private room, but it would be small in size and institutional in atmosphere. My accommodations in Berlin were neither.

By the time the conference was over in Babelsberg and we finally moved to Berlin, the housing mavens of G-4 had ranged through the suburbs adjacent to Telefunken and had identified dozens of houses which were requisitioned for the use of the headquarters' officer personnel, and although they did receive compensation, the owners and occupants were summarily ousted.

I never did meet the owner of No. 7 Im Schonower Park, our home on a cul de sac road in the suburb of Schonow, just over the line from Zehlendorf. From the contents of his library, however, it was evident that he was an architect, because he had a large selection of architectural books and manuals in his well-appointed living room. Many of these depicted and celebrated the wondrous edifices of Nazi design, such as the meeting hall in Nuremberg, the Berlin Olympic Stadium and the Reichschancellery building in downtown Berlin. It was clear that our involuntary landlord had been a profitably practicing Nazi.

As the street name suggests, the house was in a small park with many mature shade trees and wooded paths leading away in several directions. There were about five other houses in the cul de sac.

Number 7 was not a large house, but it was extremely comfortable. There was a front entry hall, a living room, dining room, pantry, kitchen and lavatory on the first floor and four bedrooms and a bath on the second floor. A coal furnace and other utilities were in the basement, which was under the aegis of a German civilian hired by G-4 to care for it. We had a phone and every possible other comfort, and no one whatever to watch over us. We hardly even felt we were in the Army!

"We" was myself and three other lieutenants with varying staff assignments at our headquarters. The one I remember best was a lad named Bill Fulljames, known for some reason as "Bully," who was Post Exchange Officer for the headquarters. This was a job with as many or more perks than mine. The PX started small, but it grew in size and elaborateness, largely through Bully's efforts. He was blond and good looking, and with a ready smile, always ready for a good time. But he was also ambitious and hard working and aspired to have his PX the biggest and best in Europe. He traveled widely, to Switzerland, for example, for watches and other jewelry, and to France for perfume and assorted luxuries. His housemates always had their choice of the goodies he brought back from these trips.

His functions came under G-4, and it proved useful during the coming winter to have his connections there because there was a coal shortage at one point from which we, however, never suffered. His access to booze and edible goodies was also limitless, which led to our house's developing a merited reputation for the throwing of elaborate parties.

Oh, yes, I almost forgot to mention that Bully was able to arrange for the services of a painfully shy but good-natured housekeeper who saw conscientiously to our needs and even graduated to a basis of friendship. I don't recall her name but a picture survives. (See photo section.)

Both our house and its comfortable and private neighborhood remained exactly as I had left them when I revisited Berlin forty-five years later in 1990.

The Reichschancellery
On that visit, one of the memorable places I most wanted to revisit was the Reichschancellery, which was a stunning building designed and built by Albert Speer in the early years of the Nazi regime and which had served as Hitler's headquarters up until the very end. I was disappointed—but not surprised—to learn that it had long since been razed, a gentle bulldozed mound being the only reminder of its former location.

The Chancellery was in the Wilhelmstrasse, whose name evokes echoes in the ears of anyone old enough to remember William S. Shirer's CBS radio broadcasts from Berlin in 1939. In addition to the Chancellery, the street housed the embassies of the other principal powers who were engaged in the ominous diplomatic negotiations which led to the outbreak of war in 1939. Thus the Wilhelmstrasse was often mentioned—seemingly with a malevolent personality of its own—as the focus of these machinations: "The atmosphere is tense in the Wilhelmstrasse tonight," Shirer would intone.

The building was faced with finely grained tan marble. Its facade featured an imposing two-story-high entry (my brother and I had our pictures taken there when he visited Berlin) adjacent to which was the famous balcony on which Hitler was wont to review troops and receive the homage of his dirndl- and lederhosen-clad subjects.

After mounting a short flight of stairs and passing through a vestibule, one entered the enormous reception hall, likewise of tan marble. It was about forty by sixty feet in area with a vaulted, gold-ribbed ceiling fully thirty feet high. The marble floor was covered by a huge and heavy wool carpet—not an oriental—with the same kind of simple and dramatic pattern which the Nazis favored in all of their designs. The only furniture in the room was a large walnut desk with torchières on either side and a stately chair behind. It was in this austere and overpowering setting that the Führer liked to receive—and as often as not, curtly dismiss—the supplicant representatives of smaller countries which he was determined to devour.

I went to the Chancellery many times (it really held a fascination for me), but of course my visits were all after the war and were to a building which had been heavily damaged both by the Allied air raids and during the Russian siege of the city. The scars of small arms fire were everywhere. The roof over the reception hall was half destroyed and the magnificent carpet—it was fully an inch and a half thick—was waterlogged and full of plaster debris. There was a closet in the wall immediately to one's left on entering, and its door had been torn away to reveal a cabinet containing hundreds of the military decorations, Iron Crosses and the like, for Hitler to award to his brave soldiers. No one who visited came away without several of these as souvenirs, and it wasn't long before the drawers were all strewn about and the only medals left were those that were soiled or broken.

On the northern side of the building, the one which abutted the Tiergarten, there was a walled garden. This was the site of the famed Hitler Bunker, the three-floor underground structure in which he took refuge in the last weeks of the war and in which he and his newly married wife, Eva Braun, finally committed suicide both by poison and gunshot. The bunker was an elaborate, self-contained structure, with conference rooms, kitchens, private apartments and even a jail cell.

The bunker was also a shambles. It had been ravaged by fire and explosives, and there were human remains in several locations within the bunker as well as outside in the garden. The aroma was quite naturally putrid.

In 1945 there was considerable doubt as to how and where Hitler had met his end. Indeed, there was even speculation as to whether he might not have escaped, and it was not until several years had passed and virtually all eyewitnesses had been found and interviewed that the details of the double suicide were finally confirmed and it could authoritatively be concluded that the married couple's bodies had been wrapped in a rug or blanket, taken up to the garden, soaked with gasoline and burned. The effort at cremation, conducted in haste by an NCO, was only partially successful, and the "remains of the remains," looking like what you might find in the bottom of your garbage can, were open to view for weeks during the summer of 1945, because while they were evidently human in origin, no one had any idea whose they were. When I finally found the sources which resolved all doubt, it was fascinating to realize that I had actually gazed upon the remains of Adolph Hitler!

Three Colonels

I have already described my first boss, Lt. Col. James P. Smith, Jr. I served under him for four months until about November when he was finally shipped home. He had a vast number of points, well over a hundred, but General Parks (another fearless leader who didn't deign to show his countenance among his juniors though his office was thirty paces from mine) decreed that he was "essential" because no replacement for him was readily available. He stayed on grumblingly, but he didn't feel so put upon that he failed to have a good time.

Colonel Smith was in his middle or late forties. Both he and I had made the acquaintance of a lady named Lisl Wellesz (pronounced "Velless"), who was a civilian employee of the Army, entitled to a junior officer's privileges and uniform. Lisl was a charming Viennese lady about forty years old whose fluent English was very expressively tinged with the accent of that city (very unlike a northern German accent), whose eyes constantly twinkled and who was full of smiles. Her job had something to do with military government—I never did quite figure out what—but she turned out to be the constant companion of Col. Smith.

Lisl was often in our office visiting the colonel, and as I got to know her, I learned that the great enthusiasm of her life was music, particularly opera, and so it wasn't long before she had fanned the flames of interest in both Col. Smith and me in attending the Staatsoper on Unter den Linden in the Russian zone. The colonel had ready access to tickets to these events and before long all three of us became more of less regulars at the performances. I would mislead if I were to pretend that a love of opera was my principal motivation (I suspected the colonel's views were like mine); the gala social scene was at least an equal attraction for both of us, and for that matter was in no way a minus for Lisl. All the same I was no stranger to classical music and did enjoy the performances.

Lisl was herself a musician and there was at least one occasion on which she played and sang a few light opera numbers at a party at 7 Im Schonower Park which Col. Smith—no doubt for good and proper reason—did not attend. She had a charming voice and delighted the invitees, who were junior American officers and their German and American dates, every bit as much as she was delighted by their considerably younger company. She was a wonderfully warm-hearted woman of whom I have always kept the fondest of memories.

That is, all except on one occasion a couple of years later when I was back at Yale completing my senior year. Three roommates and I then occupied a small dormitory suite originally designed for two students, and the rooms were both crowded and messy. One winter afternoon there was a knock on our door and two severely-dressed gentlemen entered, presented FBI credentials and asked for me. The sofa in our small living room was covered with overcoats, and as I cleared the mess and ushered my roommates out, I wondered what in God's name I had done to have earned their attention.

They then asked me if I recalled a woman named Elizabeth Wells. I pondered a moment and then responded that the name meant nothing to me. They were insistent. I still had no idea whom they were talking about. They said they were sure I knew her and finally referred to Berlin. I said, "For God's sake, you mean Lisl Wellesz!", pronouncing the name the way I remembered it. They declined to concede that they had mispronounced the name, but agreed that it was she about whom they were inquiring. They wished to know what I could tell them about her. I asked the reason for the inquiry, which they refused to explain. In the end I told them as much as I could about her, giving to the best of my ability a rave review. They pressed as to whether there were any "negative" or "subversive" associations which I could remember (the Cold War had started by this time), and I told them that the only "association" of any description that I could recall was that with Col. Smith, which I hardly viewed in that way. The two of them, who could have been monosyllabic models for Sgt. Joe Friday of "Dragnet", finally said a grudging thank you and departed.

I've always since assumed that Lisl had applied for some sensitive position in government service and was in the process of being vetted for it, and have hoped that I helped her get it.

Not long before Col. Smith returned to his wife in Ipswich, Massachusetts, I chanced to be in his office looking for a longhand memo which he had said he would leave for me. I found such a paper and was well into reading it before I discovered it was a letter to his wife; it did not start with the conventional greeting. The portion of it which I had scanned said that while he was greatly looking forward to coming home, his job had been very interesting and that he had enjoyed the association he had had with "the junior officers." He said that they "were terribly young and not dry behind the ears, but boy, are they good and they remember everything!" In addition to being wet, my ears were red when I read this passage, but it has always made me think fondly of the Colonel, especially as the years have advanced and I have better understood his comment about youthful memory.

The fact was that I did have a prodigious memory at that age. It was, I think, the product of two factors. I don't know whether the human mind, like a computer, has a finite limit as to how much it can hold, but at the time, mine, I am sure, held very little and thus there was plenty of unused capacity. Second and probably more important, everything was so new and fascinating that I sopped it up like a dry sponge. I was a voracious reader of everything remotely touching my job and found I was able to classify and arrange it in my head so that I could come up with what was relevant to a particular problem in no time at all. There were a number of occasions when this was extremely useful to Col. Smith and it helped him to avoid pitfalls or to suggest solutions to problems that had escaped others, on which occasions he would shake his head and wonder aloud how I did it. At the time it seemed easy, and as I say, it was not until years later when my memory had become like his was in 1945 that I fully appreciated what he meant.

Col. Smith's successor was a man named Beane, also a leaf colonel. My present recollection of him—that he was a pompous ass—is confirmed by a couple of lines I wrote about him at the time. Though he did not take over the job until later, I met him in September when he came for a visit. On September 13, I wrote:

> ...[T]here is a replacement coming in, a Lt. Col. Beane, hailing, naturally, from Boston, and if his reputation has any basis in fact, I am sure I will not find working for him to be a pleasure. I guess it will have to be a case of grinning and bearing. My immediate superior, Lt. Gabel, is also due to leave shortly, and it looks as though I will be left holding the bag. Col. Beane just this minute walked in the door for the first time, and my first impression is definitely negative. He looks very stuffy, and he's old enough to be a five star general. I suppose I should reserve judgment, however, until I see the man in action.

I was too patient and forgiving in those days. The other comment was in a letter of January 22, 1946:

> Col. Beane finally left today to go home. Since Col. Busbey took over, things have been a lot quieter and more peaceful. I cannot say that I regret to see the old boy go. I gave him your address because he announced before he left that he probably would be in Cleveland shortly after he got home,... so don't be surprised if he calls you up. Take my advice though and don't invite him for dinner. He'll bore you to tears.

I think my parents managed to avoid the pleasure of meeting the Colonel. I should in justice perhaps add that Col. Beane was the author of *one* gem of wisdom which I had occasion to recall in the 1970's when 55 miles an hour turnpike speed limits were in vogue in the U.S., but were almost never enforced. He and I were discussing whether it might be a good idea to put the legend "Strictly Enforced" under the speed limit signs which were being installed throughout the city. He said "No! If we do everybody who speeds and isn't ticketed will think the MP's are liars." I think he was right.

Colonel George W. Busbey was a completely different dish of tea. He was a bird colonel, a West Pointer and a career cavalry officer. He dressed, spoke and acted as a model of all three. He was a handsome man, tall, ramrod stiff with thinning gray hair combed straight back and parted in the center. He was always clad in impeccably pressed and tailored uniforms, often featuring gray jodhpurs and darkly polished cavalry boots. This awesome sight was topped off by a beautifully waxed and groomed handlebar mustache the extremities of which curved and extended upwards a full inch beyond the corners of a stern and unsmiling mouth. His appearance was so formidable that when I first saw him I said to myself, "Oh, boy, I am in for it now!" But he turned out to be a real pussycat.

At the time and for years afterwards I had the impression the colonel was in his middle fifties if not older, but on checking with the West Point alumni office I learned to my surprise that he graduated with the Class of 1924 and was only 44 years old in 1945. The discrepancy can be explained only by the overpowering austerity of his appearance and the myopia of a 20-year old.

Colonel Busbey had commanded the 16th Cavalry Group (Mechanized) which had arrived in Europe only at the end of February 1945, by which time as we have seen the serious fighting was almost over. That may represent a partial answer as to why, when many of his classmates at West Point had risen to fame (if not fortune) as brigadier and major generals, if not higher, the colonel had not risen above field grade. It must be remembered that for West Point careerists, the war represented the one great lifetime opportunity for rapid advancement. I tend to think, however, that his late arrival represented less the cause than the effect of his failure to achieve higher rank.

Whatever the explanation, I know it rankled him. He was never very vocal in his comments about his superiors, but there were times after he had gotten to know me that he could be heard to mutter something under his breath about "those goddamn know-it-all generals" with whom he had had some disagreement. Instances of this sort were not unusual. Indeed, it was soon apparent that while the higher-ups were fond of him, they did not hold him in high regard when it came to matters of judgment. In a word, while he was the kindest man in the world, he was not among the brightest.

A facet of his personality which documents both qualities was his willingness to seek advice from and be guided by someone as junior and inexperienced as I. I did have six months experience in a job to which he was a newcomer (he was new to military police work), and I think he also respected the fact that I had been in combat as an infantryman. At any rate we got on famously, and in at least one instance, he protected me from possible discipline.

The occasion was a hush-hush operation in which the MP's and some of the 82nd Airborne troops were assigned to cordon off a largish area of downtown Berlin and then to meticulously search every dwelling and building for black market or contraband materials such as weapons. The operation was intended mostly to curtail black market activities.

The curious thing about it, however, was that notwithstanding the fact that it involved hundreds of U.S. troops, I was not told about it, since the policy was to inform only those with a "need to know." And as a means of insuring that no leak of any sort would give warning of the affair, all staff officers not involved in it were required to be at the junior officers mess at Telefunken at six o'clock in the morning, an hour before it was to start.

Wouldn't you know—with my Little White House experience in Babelsberg—that I would oversleep? When I finally awoke at my regular time I tore down the road in my jeep and snuck, inconspicuously, I hoped, into the back of the room, but I was immediately espied by the Colonel, who shook his head ruefully. But he had already reported me present, and had thus covered for me. We exchanged a few words about the incident later in the day but he knew without being told that I was both mortified and contrite, so that was the end of it.

There was a curious aftermath to this raid. During the search, the MP's discovered a hoard of gold bars—about $250,000 worth—in one of the apartments they had searched. By order of the Military Government, precious metals had long since been declared taboo, and were to have been turned in. Hence the possessors of this treasure were subject to prosecution. They were arrested and incarcerated and the gold, which was in four or five bars, ten inches in length and about the diameter of a thumb, was brought into my office late in the evening. It didn't seem like very much; the cubic content of the bars amounted to less than a carton of cigarettes; but at that late hour there was no one available who could arrange for safe keeping, such as in a vault. I finally decided to spend the night in the office guarding them, and so I locked them in my desk and went to sleep—fitfully, you may be sure—on a cot in the same room. In the morning I turned them over to the Finance Officer, being careful to obtain a receipt.

The CID
Fairly early during my stay in Berlin, a seeming opportunity arose which I sensed might in the short term provide an interesting job and might get me home before I would, with my meager point total, be entitled to be rotated back. This was in the Criminal Investigation Detachment, which was a little known arm of the Army's police functions. There was a unit of CID in Berlin headed by a Lt. Kroll, a veteran, I believe, of the New York City Police Department. Kroll had almost enough points to go home, and he was looking for someone to take his place so that he could go when he became eligible, and I appeared to him to be a likely candidate, so he asked if I wanted to look the job over.

The CID was an unusual animal. It was under Provost Marshal supervision, but in practice was almost completely autonomous. The Berlin unit, consisting of about fifteen enlisted men and one officer, lived entirely apart from all other troops. The enlisted men were entitled to wear the uniform authorized for civilian employees of the Army, or civilian clothes if circumstances required. They were all college graduates and had worked for insurance companies or police departments and the like. Their responsibilities were, as the name suggests, to conduct investigations regarding matters which might result in serious criminal charges against members of the military.

It was Kroll's plan to arrange participation for me in a number of ongoing investigations so that I could become familiar enough with the investigators and their duties to take over their supervision when it came time for him to go home. Although both he and I were enthusiastic about it, it was not a good plan.

I was able to get clearance from Col. Smith and all seemed to be going swimmingly until I found out a little more about the job, and those that were doing it got exposed to me. I was sent out on an investigation with an agent named Carlucci, who in appearance and manner could have been a stand-in for a Mafia hood. He was about thirty and small, tough and wiry, and had been a detective on a big city police department. The only part of the investigation that I remember was the interrogation of a hapless GI who was suspected in the shooting of another soldier. It was a classic scene from a Thirties police film. The suspect was in a hard chair under a glaring light. Carlucci and his partner took turns questioning, using the good-guy, bad-guy technique, Carlucci of course being the latter. I was in the background observing. It was a rough examination. There was no real brutality, but there was some physical force, as for example Carlucci's grabbing the suspect by his shirt front and lifting him from his chair to demand answers to his leading questions while holding him nose to nose. Did he ever want to go home again or see his wife? Well, he'd damned well better cooperate and admit that he'd done what he was accused of, etc., etc. I made no protest, no, not me. But I sure didn't feel comfortable with what I was watching because its purpose seemed to be more to get the investigation finished than to arrive at the truth. Some vibrations of this sort must have been apparent to Carlucci, et al., because later in the day Kroll let me know he didn't think I was "right for the job," and I certainly didn't disagree.

But even before I'd been given a look, that should have been quite apparent. I was after all still barely into my twenties with only one year of college and with no experience whatever of the subject. I would have been way out of my depth!

My Police Handbook

Once we had completed the traffic plan for Berlin, the principal project which occupied my attention for some weeks was to prepare a handbook for use by the military police to enable them to deal quickly and correctly with the myriad of differing categories of people with which they inevitably came in contact in the course of their patrols. Their primary responsibility, of course, was to deal with American soldiers, but they were also "peace officers" in the broader sense, and if they found a robbery or holdup in progress, they were supposed to deal with it whatever the nationality or status of those involved. This involved endless complications.

Early on we became accustomed to calls from various consulates demanding to know why so-and-so had been jailed in the American military stockade when the proper procedure should have been for us to have turned him over to the British, who had been accorded temporary jurisdiction over nationals of that country. The city was full of such a variety of nationalities of differing status that it was not easy always to come up with the right answer.

As I answered the phone as duty officer in our office in the evening, a pattern began to emerge in my head and I began to see that if I could collect information on all the likely categories of miscreants and on the various types of offenses and also get clearances from the various government representatives in the city, it might be possible to prepare a piece that could be distributed to all the MP's and their officers that would enable them to resolve questions on the spot without disturbing my repose with phone calls. And so with Col. Smith's blessing, I set about the task.

It took me several weeks to do all the necessary research. This included extensive contacts with British, French and Russian military authorities, with the German civilian police and with a variety of other agencies, but I finally managed to pull it all together and get the resulting booklet approved by all concerned, printed and distributed. It was a thorough, concise and understandable job and I was proud of it. Somewhere in an attic I feel sure there is a copy, but I haven't been able to locate it. I'd be fascinated after a life of law practice to see what this fledgling effort looked like. I'm certain that it as much as anything is what steered me in the direction of law school.

Relations with the Russians

As a part of the military police function in Berlin I had a number of dealings with the Russians, both incidental and ongoing. As already suggested there was something of a "honeymoon period" in our official relations with them, but it never was one of real romance. I think we Americans would have been happy to have had really friendly relationships with them, such as were possible with many of the British officers, but I always had the sense with the Russian officers I dealt with that there was a good deal held back, and that they were all concerned that there was someone looking over their shoulders.

It was no secret to any of us that the secret police were doing just that. Indeed, I can recall a couple of the Russian MP officers explaining to me by expression and gesture, though never in words, that they could not agree to something because—with thumb pointing over the shoulder and a glance behind—that it couldn't be done because of those watching them.

There was, in particular, a certain Lt. Boguslavsky who played a role all out of proportion to his rank in matters relating to the military police. He was in his twenties and slovenly and unkempt, always seeming to be in need of a bath as well as a lot of care from both a barber and a dentist. He wore a loose tunic cinched at the waist with a cloth sash, and the blue shoulder boards of his rank were the only insignia of any kind to be seen. But it was clear beyond question that Boguslavsky was a member of the secret police. He did not hesitate to countermand the orders of those many grades higher than he, often with a sarcastic smile, and I can recall one instance in which a Russian general who was participating in discussions regarding the inauguration of a quadrapartite MP patrol, turned to him to get a decision as to what the final Russian position should be on some policy point. He was moreover ubiquitous, with his Russian cigarette clinging to his lower lip, at all meetings dealing even remotely with Russian-American police matters, and we soon learned that he was the guy to deal with if things had to get done.

The quadrapartite patrol was one such item. This was conceived of by the commanding generals as a means of demonstrating to both the civilian and military populations that the Allied occupiers would maintain unified policies on police matters. It had little or no practical value. In theory, the patrol might have dealt, say, with a Russian soldier's being drunk and disorderly in the French Zone. But practically speaking, even that would have been difficult because the patrol consisted of four MP's, one of each of the four nationalities, driving a set route through all four Zones once a night in a jeep. Thus if any miscreants were discovered along the way about the only measures that could be taken were to radio for another vehicle with room to pick them up.

The patrol was planned to operate with three enlisted MP's and one officer whose nationality would be rotated from night to night. Since I had been in on fleshing out the plan which the brass wanted implemented, I drew this assignment the first night out. It was immediately apparent that the concept was absurd. While I could communicate readily with the Brit and the Frenchman, the Russian had been designated as the driver and there was no way in the world to make sense with him. He swept us off into the Russian Zone paying no heed to the route which had been designated, and the rest of us wondered for a time whether we were being kidnapped. We eventually got back downtown where I reported to my boss that the patrol was a mistake. Others soon came to my view and the idea was abandoned after about ten days.

In Jean Edward Smith's biography of Lucius Clay, the latter is quoted as saying that as U.S. Military Governor in Berlin he recalled no difficulties with the Russians with regard to access to Berlin until 1947, which is when the possibility first arose that the Russians might blockade the city. (See *An American Life*, page 275.) I remember it somewhat differently. It is true that there were never any really serious disruptions of traffic flow, but there were enough minor ones to keep me, at least, from feeling altogether comfortable 110 kilometers inside the Russian Zone.

For example, eastbound U.S. military convoys awaiting clearance at the Helmstedt checkpoint on the autobahn would be kept waiting for hours with no explanation, and when clearance was finally forthcoming it would be with no apology. Similarly, if a U.S. vehicle strayed even slightly from the autobahn's route, its occupants would be endlessly detained and the treatment they would be accorded would sometimes even approach the brutality which we often saw Russian MP's using with their own soldiers, which was considerable. The same was not unusual when GI's got into difficulties in the Russian Sector of Berlin; the Soviets did not share American concepts of "due process," even the limited ones which were in force in the American Army, and it might be several days before we would hear of their detention and could succeed in obtaining their release.

There was never any confirmation, however, that any of this was maliciously intended or that it was the result of any deliberate policy to behave abrasively towards us. It seemed more likely to be ascribable in the main to cultural and social differences.

There was a certain amount of socializing with the Russians, but it was limited almost entirely to lavish formal occasions which they loved to host. There were, for example, the performances at the Staatsoper, the opera company whose stage was one of the few public buildings left standing in their sector on Unter den Linden, and to which they invited members of the western staffs to demonstrate their love of the arts. I don't recall any particular performances, but I certainly do remember the wining and dining that accompanied them before, after and during intermission when seas of vodka and crates of caviar would be spread before us and anyone who was a guest of a particular Russian would have to match endless toasts with his host.

There was another occasion which did not come back to mind until my visit there in 1990, when we visited the Russian War Memorial which they erected in the Tiergarten, just west of the Brandenburg Gate. As we watched the honor guard standing in the rain, the sentinels, who to my daughter Kate looked more like effigies than real soldiers, suddenly began their stiff-legged strut down the stairs in the ceremony of the changing of the guard, and I immediately recalled that I had been at the monument on the occasion of its dedication in 1945, when exactly the same ritual had been inaugurated. One slight difference, however, was that the 1990 soldiers immediately showed up behind the fence about twenty yards up from the monument attempting to sell bits of uniform and badges to western tourists.

Paris: Martine
The traffic routing plan which Gross and I had prepared and which Otto had superimposed schematically on a large Berlin map needed to be reduced in size for printing and distribution, and it turned out that the equipment necessary to accomplish this could not be found in Berlin. Gross, whose assignment in Berlin would be over when the job was done, agreed to take the large map to Paris where the Army had established a large map-making operation. However, on his arrival there he had developed severe back spasms and our project languished while he was undergoing treatment in the hospital there. Since I was the only

other one who knew the detail of it, I was deputized to go to Paris to supervise its completion and bring the finished product back to Berlin. It took five days to get the job done, but fortunately it did not require much supervision, and I was largely free to do as I pleased, and to say that I was pleased gravely understates the case. I was in love! Here is only some of what I wrote on my return on September 24:

> About an hour ago I got back from Paris, after having had the most wonderful time in years...
>
> To begin with, the weather couldn't have been better. Paris in the spring may be wonderful, but Paris at the beginning of autumn is fantastic it's so beautiful. During the day the sun was bright and warm, always with a cool breeze that allowed you to wear a jacket and be comfortable. It was weather that made one feel good to be alive and walk around. Paris cannot be over-described! The girls are pretty and still manage to retain a degree of their world-famed chic; the store windows are full just to the right degree, whether or not the stores themselves are. The crowds along the Champs Elysées are gay and happy, and interesting as ever. The contrast between my impressions of Paris and what I saw in Berlin on my way back from Tempelhof Airdrome is like the difference between day and night. It depresses me, but at the same time it makes the satisfaction of enjoyment of the last five days complete, and I look forward with tremendous eagerness—which is almost restlessness—to the day when I may again go there... Paris, like no other city, is a place full of the good things of life. It is the example to the world that life can and should be enjoyed...
>
> I had better start from the beginning instead of raving like this.
>
> I landed at Orly Field Thursday afternoon, and by the time I had got myself settled at the Crillon Hotel (now a Red Cross Officers' club), the evening was about half over, so I went to a dance which was being held at the hotel. It was a very corny affair, the orchestra a French one, and judging from the way they played it was hastily assembled about five minutes before the dance began.
>
> For me, however, it was far from being a flop. The girls were

French, and the affair was chaperoned by three Red Cross dowagers whose professional doughnut-and-coffee smile was dropped in favor of an expression denoting the expectation that anything might happen and the readiness to take immediate corrective action if it did... At any rate I asked a very attractive French girl to dance. During the course of the evening it became evident that she was something out of the ordinary—not what one might expect to find at such an affair (though backgrounds are supposed to be rigorously researched by the militant Mesdames of the Red Cross). We danced every dance together, and when the dance ended at a conservative eleven o'clock, I escorted the young lady home. We walked along the Seine from the Concorde to the bridge opposite the Eiffel Tower. The night was cool and clear with the biggest and most glorious full moon I ever saw, and a million stars pinned around it, and half a million more shimmering in the river. Dear God, what a night! ... It was as though all of nature was alive, each element eager to make its contribution to the beauty and peace.

We stopped now and then to lean on the quay wall and listen and watch in silence, and finally crossed over the river and walked through the Champ de Mars, on the edge of which her apartment was located...

I managed to walk home—how I don't know, because my knees were like water.

On the nights following we went to the opera (Romeo and Juliet) and to a French play both of which we enjoyed immensely. For the first time I had a chance to see Paris a little more at my leisure, and with the most charming and entertaining guide imaginable. We did the Louvre, Notre Dame, the Sacré Coeur, the Sorbonne and the rest. Her parents were at Fontainebleau for a couple of weeks, so I didn't get to meet them, but it was lucky, on account of the fact that they are of the old school and do not approve of her going out unchaperoned. They have a beautiful apartment, [quite] large... Her father is affiliated in some way with the Continental Can Company, and her uncle, who was also out of town was (before the war) ambassador to Berlin... The family is very well-to-do, though that means very little in these days when prices are prohibitively high.

But more important than all of that is the fact that she is beautiful, vivacious, frank and very sweet.

The whole thing was so perfect it hardly seems real any more. They are days lived in a faraway dream and it is hard to recapture even a part of their essence, but she is still there and will be waiting for me when I get there...

Anything else I did in Paris, such as business, is purely incidental, and is put in a file marked 'Items of Small Importance'... I hope you have half as much fun reading this letter as I had writing it—at least you will get a laugh out of it (if I know my father). And despite your warning to me before I left the States, Mum, I might take matters into my own hands. That is not a threat—just the acknowledgment of a possibility. [Before I left the states my mother had said, facetiously I think but am not sure, that she would disown me if I married a French girl.] Anyway, I was very happy for a while and you should be happy about that.

P.S. On reading this over, I note that I failed to mention the name of the new star in the firmament—Martine François-Poncet—Now you know all.

I had been in love before, or thought I had, but never like this. Martine was nineteen, a literature student at the Sorbonne and she truly was a beautiful girl, with classic, almost Grecian, features and a disarming way of looking you straight in the eye. She dressed in a simple, unadorned fashion favoring dark blues which was nonetheless exceedingly stylish. Both her surroundings and, as I was later to learn, her family, were likewise stylish, if not indeed aristocratic. Her apartment was decorated in the classical French mode, with ormolu fixtures, Louis Quatorze furniture and Aubusson rugs.

But what a magical interlude it was! The evening in the ballroom at the Crillon was like sudden lightning. I saw her on the dance floor dancing with some other lieutenant. I cut in. We introduced ourselves, laughed at the orchestra and the Red Cross ladies and refused the overtures of all other officers who wanted to cut in. We spoke in a tumultuous mixture of French and English, while leaning back at the waist to study each other's reactions. It seemed truly miraculous that we had found each other because there seemed to be no subject on which we did not agree.

On the walk along the Seine I learned that she had ventured to the Crillon in disobedience of parental strictures but with the complicity of her old nurse who greeted us with a smile of toothless pleasure and approval at the door of the cold apartment and then quickly disappeared. It did not matter that the apartment had no heat as we recognized that whatever else we might have had planned, it was now inevitable that for the next four days, we would spend our waking hours together.

And so it happened. Martine did whatever was necessary to cut her classes at the Sorbonne while I delegated oversight of the map-making project to an obliging sergeant. We saw the sights, we held hands and kissed in the streets and reveled in the pleasures of Paris, not the least of which was one memorable dinner in a small garden restaurant near the Place du Tertre on Montmartre which we happened to wander into and where I for the very first time gained a wholly unexpected insight into the brand-new world of French cuisine. I was of course in a state of bliss before I walked into the place, but at Martine's urging, I ordered "rognons de veau, sauce diable," having no idea that I was about to be served veal kidneys in a subtle mustard sauce (nor, if I had been told, what exactly a veal kidney was), and they were sensational, altogether novel textures revealing undreamed of complexities of flavor! I had no idea that food could possibly be this interesting and delicious. Another chamber of delight had been opened to me by Martine!

Our parting was sad but joyful as I promised to move heaven and earth to arrange another trip to Paris in the shortest possible time.

Unfortunately, documenting the course of our romance over the next few months is made difficult by the fact that while the file of correspondence maintained by my father seems to have been relatively complete through September of 1945, it inexplicably becomes quite sparse for the remaining months of my time in Europe, with only five letters having been preserved over the seven months. One unhappy result is that there is no further mention whatsoever of Martine, so what follows will have to depend on memory alone.

On my return to Berlin, we corresponded almost daily and our affair continued with seemingly every bit as much intensity as had been the case when we parted. In addition, I focused not only on enabling myself to revisit Paris, but also on getting myself reassigned there.

At some point during the winter, my father informed me that a close friend of his who had been a businessman in Cleveland and had volunteered for public service in the war effort had been placed in charge of the office in Paris (I do not remember its official title) which was to be responsible for the disposal in Europe of the immense amounts of surplus property owned by the Government there. The man in question was named John Virden, and he was in the process of accumulating a substantial staff to help him carry out his task. I quickly got into communication with Virden who invited me to come to Paris for an interview.

Without telling anyone in my office what I was up to, I managed to get permission for the trip, met with Mr. Virden in his office at one of the hotels in the Avenue Georges Cinq, and after a cordial few minutes was sent to be interviewed by a major who was one of his principal deputies. I remember feeling that the interview had not gone particularly well, that I seemed somewhat out of my depth dealing with the large marketing program that was under way and that my command of French, in which the interview was largely conducted, seemed quite shaky on the day in question. But in spite of these misgivings, I was promptly told by Virden that he would be happy to request my assignment from Berlin to Paris, but that in accordance with Army protocol he preferred not to do so until I had returned to Berlin and had obtained assurances there that if such a request were to be received, it would be acted upon favorably.

In any case, on the somewhat iffy premise that I might be coming to work in Paris, I went to dinner with Martine and her parents at their apartment in the Avenue Charles Floquet, which if not the most desireable address in Paris, certainly had to be one of them. It was on the left bank across the Seine from the Trocadéro, was dominated by the Eiffel Tower and adjacent to the Champ de Mars, a wide esplanade surrounded by gardens. Unlike almost all other apartments in the city whose walls are built flush to their adjacent sidewalks, the apartments next to the Champ de Mars were surrounded by gardens and landscaping and had as a result an air of quiet and privacy which was quite unique.

I was announced by the concierge and Martine came downstairs to greet me. We embraced fondly and held each other for some moments and then proceeded upstairs, where she introduced me to her parents and her uncle André who had been the French ambassador to Berlin. The reception which I was accorded, like the luncheon which followed, was perfectly proper but distinctly cold. Martine and her mother were both attired with simple but clearly expensive elegance, while her father and uncle were clad in cutaways, wing collars and dark ties with pearl stickpins in them. They were perfectly polite and even tried to be cordial in inquiring into my education, background and present activity, but it could scarcely have been clearer that they would instantaneously have sided with my mother if asked to vote on whether union between Martine and me was desirable.

I struggled through the meal as best I could—my French seemed again to leave me in the lurch—until at last it was over, and the two of us were able to escape to the outdoors. I don't know what time of year it was, but neither the season nor the weather was anything like it had been in September. It was cold, raw and damp, which did little to revive my spirits as Martine clutched my arm and tried to reassure me. We spent the balance of the day together and I eventually returned to the Crillon for the night.

Over the course of that night, I developed a high fever. I reported in to a medical officer who immediately ordered that I be sent to an Army hospital in a Paris suburb called Villejuif. I don't recall any particulars of my illness other than that it took me a few days to shake the fever and recover. When I was at the point of being discharged I called Martine and explained what had happened and told her that I now had to return to Berlin. She was desolated and asked why I had not called her earlier so she could have visited me at the hospital. It had simply not occurred to me that a French civilian would be permitted to visit a patient in an American military hospital, but she proved that it was by appearing immediately at my bedside, to my delight and the awed astonishment of everyone else. But the visit was both sad and brief as I had to head out to Orly airport.

On my return to Berlin I presented the matter of a transfer to Col. Busbey, who could not have been nicer. He said that he was disappointed I wanted to leave him, and that he had been well pleased with my work for him, but that he had never stood in the way of an officer who wanted to move on. He also added that I had better check out the matter with the personnel officer at G-1 because there might be a need for my services elsewhere in Berlin which would keep G-1 from releasing me. I thanked the colonel for his kind words and assured him that it was not my dissatisfaction with him or my job in Berlin which led to my request, but rather that the opportunity in Paris seemed to me uniquely attractive. (I don't believe I said anything about Martine.)

I made an appointment with the major in question, a humorless bureaucrat with a black mustache, and this worthy took precisely the position predicted by my colonel, so that ended that, and I stayed put. I have many times wondered what would have happened had it been otherwise.

Though we did correspond for a time after I got back to Berlin, that really was the end of our affair. I don't know why it unraveled so quickly and completely nor why I "fell out of love," but that exactly is what happened. I doubt that the aloofness of Martine's family could alone have been the cause, though it no doubt didn't help. It may have been that I sensed a possessiveness developing and perhaps I didn't feel like being possessed quite yet, and I think too that there may have been an element of "being in love with love," but I am just guessing. There also may have been a developing awareness in me of how large the gulf of difference was between American and French customs and habits, notwithstanding my fondness for Martine and her country. I don't recall either how the affair terminated. I don't think there were any formal "good-byes" either in person or by letter; rather it just seemed to sort of "fizzle out."

Some years later, in the early Fifties, I became friends with a Parisian named Phillippe Richer who said he had known Martine well in the interim. To my astonishment he described her as cold, humorless and conceited, none of which qualities was remotely descriptive of the girl I knew. I found his account distressing for more reasons than one.

Hannah

I was involved in one other romantic liaison which merits comment. That was with a German girl named Hannah, who came into my life well after Martine and I had drifted apart. She was about twenty, blond and blue-eyed, a prototypical Rhine maiden. She was stunningly beautiful, with regular features, bright red lips and laughing blue eyes, and she spoke English well. I don't remember much of Hannah's background. She was not a Berliner, having come to the city with her mother who took some sort of government job during the war. Hannah now worked in a clerical job for someone at Telefunken and was her mother's support. Just why she had set her sights on me I don't recall; she was a world-class beauty who could easily have commanded the attention of someone much more exalted than I, though by this time I had been promoted to First Lieutenant.

For a time Hannah and I were socially inseparable, and she spent many a long evening at 7 Im Shonower Park, including quite a few that did not involve one of our parties. We would enjoy each other's company in the silly ways of youth, joking and laughing and kissing like two puppy dogs. Then one evening we found ourselves recumbent on our living room couch and doing anything but resting; indeed there was every evident prospect that our relationship was about to escalate to a new plateau. Suddenly she drew back from our embrace, looked me in the eye and said that she thought we should get married. I felt like a dog who had been hit with a pail of cold water. As we sat up, mussed and panting, to review the situation, it became clear that this was not a ploy: she was firmly fixed on getting married and going with her mother to the States as Frau Alexander Hadden. As gently as I could I told her that while I was very fond of her, I had had no idea that she viewed our relationship so seriously and that I didn't feel I could because I still had years of education ahead of me and was in no position to get married.

She was obviously startled and disappointed at this outcome, and I felt for a time that she had tried to spring a trap on me, but it was as friends that our relationship ended, and I eventually came to feel a grudging admiration for her willingness to use all tools available to flee the bleakness of post-war Berlin. I have no doubt whatever that she promptly went back to the sea to cast her line in once again and would be astonished if she did not succeed; the odds were powerfully in her favor!

Sailing on the Wannsee
Our pleasures were not exclusively bibulous or nocturnal. During the Conference in Babelsberg, Bully and I discovered that an assortment of pleasure yachts were moored at a couple of yacht clubs on the Wannsee, which is another of the series of lakes of which the Griebnitzsee is a part, all of which extended in a general north-south direction at the western edge of the American Sector and north into the British. The yacht club in the U.S. Sector had become an officers' club, while something similar happened to the one in the British sector at the north end of the lake, and a series of yacht races was instantaneously organized. They were wild: we were becalmed; we were swamped; the rigging tore or broke; and we almost invariably lost the race, but we always had a good time, in part because it was deemed necessary that the ship's stores include champagne. My letters describe a number of these adventures, but the following, from a letter of May 26, 1946, will provide a sample:

[After lunch] we proceeded out to Wannsee to go sailing. The weather for sailing could not possibly have been better. The wind blew so hard that at times I was sure it was about to tear off the rigging. But the air was warm and I was quite comfortable in a pair of shorts. The English held their first race of the season under these ideal conditions. There were about ten boats that started, of which only four finished, so you can imagine what kind of a wind it was.

We were the only American boat in the race unfortunately. News of these races does not get around very easily, mostly because the English racing club is about ten miles down the lake from ours. The race started at three o'clock, and we had about 75 minutes to make the ten miles from our end to theirs. We got there just in time to be given a number and to get our instructions and hear the starting gun. We got off to a good start and started on the first leg, which was about a seven mile one. Not more than five minutes out, one boat which was giving us stiff competition hit a squall which was evidently unexpected, for their mast quivered once or twice and then snapped with a loud crack about six feet off the deck. There were no more casualties for about a half an hour as we completed the first leg. About three or four boats that seemed to be faster than ours slowly drew away from us and beat us to the next marker, but as one of them made the tack, his sail whipped over in a particularly vicious gust and tore in three places, one of which tore completely loose and went on down the lake. We came about very neatly and started back up into the wind with the keel out of the water and the lee rail under. The waves were about three feet high and the spray from each one of them carried back into our faces until we had to start bailing to keep from being slowed down.

…[W]e came down the home stretch with one other boat hot on our heels. We had to round one marker and then pay off down wind to the finish line which was about five hundred yards [away]. We were still ahead of the British boat when we came up to the buoy, but he was above us. If we had wanted to, we could have crowded him so he would have had to go above the marker, but since it was the first race, and since we wanted to be invited to the next one, we chose to give him room, and he beat us by about a length... It was such a thrilling race that we didn't particularly mind losing by such a close margin... Tonight the living room is draped with the jib, which we had to bring in because it started to rain just as we came in.

The Trip Home
Not one of my letters from Berlin fails to mention whatever latest development had occurred with regard to the point system or the probable date of my departure. But at last and somewhat suddenly on a day in June 1946, I was informed my time had come.

Preparations for departure were hectic. I had only three days to pack and ship my gear, some of which took the form of souvenirs such as a large Telefunken radio which at the time represented the state of the art. I also had to do whatever I could to shift to my successor responsibility for my duties at the office, and to arrange for new ownership of a female police dog that I had acquired as a pet over the winter (I would have scant memory of her were it not for mentions of her in letters). There was time neither for a farewell party such as we had had for our housemates when their homecomings loomed, nor for any kind of retrospective appraisal of what my Berlin experience had meant to me. If there had been, I'm sure my reflections would have been tinged with more than a little sadness.

Berlin was a city of unrelieved bleakness and much human suffering. Its appearance and especially its smells were starkly offensive and depressing. But for me it had been an eye-opening, mind-stretching and exhilarating experience. As regards living arrangements, I don't know what more I would have asked for. My life was comfortable, but it was not sybaritic and I would not have wanted it so, because above everything, it was safe, and I doubt that I could have savored that safety, as I did every single morning when I awoke, if I had had nothing to do. What gave the safety real dimension was that it enabled me with a clear and untroubled mind to immerse myself in a day of interesting and apparently useful activity.

At the social level, what more is there to say? Life was a ceaseless round of new and intoxicating experiences which engrossed my attention at every emotional level. I would have had a sensory overload if I had had more, and maybe I did even as it was!

But it was perhaps at the professional level that the experience was the most rewarding. I had been plucked as a virtual teenager from a filthy foxhole, dusted off and cleaned up a bit and given a little training which would turn out to have no relation whatever to what I would now be asked to do, and guess what? Not only could I do it and do it well, but my contribution even turned out now and then to be really important. This was heady stuff indeed!

Another factor in the picture, as illustrated by my brush with the CID, was that in terms of opportunities: the sky seemed to be the limit. If you were bored with what you were doing or thought you saw greener pastures across a fence, it hardly seemed to matter that you knew nothing about criminal investigation, or about the marketing of surplus military equipment, if you played your cards right you might still have a chance at that slot.

It is probably no wonder when I got back to college for my junior year (I got a year's college credit for my eleven months as a grasshopper at Illinois), that I had no patience whatever with the extracurricular activities that were supposed to represent "bright college years" and could hardly wait to get out.

In any event, I took a train to Bremerhaven, which was the port for U.S. occupation activities. Along the way somewhere I was put in command of a package of "returnees," about ninety-five enlisted men, and after a few days at a sort of reverse repple-depple where a ton of paperwork was transacted, we were ordered to the docks where a Liberty ship named the *Montclair Victory* awaited us. Just before boarding its rusting 10,000-ton bulk, I was required to disburse to my men their final European payroll, which in many cases was substantial. I counted out about $35,000 in U.S. currency, none of which I had seen for almost two years! The cash disbursement went smoothly, except that when we got done, the sergeant who was helping and I were left with some $300-odd dollars, without even the remotest idea of who might have been shortchanged. With virtually no discussion whatever, we decided to split this unexpected bonus down the middle and to say nothing to anyone about it.

I did not think too well of the Army's timing in distributing this payroll. It constituted an invitation—which was immediately accepted—to a high-stakes non-stop poker game in which a handful of men ended up with many thousands of dollars and many more were totally cleaned out. Why wasn't the payroll delayed until we all got home?

Apart from that the trip was totally uneventful, the sea smooth with nothing to remember until we got to New York harbor. There, our ship pulled into a berth in Hoboken on the New Jersey side, where below us on the dock were two gaudily attired and overweight girls—they appeared to be identical twins—who, with recorded music and a loudspeaker, had been hired by the Army to serenade our homecoming. We listened to "When Johnny Comes Marching Home Again," "The White Cliffs of Dover" and "I'll Be Seeing You," etc., etc. I found it mawkish and pathetic. I don't know what I expected, but nothing would have been better than these two girls.

The mood of disappointment was not enhanced when we boarded a dirty train and were displayed the filthy backyards of the slums of Hoboken, Newark, Trenton and Philadelphia on the way to Ft. Meade, Maryland.

There, effective July 4, 1946, three years and three months after being sworn in, twenty-one months after leaving the U.S., and thirteen months after being commissioned as a lieutenant, I finally once again became a civilian.

— Not Me! —

Author and Bill Fulljames' fox terrier puppy, Berlin, Spring 1946.

— Not Me! —

Lisl Wellesz and our housekeeper, Berlin, Spring 1946.

Author at Ping-Pong, Berlin, Spring 1946.

Author and housemates, 7 Im Schonower Park, Berlin. Bill Fulljames on the left. Spring 1946.

Author and brother, Nicky (John), on the steps of Hitler's Reichschancellery, Berlin, Winter, 1945.

Afterthoughts

MY daughter Kate read the manuscript of this book when it ended with the chapter you have just read, and she penciled in the margin, "What was it like getting home—you can't just gyp us out of that!" As it happens, my memories of the event are quite vivid. I took the train from Ft. Meade to Cleveland (the Army had not yet acknowledged that travel by plane was possible), and the actual scene at the train station was remarkably similar to the filmed version of my homecoming which had solaced me so often as I had watched it in my foxhole. Now, however, there was an added dimension which I never could have imagined during that winter, now already a year and a half past.

I wore my slickest uniform. It included a dark green Eisenhower jacket (see photo section) which I had had tailored from scratch by a Berlin tailor whose single second floor workroom was suspended in air in a building on the Potsdamer Platz, all of the surrounding rooms including those on the ground floor having been blown away. It cost me only two packs of cigarettes but it fit me like a glove. My trousers were officers' "pinks"; they were really gray but had pinkish highlights. On my right shoulder was the flaming sword and rainbow patch of the U.S. Berlin District, and on my left breast two rows of service stars and ribbons, not gaudy but adequate. The gold crossed rifles of the infantry were on my lapels, while the silver bars of a first lieutenant were on my shoulders. My dark green service cap carried the light blue piping of the infantry. Most important of all were the Bloody Bucket patch of the 28th Division on my left shoulder and, above the service ribbons on my left breast, the Combat Infantryman's Badge.

None of this finery had been featured in my foxhole reveries, but now that I was actually living the scene, I felt every inch the conquering hero as I stepped off the train into the waiting embrace of my parents. And I am sure that they, especially my mother, were almost swooning with joy, pride and relief at my safe return.

For a few days I was squired about in uniform like a new bridegroom and shown off to friends and relatives, but it wasn't very long at all until the novelty of the experience began to wear off, like a balloon with a fairly rapid leak, that my military trappings and all their associated memories soon came to seem irrelevant.

Further contributing to the deflation was the realization that nothing about life at home had changed in the three and a half years I had been gone. My room was the same, though the clothes in the closet looked strange and didn't fit me anymore. (I now weighed 185 pounds, and my 18-year-old sister Betty remarked that my legs looked much better because "they're not so skinny now.")

The suburban trolley cars still clanged up and down on the boulevard outside my window. Mealtime rituals were the same, though I was now permitted to participate in the cocktail hour, dear to my father, which preceded dinner. The formalities of conversation, of which he was always in complete charge, were for a time focused on learning of my adventures overseas, but it was not very long before the effort seemed to flag, mine to try to explain to them and theirs to try to understand all that had happened to me. I don't think I even tried to relate anything about combat other than to answer my father's questions about where I had been and when; he had kept a map file on which he had tried, not very accurately, to trace my movements. But our failure to communicate—it almost seemed that we were talking different languages—went well beyond that. I was finally able to come clean—and to make joke of—the fiasco in Babelsberg when I had twice been discovered in bed at 10:30 in the morning and was fired from my job, and there were other stories to be related on which I could put a humorous twist, but to convey to them any sense of what the experience meant to me and especially what combat had been like I soon realized was impossible.

It was more my fault than theirs. I lacked both the energy and the ability to make it come alive for them. But I also felt that they didn't have the patience or the interest to listen to the lengthy explanations which would have been necessary to make them understand. It was really very much the same as it had been in Europe when I threw up my hands at trying to explain things in letters. And another complication was that they tended to treat me in ways that failed to acknowledge or understand that I was not the same person who had last lived in their house. I soon began to feel that the atmosphere was claustrophobic, and after doing what was necessary to assure my return to Yale in the fall, I arranged with a couple of old friends, who had been deferred from military service for medical reasons, to retreat to the wilds of northern Ontario for a three week canoe trip. I was now able to portage a canoe for a good distance—a task which had been agony when I had been a camper four years earlier—without discomfort, and I found that I had to do virtually all the work of camping because of the ineptitude of my buddies, but I actually enjoyed it, and the solitude and beauty of the lakes and woods were, as I had hoped, a balm to the soul.

A Green Beret Captain named Collins who had repeatedly "re-upped" for combat duty in Vietnam was interviewed on March 26, 1992 in *USA Today*. He said he had no wish to be critical of those who had sought refuge in Canada or otherwise opted out, but, "They simply missed the most profound experience of their lives."

There is truth in this observation. For me it was not quite the same truth as intended by Collins, since he seems to have been one of those who, in Robert E. Lee's phrase, became "too fond" of war. But the real reason why the experience of combat is indeed the "most profound" in the lives of all who survive it, is that there is virtually no other way to learn and be certain of what you are really made of.

It will have been noted that this was not a lesson that I lusted to learn. The title and theme of this book are ample testimony to that, even though some of the "Not Me's" have been semi-facetious. It was always clear that I was not going to be a hero. But *after* I delayed my military service for a year, and *after* I avoided flying duty in the Air Corps, chose college life in the ASTP, and shunned the OSS, there finally came a time when no further outs were available, at least none that would not have been even more unpalatable than the infantry, even though I well understood the inevitability of combat. And so, claiming absolutely no credit for it, that was where at last I found myself.

And there, in spite of the doubts and terrors that assailed me in Hürtgen and in the Ardennes, I found that not only was I able to assimilate enough skills to greatly enhance my chances of survival, but also that I could, in spite of enormous emotional stress, perform effectively and even aggressively in moments of crisis. There has been no experience in my subsequent civilian life that has been even remotely comparable.

Thus it is perhaps no wonder that my wartime experiences have once again come to mean so much to me, or that I should agree so wholeheartedly with a fellow combat infantryman who also lived through the Ardennes and whom I got to know recently. Notwithstanding a long and conspicuously successful business career, he said, "Sandy, it's taken me a long time to realize it, but what I did in the war means more to me than everything I've done since." Nor is it surprising that such a strong and immediate bond should have been felt by those of us who met in 1992 in Minnesota, or that I should have come to have so much enjoyed the experience of recording my recollections here. It has been with growing eagerness that I have sat at the word-processor to discover what long-forgotten memories would be evoked that day. It's been a rediscovery not only of those memories, but of a good piece of myself, complete with abundant warts.

A final word to my offspring and to theirs as well. While my outlook today remains fundamentally quite cynical about the ability of mankind to manage its affairs in a manner that will give reasonable assurance of its long-term survival, I have been pleasantly surprised that half a century (and not just the five years that I hoped for in 1945) have now elapsed without a World War III. That the world has succeeded in posting such a record in the intervening years is hardly a testament to the wisdom of its leaders, given the enormous glitches represented by Korea, Vietnam and Afghanistan, to name only three. The real and only reason is that those leaders realize that the weapons which we have created for ourselves have now for the first time put in their mouths the salty taste of dread which in prior wars was reserved only for the likes of me in the front lines. This powerful new psychological factor may just allow us to wiggle through for a while longer, at least until some madman like Hitler or Saddam Hussein (his name could as easily be Jones or Murphy) gets his hands on a few H-bombs and decides, as Hitler almost did in Germany, that "If I can't be boss then no one will." I wish I did not believe that that or something almost like it is almost inevitable.

There was a time when it seemed impossible that I would survive to see the dawn of peace in Europe. I was wrong about that. Maybe I'll be wrong about this too.

Journal of European Trip

August 18 to September 6, 1990

SATURDAY, August 18, 1990—At last! To recap briefly our transatlantic journey, Kate, Susan, two six-pound poodles and I left Boston Logan Airport at about 11 p.m. on a non-stop Sabena flight to Brussels. Kate says "There should be a Sabena contest—which passenger looks crappiest of all?" We finally arrive at 11 a.m., bleary-eyed. No one slept except the dogs, who did just fine. We were in the last row where the seats could not be leaned back. Food awful. Mini-packet of Smucker's jam was the best thing about it. Crammed with folks.

We will lay our heads tonight in the small town of Ligny-en-Cambrésis just over the French border, but en route we find the wonderful city of Mons, Belgium, totally unresearched and unanticipated. A fascinating museum full of (1) artifacts of both World Wars, (2) pottery ("faience"), both local and world-wide, (3) fossils, and (4) numismatics—distributed over three large floors. A bizarre cathedral surmounts the high hill in the town—le Collégiale de Ste. Wantzenau, with a gilded carriage in the nave ("Le Car D'Or").

The rain abates and after a couple of miscues we make it across the frontier (where the French douanier waves us through with a Gaelic shrug dismissing our proffered passports) to Ligny, a distance of perhaps 100 kilometers from Brussels, but to the driver—me—it seems a lot longer. The drive through Belgium is unremarkable at least to my numbed psyche, which however revives remarkably on arriving. Ligny is a town of perhaps 1,000 souls, and smack in the middle of town in a property of about five acres is our hotel, the Chateau de Ligny, built in the thirteenth and seventeenth centuries. We are instantly in the warmly welcoming bosom of rural France!

We cross an ancient and decayed moat into a cobbled courtyard which is embraced by the tan stone walls and slate roofs of the small chateau. Flowers adorn the window boxes, and the cobbles glisten wetly as the skies clear.

We are taken in tow by a tiny chambermaid who cannot be dissuaded from helping us lug our large duffel bags up the stone staircase to our circular tower room on the second floor.

We are installed for dinner, dogs under the table, in a small dining room. It turns out we are the only guests in the hotel, which has only six sleeping rooms, but apparently does a land office dinner business on Friday and Saturday nights, when a larger dining room is used. The smaller room is paneled in oak and has only three small lace covered tables.

What a meal! We have "croustillant de ris de veau" which turns out to be crisply deep-fried sweetbreads, and they are perfection! Even Kate, who has never allowed such repugnant morsels to pass her lips during her 21 years of life has asked for several bites. Fantastic!

We fall like stones into instantaneous sleep to awake at varying intervals during the night as we adjust to jet lag.

Monday, August 20—Up at a fantastic 8:45 a.m. to find the skies mostly clear, temperature 65 degrees. Breakfast is served in the cobbled courtyard of the chateau, again on a lace tablecloth and features croissants gooey with butter—wicked and wild!

Then off to the west through the 1915 battlefields of World War I in the valley of the Somme. While I knew that our route would traverse this area, I am not prepared for its impact. We pass no fewer than ten cemeteries which abut the highway and see signs directing travelers to another twenty. At one simple and moving monument close to the road is a pillared colonnade bearing the legend in both French and English:

> To the 7,026 members of the British Expeditionary Force who lost their lives in the battle of Cambrai, September 23-October 2, 1915, for whom no identifiable remains could be found, and for whom this is the common sepulcher.

We come away with tears in our eyes.

We now travel through gorgeous rolling countryside with poplars of various sizes, shapes and pollarded styles marching in file along the road and across the horizon. Prosperity most evident, with one or two cars in every farmyard.

We arrive soon at Amiens where we marvel at the height and brilliance of the cathedral. Only a few stained glass windows are in place, but those present are sparkling, as are the black and white marble floors, patterned in a multitude of geometric designs.

Stores are mostly closed, we can't figure out why. (We later learn that it is the custom in this part of France to close on Mondays rather than Sundays.) We finally find a small grocery store in the picture postcard town of Aumale and we make a picnic en route to Rouen, where we prowl around the old half-timbered town near the clock tower and cathedral, which we wish we had seen before, not after Amiens. Nimmo (the teen-ager of our six-pound poodles) becomes excessively fond of a small brown dog in a sidewalk cafe, which requires that we remove to the auto and drive on.

We make it to the Chateau de Goville in Le Breuil-en-Bresse, Normandy, just west of Bayeux, at about 6:45, where we have a pleasant room in the chateau-style establishment, built in the nineteenth century and made into a hotel-restaurant only within the past three years. It appears to be run by a group of friendly gentlemen. Fancily-decorated first floor rooms, quite eclectic, but some attractive oil paintings, bibelots, etc.

On checking in I am told by one of the gentlemen at the reception that I had a phone call during the afternoon from someone who did not leave a message and said only that he was an old friend of mine from long ago and he would call again later. Not long after being installed in our rooms the phone rings and I find myself talking to Michel Bucaille, the son of René and Suzanne whom we are scheduled to see tomorrow in Carentan, and who was a lad of twelve when I passed through as a soldier in 1944. There are essentially two things he wants to communicate: first, that he and his wife Claudine would very much like to have us as their guests at their home in St. Lô the day after tomorrow, and secondly, that he wants us not to be surprised when we meet him by his physical condition, which he thinks his parents, who are most anxious to see us tomorrow, are unlikely to mention to us. He then proceeds to explain that as a fourteen-year-old in 1946, shortly after the war was over, he was badly wounded while on the way to soccer practice, and that both his vision and one of his arms were permanently impaired as a result. He emphasizes that the matter is of no great consequence as far as he is concerned and is confident we will feel similarly. All of this comes at me in a torrent of French, much too rapid for my rusty ear to assimilate, especially the details concerning the circumstances and extent of his injuries, which somehow involved German prisoners of war and a grenade. I elect not to press for these and we make a date to see them two days hence in St. Lô.

Fatigue is upon us and we elect to eat in the hotel dining room, which turns out to be a mistake, meal not up to the standards to which we have so recently become accustomed and service so slow that we don't make it to bed until 12:30 a.m., still somewhat on eastern daylight time.

Tuesday, August 21—Château de Goville. A day both memorable and moving.

Manage to dynamite Kate from her sack (of whose quality she complains bitterly) at 8:45 a.m. We had ordered breakfast "sur la terrace" but are counseled against it by one of the proprietors on the grounds that it is too cool. It's about 65 degrees but a little breeze and fog are blowing in from the ocean so we go indoors where two boiled eggs "en coque" were ordered last night. Illicitly novel and delicious!

Off after breakfast to Isigny (five kilometers east of Carentan) to acquire picnique, cash travelers checks, etc.

One of the most enduring of my memories of 1944 (and accordingly, one of the larger reasons for the present trip) is of my sojourn at Carentan and my meeting René Bucaille and his family. About a month before our departure, I wrote to "La Famille Bucaille, Carentan, France" not having any better address and not knowing whether there would be anyone to reply, let alone someone who might remember me. In short order I got a letter back from Suzanne who said in part:

> Of course we remember you, and we remember those heroic times. An entire lifetime has elapsed since, with its joys and sorrows, but your letter instantly brought to life those days of our youth. We will be overjoyed to see you and we will talk more about those days. I hope your mother is still living? I remember very well having corresponded with her and I have even saved a letter from her which I will be happy to show you.

At about 11:15 a.m. we present ourselves at 16 rue Sébline, Carentan, a tidy townhouse near the center of a totally changed Carentan in which I recognize nothing! Much grown. Big warehouses, chain stores in the outskirts.

We are welcomed at the tidy door yard by Suzanne Bucaille and are invited into the living-dining room to the right where René is in his wheel chair ("chaise roulante"), and in spite of a stroke which has paralyzed his legs, he seems in good spirits if somewhat subdued. Not Suzanne! A bright and cheerful 78, she couldn't be more welcoming if she were our grandmother. We sit around the dining room table and are served hors d'oeuvres and champagne, with which much toasting takes place. She soon brings forth a small envelope and as we watch, she inscribes a dedication (in French): "For Sandy, Susan, and Kate, these 'relics' recall our black years, unforgettable. With the fond memory of their French friends. Carentan. August 21, 1990. S. & R. Bucaille."

On opening, the envelope reveals three letters addressed to the Bucailles. Two from me dated November 10, 1944 (the day before I joined the 28th Division in the Hürtgen Forest) and September 14, 1945, and one from my mother dated September 29, 1945. My 1945 letter contains a postcard photo of me wearing the Combat Infantry Badge taken, I believe, in the winter of 1945 on the occasion of a three-day pass from the front to Verviers, Belgium, before I went to OCS. I start to read the inscription on the photo out loud and Suzanne finishes it for me—she knows it by heart: "Aux premiers et meilleurs amis français d'un pauvre soldat américain, le 13 septembre 1945."

We exchange reminiscences among which are my totally erroneous impressions as to the location of their house, which is the identical one in which I partook of their rabbit stew and other warm hospitality forty-six years ago. I remember with total clarity that 16 rue Sébline was on the northeast side of town, whereas it is actually on the west, and it hasn't moved. Also the field on a hill in which our unit was encamped in 1944 is now totally covered by an apartment complex. Carentan has become a bustling small city of 7,000 people, up from 4,000 in 1944.

Suzanne Bucaille recounts how they had fled on foot from Carentan to a town near Tours, 200 kilometers distant, where they had stayed for two months, returning to Carentan in September, not long before I landed on the Normandy Beach. While they had met American soldiers before that, I was the first one with whom they became friends.

Susan, Kate and Suzanne are on the same wave length instantaneously. Warm friendships are formed such that when, after an hour's visit, we deem it prudent to depart, tears start flowing copiously and long-held hugs are exchanged. Our visit has seemed all too brief but Suzanne has gestured that René is tired, and so we say goodbye and promise to be back much sooner, after a flurry of photos. This prediction turns out to be more accurate than anyone thought when we discover after putting one kilometer of distance between us that I have left my camera behind. When we return we also find we have left a gift bottle of wine tendered by the Bucailles. As we depart the second time, Suzanne asks us to convey her love to Michel and Claudine when we seen them tomorrow. I decide not to ask her to clarify the details concerning Michel's 1946 injury.

Finally we are off north to Utah Beach where I think I may have landed in 1944. It doesn't, however, look at all like what I remember, being quite flat with little or no bluff of the sort I can remember climbing. There is a museum there covering the events of D-Day, with a multimedia presentation which conveys some of what happened, illustrated by an illuminated map, which makes it all clearer.

After a picnic lunch on top of a German pillbox a quarter mile back from the water, we go back inland to Ste. Mère Eglise, and en route I tell the ladies that in the early morning hours of June 6, 1944, an American paratrooper from the 82nd Airborne Division ended his parachute descent hung up on the church steeple in the town. No sooner have I got this sentence out of my mouth than we turn a corner and there to our astonishment, hanging from the steeple is what turns out to be—in effigy—the very same soldier! (We later learn that he did escape with his life.) Ste. Mère Eglise may have been badly damaged by the landing but its tourist future was surely made by its place in history. Crowds of tourists of all nations teem in the town square.

With my head in a considerable quandary as to my 1944 landing place, we proceed to Omaha Beach to verify impressions there. We drive south back through Carentan and then east along the coast road, which now discloses, at ebbing tide, a prosperous summer resort and wide flat beach, with 200 yards of sandy width, well used by wind surfers on wheels! Looks like fun.

The configuration of the beach and countryside, which alternates cliffs and bluffs of perhaps 75 to 125 feet in height, verifies conclusively that Omaha was where I alit. I remember walking up a small glade to the plain above and that's what I now see.

Along the coast a little further east we come to the American cemetery at St. Laurent-sur-Mer, one of the most moving places I have ever visited. There are about 7,000 Americans buried here, with white marble crosses and stars in rank and file stretching across immaculately tended lawns of putting green velour. There is also a semi-circular marble colonnade and reflecting pool at one end, with a large mural map showing all areas of the Allied landing, the sweep across France toward Germany, the Germans' Ardennes counteroffensive (in black), the Allied elimination of the German Colmar "pocket" and the final campaign into Germany. The whole ensemble is marvelously conceived and impeccably maintained. And what is as touching as any aspect is the horde of awed tourists who come to pay their respects. They seem to be largely French, but there are many others including numbers of Germans. One wonders what goes through the heads of these latter. After shedding further tears (its been a tough day on the ducts) we make it back to Goville.

We go into Bayeux for dinner at Le Lion d'Or, a Michelin one-star restaurant where the food and service are an improvement over Goville, but still not sensational. Home and to bed.

Wednesday, August 22—Today after an appropriate playtime for Nimmo and Farnèse, the management's whippet, who tear in circles around the Chateau, we are off to Mont St. Michel, a drive of about an hour. Our hearts sink as we near the massif that looms from the sea. The line of cars and busses is colossal. We finally inch out onto the causeway to the island to find every inch of margin occupied by parked cars. Closer in we find a "parking payant" (10 francs) off on the tidal salt flats, where there is a sign calling attention to the fact that the tide will rise at 20h., and all are counseled to remove autos before that time.

So we park and walk and jostle the crowds (Attila and Nimmo in our arms so as not to be trampled under foot), which in the constrictive passage between postcard and souvenir shops, move about five feet per minute.

We finally have lunch at "Terrasse Poulard," having the obligatory omelet. Dry and *burned!* (The horde is so great we don't complain; at least we ate.) We move up to see the sights only to learn that dogs are not permitted in the religious edifices at the summit, so I take them down while Susan and Kate have a look. The crowd always presses.

"Not worth the detour" is our unanimous opinion, at least at this time of year, though as a spectacle it is still sensational.

That night we stop in St. Lô for drinks and dinner with René and Suzanne Bucaille's son and daughter-in-law, Michel and Claudine and their two sons, Phillippe, age 12, and Stephane, 18.

They have a spic-and-span three floor apartment just off the main street, which is Avenue Le Clerc, theirs being Avenue Générale Dagobert. The town of St. Lô was virtually destroyed in the Normandy breakout in July 1944, and as rebuilt, it is tidy but very plain.

Michel and Claudine have invited us for dinner and they do it up with elegance. First we have champagne and hors d'oeuvres at their apartment. Michel Bucaille is a "kinéotherapeute," or physiotherapist. His office is on the ground floor of the apartment, which we are now proudly shown. During the tour, intense mutual interest is displayed between Attila and Nimmo, on the one hand, and the Bucaille's family dog Uti ("un Fox," meaning fox terrier) on the other. There appears to be no language barrier whatever between them.

After a pleasant hour in their apartment we go, they in their new BMW with Suzanne driving, to an excellent restaurant in Balleroy, the town where Malcolm Forbes' chateau is located. We eat and drink everything in sight. Endless bottles of Bordeaux. Nothing is spared, and we talk about everything under the sun, determining in the process that our opinions are remarkably similar about most things, including the correctness of the U.S. position in Iraq-Kuwait, which is still in its formative stages. Michel (the family spokesman) voices the view that it would be well if it were brought to a close promptly.

In light of Michel's explanation to me yesterday on the phone, we are all naturally curious concerning his physical condition and on meeting him this evening, I note that he extends his gloved left hand and I have to reach to shake it, not vice versa. Later, at table, I see him methodically rotating his plate in stages so as to be sure to get at all the food, and finally I see him address the waitress on his left when she had already moved away behind him. I conclude that he is virtually blind.

At any rate, he and Claudine can scarcely be more accommodating hosts. We much enjoy their company. With a giant handicap Michel has obviously made a big success of his profession as a physical therapist and proudly shows it. We invite him and his family to stay with us in the U.S., and, after fond good-byes, we finally go home to bed (fortunately only seven kilometers away thanks to their choice of restaurants) at midnight.

[The above description of our evening with Michel Bucaille and his family requires considerable amplification both to do the man himself full justice and to fill in some of the blanks about him that nagged at me even after our return to the United States. I was still uncertain as to the circumstances and extent of his injuries, and wanting to be able to record those facts here with full accuracy, I wrote to Michel not only to thank him for his wonderful hospitality but to ask if he would be willing to provide clarification, even though it might be painful for him to revisit the events of 1946 which he had so successfully surmounted. I also wrote to his mother to express to her how touched and grateful we were for the wondrous reunion we had had with her and her husband. About a month later I got a marvelous letter back from Suzanne thanking me for mine and for the photographs I had sent and closing with the notation that Michel had greatly enjoyed my letter and had promised himself "to answer it in due course in his own way—I think he plans to do it in a somewhat unusual way—it will be a surprise." Lo and behold a short time later came a notification from the Post Office of the receipt of a registered package which turned out to be an audio cassette, totally unidentified as to origin except for a French postmark. On the way home from the Post Office I popped it in to my auto tape deck and found it to be a recording by Michel, quite conversational and discursive in tone and substance but obviously intended to respond to my questions.

Among other comments in my letter, I had said at how amazing I had found it that a young lad of twelve should have remembered me so clearly and that now at age fifty-eight he should attach such importance to renewing our old acquaintance. He responded to this comment and my other questions in the following way:

> I am not surprised that it is difficult for Americans, not having been subjected to the occupation of the repressive Nazis, to imagine how intensely my family and I anticipated and desired the coming of you Americans which we all knew was imminent. We listened regularly, and at considerable risk, to the BBC broadcasts in French and to the pronouncements over that medium by General DeGaulle from London. My father kept a secret map in our house with notations and movements of the Allied advances clearly shown and adjusted as necessary. At school, I had an intensely patriotic music teacher who made sure that all the students knew the patriotic songs, including particularly the 'Marseillaise,' which we would sing on Armistice Day, November 11, after posting a sentinel to be sure that no German soldiers

were passing in the street outside. We fled south when the invasion took place, and had returned to Carentan only a short time before you landed in October, 1944. Hence, although I then and later saw hundreds of American soldiers, you were the first one to whom I could attach a face and a name and with whom I could converse. Moreover, in light of my subsequent accident, events and persons whom I could remember having seen before it took place retained a clear focus for me.

As for the details of my accident, while it is not something that I like to dwell upon, I am not surprised that you found our initial telephone conversation difficult to understand and am glad to provide the details so that this chapter between us can finally be understood and closed.

On a Tuesday in January of 1946 at 2:15 in the afternoon, several classmates and I were on our way to a football practice down a country road near Carentan when an object sailed over an adjacent hedgerow and landed at our feet. One of my friends picked it up and I instantly told him, "Don't touch that; we don't know what it is," and as I took it from my friend's hands, it exploded. My friend had recoiled out of the way and was injured though not gravely, but I was badly stunned, was covered with blood and fell into the nearby ditch. I was picked up by some American GI's who immediately took me for emergency treatment to a nearby American military hospital, where I was bandaged like a mummy and then taken in an American ambulance to a French civilian hospital in Cherbourg. There followed a series of nine additional operations in Paris, Nantes and other locations over a period of years, the end results of the treatment being as you observed them (blind in both eyes, a partially amputated hand and a residual limp).

My father naturally did everything possible in the aftermath of the atrocity to ascertain and pursue the perpetrators. It appeared that under supervision of some American GI's, a group of German prisoners of war had been engaged in sweeping the field on the other side of the hedgerow to free it of mines. The thrown object, which was about 15 centimeters in length and five in width, must have been some form of grenade. In the ensuing investigation, it became apparent that there was no way to extract from the German prisoners the identity of the culprit, since they were all subject to the protection of the Geneva Convention and could not be compelled to answer such questions. I continue to wonder to this day whether the act was deliberate or merely careless.[28]

But I very quickly determined that I would not permit the impairment, terrible though it was, to prevent my leading a useful and enjoyable life. I give great credit to my parents who managed to equip me, even at age fourteen, to be able to confront a crisis of this sort, to rise above it, and even to derive strength from it.

His cassette then went on to describe his subsequent life, the great satisfaction he takes from his profession which brings ease and comfort to his clients, and also to a supplementary career in which he has served as officer of an administrative tribunal which regulates employer-employee controversies in western Normandy. Michel completed the cassette by patching in a recording of a song by Michel Sardou called "L'Ericain," a slang contraction of the French word for "American" which, in a highly entertaining way, twits Gen. DeGaulle and other latter day French politicians for their anti-American stance on various political issues, and calls attention to the fact that the "Ericains" were dying in Normandy and occupying Germany when the French politicians were nowhere to be seen.

Thursday, August 23—A long day of driving. Around the ugly, stinking, hot Parisian banlieu on the "autoroute périphérique," which is worse than Boston's Route 128 in terms of traffic and stop and go. (On making our auto reservation I had been told that air conditioned cars were not available, but were in any case unnecessary because the climate would not require one!)

---

[28] I do not share this doubt. If the device did not detonate on impact with the ground, it could have done so thereafter only through the functioning of a deliberately activated time-delay fuze which is a part of every grenade. Moreover, the intense hatred of French civilians by German prisoners of war is well documented: the Germans could not understand how the French could appear to treat the invaders cordially during the occupation and then with hatred and contempt after they had become prisoners. See Helmut Horner, *A German Odyssey* (Fulcrum Pub., Golden Colorado, 1991).

This is a day to forget except for Reims and a picnic which we enjoy in the town of Epone, on the Seine about twenty miles west of Paris. We stop in the Mantes-le-Joli (a misnomer if there ever was one), a working class polyglot town next door to buy the necessaries in a well-endowed charcuterie, and were despairing of finding a bucolic picnic spot when Kate espies a sign for the "Parc du Château." The gardener graciously moves his hose and urges us to move our car into the shade "pour les chiens." So we munch comfortably under the trees and manage to stay reasonably cool.

At Reims we stop to savor the cathedral. We now have some expertise and find it superb in some respects (transept, rose windows and high straight main axis; also *cool* inside) and disappointing in others. Can't beat Amiens or Bourges, for my money.

Friday, August 24—Achouffe, Belgium. Our hotel, picked out of the Belgian Michelin Guide for its bucolic setting, turns out to be a mistake. Our room, said to be for three people, consists of a double bed with springs in the shape of a hammock barely big enough for the two of us, while Kate's "bed" consists of a mattress on the floor on which we must tread en route to the john. It creaks noisily with each step. Sleep is not enhanced by the scullery boy who every morning clinks glasses on metal for five minutes directly below our second story window, nor by tractors and motorbikes which charge down the hill under that window and gun themselves up the opposite hill under the other window. Well, at least we have cross ventilation. The food is very uneven (steak drowned in a vinegary béarnaise last night).

But we are nonetheless rested (perhaps I speak only for myself), and we head south on a new autoroute to Bastogne to visit the Museum of the Ardennes campaign there. We drive into town first and find Bastogne, like even the least consequential Belgian or French hamlet, thriving and prosperous, amazingly so. My memories of a bleak town square surrounding a frozen fountain cannot find an echo anywhere. Bustling stores and banks with computers in each one and the streets jammed with autos.

The museum is located on a hill outside town in a round or octagonal building. It is quite fascinating. There are two life-size dioramas, one of a German Army unit or group with representative uniforms, vehicles, arms and equipment against a snowy scene and on the opposite side of the building an equivalent American group. Along the margin of these displays are glass cases housing a encyclopedic ensemble of weapons, rations (K's and C's!), life size mannequins in uniform, etc., etc. Off to one side there's a small theater where a multimedia black and white show depicts the events from December 18-19, 1944 through the first week in January 1945.

I am quite surprised to learn that the Germans perpetuated their attack for many days after the relief of Bastogne by the Third Army on December 26, 1944 and by U.S. air drops when the skies cleared a day or so before that. Indeed, much of the worst of the casualties appear to have been incurred in the first week in January. The total numbers were also large—something like 75,000 for the Americans, 3,000 Belgian civilians, with the German number unknown.

The museum is the brainchild of a native of Bastogne, Guy Franz Arend, who, largely single-handedly, conceived and brought it into being. In addition to the multimedia presentation there is a circular amphitheater seating fifty people on the floor of which is an illuminated map which shows the American and German positions as they changed from day to day during the battle. It is quite informative but is limited almost entirely to the immediate area of Bastogne and does not integrate that engagement into the larger picture or to include the harrowing events to the east during the first two days of the breakthrough.

After an hour and a half at the museum and its associated memorial (which is a disappointment after the Normandy cemetery) we head off to the east.

Our first stop is Clervaux, concealed in a deep cleft in the Ardennes uplands created by the Clerve River. It was here in mid-December 1944—after a month of life in a foxhole—that I enjoyed the unparalleled luxury of an extended hot shower followed by a complete set of clean clothing. Once more I can't say I remember a whole lot about the town except for the castle which sits on a rocky prominence in its center surrounded now by quaint buildings, many of which have been rebuilt or were newly built after the war. The town swarms with tourists amongst whom we enjoy lunch on a terrace square, as the dogs loudly protest the existence of others who dare to promenade nearby.

Then to Weiswampach, Ouren and Lutzkampen, following the route I marched to the front in November 1944. I am astonished to discover that the road from Weiswampach to Ouren is downhill—my recollection of panting and huffing and throwing away extraneous equipment on an upgrade is clearly wrong.

It figures, of course. Ouren is at the bottom of a valley and very peaceful, set about by summer camps dedicated to international friendship. There seems to be very little to photograph in Ouren so we head east into Germany. The map shows no customs at this border point but a congenial barkeep in one of the auberges tells me that there is free passage and we go up a one lane blacktop road towards Lutzkampen, about three and a half kilometers away. This *is* uphill, steeply. It is clearly what I so distinctly remember. Once at the top the lay of the land differs only slightly from what I remember. Lutzkampen, of course, was between the American and German lines and was heavily damaged and totally deserted in November-December 1944.

I find a farmhouse just west of the center of the village in a location which seems to duplicate what I remember as a command post occupied by the company in 1944. If I am right, it has of course been rebuilt because the command post was destroyed by a German tank on December 16, 1944, which was when the Ardennes Offensive started. I try to find the company reserve position in the woods to the northwest but a much larger proportion of the area seems now to be wooded than I remember and there is no way to know which of the "woods" I now see are the ones I remember.

We drive down into a farmer's field in the valley which looks towards the east and in which I remember our foxholes were located on the morning of December 16, 1944. There is no way to know just where they were. I know I'm more or less in the right place, but there are no clearly identifiable landmarks, and certainly nothing in the way of an indentation or depression in the earth which might possibly be "my hole." I didn't expect that there would be, but somehow I'm disappointed.

We drive east through the town, which appears just as prosperous as its Belgian and Luxembourg neighbors, towards where we know that the Siegfried line was. Now, however, the only remnants that can be identified are traces of "dragon's teeth" hidden in a woodland area off the roadside. I am amazed that such formidable works of reinforced concrete can have vanished so nearly completely, and conclude that the government must have made a huge project of their removal.

After taking numerous pictures, including panoramic views, we head back to Ouren (more pictures) and Weiswampach, where Susan has detected a Villeroy and Bosch china store and where I eventually drink all four Cokes I have ordered because the girls don't know where to find me, but it's hot and I am thirsty.

In late afternoon we head back to Achouffe, scout around for a different place to eat and finally dine again at our own hotel, the Hotel de la Vallée des Fées. ("Hotel of the Valley of the Fairies.") It is a strange place as they don't make up our beds until I ask at 7:30 p.m. There is a llama on a tiny island in a very small pond—the island perhaps twenty yards in diameter. The grass around the hotel has not been cut in three weeks. There is a nice lady who appears to run the place but she's only there occasionally and the result is a very sloppy operation.

Saturday, August 25—We set out once more to Beho and Rogery, Belgium, which my correspondent Cliff Hackett holds to be the location where we (the remnants of Baker Company of the 112th Regiment) were ambushed by a German tank column on December 23, 1944, my 20th birthday, Though I know by now that I will probably recognize nothing, I am anxious to visit these towns to try to clarify the gaping discrepancy between my quite clear recollection and the chronology prepared by Cliff, our company historian, who identifies them as the place in question. I find that Rogery, where Cliff states that we "guarded three railroad bridges," is largely flat, has no waterways and, though there is one abandoned railway line, cannot be made to conform to his description let alone my recollection.

What I thought before and now still think after visiting is that the events described—German ambush, etc.—did not take place there, but 10-15 kilometers further north along the Salm River, possibly at Trois Ponts—a name I remember from the time and whose layout roughly approximates the territory I remember.

The recollection which I am trying to square with the reality of the topography is that we were near a church, castle or other ruin on the top of a hill, overlooking a valley to the north, on the far side of which, moving from east to west, a column of American tanks appeared and soon began firing on us.

But as I find after we travel the necessary distance, this vision does not correspond to Trois Ponts either, although I look hard. I conclude that this enigma is to remain exactly that and that I will never be *really* certain of the truth in the matter. [Eventually, after a great deal of additional reading and the comparing of notes with the survivors of Company B who attended our Minnesota reunions, I reach the final and somewhat reluctant conclusion that Rogery *must* have been the location of the events of December 23, 1944, no matter how great the discrepancies between its topography and my memory; the written record, both American and German, is simply too categorical not to be correct.]

We then motor to La Roche-en-Ardennes, where we lunch at La Claire Fontaine, which turns out to be one of our most memorable meals. The dining room is most attractive: we look out over a garden fronting on the Ourthe River, and the food, served by a rather forbidding spinsterish lady of forty, is exceptional.

We spend the afternoon taking in the sights of La Roche, which is celebrating some sort of fair. It ain't much, except there are dogs of all sizes, colors and temperaments everywhere. Ours find the experience very intense. In company of many others, we climb the old fort in the middle of town. And then we head back to Achouffe, stopping en route in Madrin, a hamlet to which Michelin attributes three good restaurants, two of which, with lovely views to the southwest, are booked solid. We end up at "Les Ondes," a restaurant with an all female cast, which turns out to serve a quite respectable meal.

Sunday, August 26—We are finally permitted to leave Achouffe, driving south through Houffalize (we call it "Fouffalize" in honor of our cat Foo-Foo), then on in ever increasing warmth along the Sure River, demarcating the German-Luxembourg border, and the Moselle River, where endless slopes of grapes are now discerned.

We continue to find ourselves harassed by the unseasonably hot weather—humid, heavy, much haze, preventing any distant views. It has been like this since we arrived—Normandy, and Belgium and now back in France. Strange meteorological doings!

We whiz down the autoroute, breaking for lunch at a place called Le Horizon on a western hill overlooking Thionville. I stupidly fail to check my green Michelin Guide to reconnoiter the Maginot line fort of which we had been told. So we miss it. I see later in the guides a long article about Verdun which I would love to come back to and look at sometime, but not this one.

On into to Lorraine. At Nancy, a heavy thunderstorm which turns out to be quite local and then very quickly we are at Trois Epis, in Alsace.

Now here at last is a place that really does look like the one I remember! The jewel-like (inside) small church is unchanged. The Grand Hotel is grander but the older part is as it was. Tobacco and news store likewise. Of course many new buildings, especially a large hospital complex apparently devoted to nurturing the health-impaired members of the French Teachers Union, courtesy of the state.

On arrival we find a message from old friends Conny and Bill Quinby who are participating in a tour and seminar sponsored by Princeton and which is sojourning in Trois Epis for a few days. They are attending a lecture until 8 p.m. so we have dinner in the Grand Hotel's quite grand dining room, and end up being very disappointed in the food and service. Unfortunately we don't find out until later that there is another simpler dining room next door in an annex to the hotel (called "L'Auberge," in the original pre-1945 building) at which we might have done better. The grand dining room is one of those where the waiter puts the wine bottle at a distance and then does not pour it.

After dinner we make contact with Conny and Bill. They are attending a sort of loose question and answer session with their Princeton group (totaling fifty, but only perhaps twenty this evening), led by André Maman, Princeton's foremost French professor who is an agreeable wit and raconteur. I am introduced to the group by Bill and find the session interesting and entertaining. Among other pearls cast by André is his assessment of the importance of wining and dining in France: "We are trained not to be too friendly with strangers, and a meal with wine lets us communicate without an open-ended relationship. Also, when we have failed or been disappointed in some significant way, it can't be so bad that a good meal and a bottle of wine can't correct it."

Monday, August 27—The ladies are pleased at my suggestion that they have the morning to themselves, so after the most agreeable breakfast on the balcony of the Auberge (red-checked table cloths, a stunning if hazy view over the plain of Alsace and quantities of bread, jam and tea) I set off on researches.

I inquire at the news and tobacco store opposite the hotel if anyone is known to reside in Trois Epis who might have been there at the moment of La Libération and am given two names, one of a Monsieur Adam. When this name is pronounced in French it gives me a bit of a turn because it sounds very much like the way my own name is pronounced; I don't find out how it is spelled until I search out M. Adam's house. This I do by walking up the hill—now a municipal parking lot—down which we came screaming with bayonets fixed on the morning of February 3, 1945 to liberate the town. I find M. Adam's house on the reverse slope of the same hill. The tidy establishment is named "Maison Adam" and carries a painted sign on the front gate indicating rooms are for rent. Though the front door and many windows are open to the summer sun, no one answers my ring, so I proceed back into town and down the main road for half a kilometer to the "Restaurant Mon Repos," which is operated by the other person whose name I had been given, a Mme. de Mangeat. This elderly lady emerges from her kitchen after two rings, listens to my inquiry, which brings a broad smile to her face, and then embarks on an excited recital, which goes something like this:

> Of course I was here. Of course I remember! What a glorious day! We knew you were coming and the Germans knew you were coming, too. We even knew which way you were coming. There is a 'Route Forestière,' which forks to the left into the woods off of the road from Ammerschwihr about one kilometer below town—that's how you came up. I was here with my husband and little daughter, age one and a half. There had been much bombing and artillery, and we had hid in a cellar nearby [pointing] and it was just at its entrance that we saw our first Americans. Oh, how happy we were!
>
> The town has changed so much since. There is the big hospital for teachers. [Indeed, it covers almost all of one side of the top of the hill in the center of town.] But the news dealer's store was there as was the Auberge and the church. The rest is all different.
>
> The Germans that were here included many SS with other troops. The SS were here to watch over the other troops. By the time you got here most of them had fled, but there were some who preferred to be taken prisoner. How wonderful it is to remember that day! No, M. Adam wasn't in town on the Jour de la Libération. He was a prisoner in Germany.
>
> Thank you for coming to free us!

Greatly exhilarated by my exchange with her I drive down to Sigolsheim to find again (this time it's no surprise at all) that all is totally changed. The town was nine-tenths rubble in 1945, and now has been totally rebuilt with a repaired church tower as the only pre-war building which even partially survived. The new town is tidy but with none of the warmth of the half-timbered structures that are so characteristic of the other wine-growing towns of the region. I ask in a cafe and a young lady directs me to the butcher's shop across the square. That young lady hasn't a clue. So I wander into the "Centre Coopérative Viniculturelle" a large and imposing structure with spacious sales and tasting rooms at the front. There a middle aged gentleman ponders my question reflectively for some minutes, and finally invites me into his office where he places a phone call, talks to a lady whose name I don't catch, asks to speak to her husband, to whom he explains that he has in his presence "un ancien combattant américain" who had been in Sigolsheim between mid-January to the first week in February of 1945 and who had then gone up to liberate Trois Epis, and could his hearer recall anyone who had been here at that time? He then listens for a while responding at one point "Pas vrai!" ("Not true!"). On finishing his conversation he tells me that he has been talking with M. Bernard Dietrich (pronounced "Dee-et-reek") who was indeed in Sigolsheim (pronounced "See-gol-sime") in those days, had been a member of the French First Army, and went up to Trois Epis on the very day that I had. He is said to have pictures of the time and is awaiting my arrival.

With profuse thanks to my intermediary, I jump in the car and go around the block to the Restaurant De La Viniculture, where my host Bernard awaits me with a large smile on his face.

What a time we then spend together! It is lunch time and his restaurant is jammed with people, perhaps twenty-five to thirty at tables and perhaps another eight or ten standing at the small central bar. We sit at a table where he brings out a large photo album which is filled with 8" × 10" black and white photos of Sigolsheim taken in the winter of 1944-45. They show what I remember, but I cannot identify from the pictures of the rubblized town the cellars in which I was quartered, the outposts we manned in the vineyards, nor the German bunker that we attacked to take prisoners. There is no way to identify those winter 1945 sights in the summer of 1990.

Not many minutes go by before Bernard invites "la famille" to join him and his wife as "nos invités" for lunch, so I tool back up to Trois Epis following the self-same Route Forestière described by Mm. de Mangeat (now black-topped, however) a ten-minute drive at most, which I cannot help but comparing to the night-long trudge of forty-five years ago (1300 feet of difference in altitude), and we soon coast back down to Sigolsheim where introductions are made and we settle down to an impromptu lunch of tuna, cuisse de lapin and steaks, served with a gray riesling for me and a red wine plus a pinot gris rosé for the ladies. We eat industriously while Bernard says "je ne suis pas grand mangeur" and has a small steak with some frites. His story unfolds and is contributed to by his wife Martha when her kitchen duties allow.

He was inducted into the German Army in 1940 at the age of eighteen. As a native Alsatian, he was totally fluent in both German and French. He spent the first eleven months in Germany at the end of which he was given an Ausweise—a pass—to come home. He deserted shortly after his return and became part of the French underground in the area of Lyon. His parents were arrested by the Germans in reprisal, taken to concentration camps in Germany where they perished. He was taken out twice by submarine across the Mediterranean to Africa for training and instruction. On return to France, as he puts it to Susan, "Nous avons fait des choses méchantes." ("We did naughty things.") During this period he was under the orders of the Free French Government in London. When the Normandy invasion of France took place, he joined General Leclerc's First French Army and eventually participated in the reduction of the Colmar pocket (a German salient extending into Western Alsace which had been bypassed by the initial Allied drive to the Rhine). Bernard was in and about Sigolsheim during December 1944 when it was liberated, also when it was retaken by the Germans shortly thereafter and still later when in early January 1945 it was retaken by the American troops who were relieved by my 28th Division about January 15, 1945.

Even more coincidentally, it turns out that both of us were in Trois Epis the day it was liberated—February 2-3, 1945. He recounts having visited Mme. de Mangeat at Mon Repos that morning and having had her daughter sit on his knee only to have her go "pi-pi." It has since been a standing (what else?) joke between the three of them—she's not allowed to sit on his lap even today.

Martha's rancor for the Germans is if anything deeper and more intense than her husband's. We speak of how the young people of today don't know, don't understand and don't care about the German occupation. It is not clear whether the Dietrichs regard this as an improvement. Bernard mentions the tension that sometimes enters the room when a German tourist visits the restaurant. Martha says, "No one who didn't live through it can understand how terrible the Germans were."

I ask how it came to pass that with town and family names all in

German, they had such a strong French allegiance. They answer by anecdote rather than directly, mentioning Bernard's dead parents, other hostages taken from virtually every family in town, most of them killed, and the hatred handed down from their forebears resulting from the German annexation of Alsace-Lorraine after the Franco-Prussian War. Bernard said that he and Martha—she from Bennwihr, the next town 4 kilometers to the east—had wanted to get married on his return from Germany in 1941, but their parents had ruled against it, saying they should wait until their marriage would not be performed under German law and thus be an acknowledgment of the legitimacy of the German government. They finally were married in 1945 when Bernard's colonel authorized it as a means of keeping him from having to go to Indochina.

An amazing insight into the life of the French in these wine-growing Alsatian towns is that they all grow up speaking "Alsatian," a dialect which sounds a little more like German than French, but which is neither. It drove the Germans crazy, as Bernard says with relish, because they couldn't understand it. He says even the dialect in Bennwihr differs from that of Sigolsheim, only four kilometers away. And notwithstanding the leveling effect of radio and television, all of the kids still grow up knowing the local Alsatian as their first language.

We finally leave the Restaurant De La Viniculture totally sated with food and exchanging names and addresses and fond hugs and kisses all around and with promises to send photographs and letters, which we certainly will do.

Off then to Colmar where we walk around the old city which for some reason (possibly associated with the emotional high and plentiful wine at lunch) does not impress as much as we expected it to. One attractive feature, however, which Colmar shares with a number of other cities which we later visit (Strasbourg, Cologne) is the existence of large "pedestrians only" areas in the center of the old city.

We finally get back home to Trois Epis where we again savor the glorious view over the Alsatian plain from our window and the cool air of its 2,000 foot altitude.

We decide not to eat at the Grand Hotel, having made a reservation for five at the one-star restaurant Le Caveau in Eguisheim. Time for our departure comes and goes without any sign of the Quinby's who have spent the day in Strasbourg with their busload of Princetonians. We cancel Le Caveau and finally go instead to the other larger hotel in Trois

Epis, Le Marchal, where we get in just under the wire at their 8:30 p.m. closing time and have a pleasant if not particularly memorable meal, enlivened at its end by Bill and Conny's arrival, with whom we share our days' experiences.

They were detained in Strasbourg by a lengthy reception in honor of their group given by the American Consul General. Bill is greatly interested in what they have been learning about the multi-layered new government of Europe which is emerging and which, though heavily bureaucratic (40,000 employees already) is generally acknowledged as an effective instrumentality.

Tuesday, August 28—Today we drive around Alsace, attempting first the monstrous chateau at Haut Konigsbourg, which was rebuilt by Kaiser Wilhelm II in the early years of the twentieth century and which is huge and ugly. It sits atop a Vosges crag at about 3,000 feet, and its approaches are swamped with hundreds of autos and buses. We trudge up to the entry only to discover that it's closed for the lunch hour, it being a little past noon. With small regret we go back down and repair in a raging thunder storm to the only restaurant that can be found in the town of Ste. Marie-aux Mines, famous in past years for its silver mines (and also, as I do not learn until later, as the town in which Pvt. Eddie Slovik, the only American soldier to be shot for desertion during World War II, was executed by a 28th Division firing squad in February 1945). The restaurant, called the Café des Chasseurs, though unprepossessing, turns out to be most satisfying, with the same simple fare and atmosphere of Bernard Dietrich's place in Sigolsheim.

Then back home over a very picturesque back road to Trois Epis, where this time we have left the Quinby's to make the dinner reservation, which they have done at a two-star place in Ammerschwihr, six kilometers away, called "Les Armes de la France." In Conny's handwriting on the note she has left for us announcing this choice it seems to be spelled "Les Amis de la France" which causes some confusion when we inquire of some Ammerschwihr teenagers where it is located, but we do find it located most handsomely on the second floor of an old Alsatian mansion. As has been our unfortunate experience in other highly-touted restaurants, the food turns out to be undistinguished and the bill enormous. We resolve to avoid prestigious joints in the future.

Wednesday, August 29—We take our leave somewhat latish, as seems to be our custom, and head northwards along "La Route du Vin," through the most incredible series of picturesque old towns nestled in the foot hills of the Vosges mountains. Ribeauvillé, St. Hippolyte, Bergheim, Kintzheim and Ittersweiler, to name a few. They tend to be no more than three to four kilometers apart, each with its own church, town square, ruined castle above, and incredible quantities of flowers everywhere, on walls, in window boxes. Reds, magentas, purples and blues all mixed together to marvelous effect. And the towns all brimmingly prosperous. Everyone is in the wine business in some fashion with a sub-specialty of eaux de vie. I'd love nothing more than to spend a week poking in and about these luscious locations.

We end up in Obernoi, towards the north end of La Route du Vin. It is on the Alsatian plain, considerably larger and hence not as atmospheric, though the center of town is ancient and quaint and dominated by a medieval clock tower.

We speed north on an autoroute around Strasbourg to a northern suburb called La Wantzenau, which is actually detached from the city in farming country rapidly turning industrial. (It is not until much later that I become aware of the curious coincidence between the name of this town and that of the cathedral in the Belgian town of Mons—see entry for August 19, above; there has to be some explanation, but superficial checking has not revealed what it is.)

We lunch excellently at Restaurant Schaeffer on the banks of the Ill River, whose patron informs us with unconcealed zeal, when we ask him directions to Le Moulin, where we have room reservations, that their cuisine is closed on Wednesdays.

Eventually we find Le Moulin and are immediately pleased. It's an old mill of bygone days which bridges the Ill River and has a copious flow of water beneath it due to local thunderstorms. It was rebuilt in the Fifties into a thirty-room rustic hotel, with an attractive restaurant which we of course are unable to try. The innkeeper's wife is a charming lady who looks like Oona O'Neill. We have the top (fourth) floor bedroom, a bi-level affair with two bathrooms and windows on three sides. Kate occupies the mezzanine with one of the dogs. It is still hot and humid and we are grateful for the breezes which blow through the room. Unanimously voted the nicest hotel yet.

After a brief repose we sortie for dinner at the Le Restaurant Zimmer, a handsome room with an excellent dinner served by a red-mustachioed waiter who attracts the eye of my wife though not my daughter. We sigh because this will be our last French meal.

Thursday, August 30—Up and out at our usual 10:30 after a very pleasant breakfast in the garden by the river. (We've become addicted to oeufs à la coque—and also to asking for espresso coffee, the French breakfast version leaving our coffee drinkers cold.)

Up and away into Germany. We cross the Rhine and accost the Black Forest which turns out to amaze and please us. Unlike its mirror image Vosges—which it does copy in terms of topography—the hillsides are cultivated quite high up the steep slopes where beflowered farmhouses cling to them, lending a distinctly alpine appearance. But then we go to the 2500 foot level and into the high pines. We come to the Altestrasse von Schwartzwald, also known as Route 500, which runs along the crest of the Black Forest range, and then turn north towards Baden-Baden.

Hunger overtakes us and we stop at a rustic Gasthaus in the woods to puzzle over the German menu, which is only slightly clarified by my Berlitz German phrase book, and not at all by the waitress or hotel keeper, who once and for all lay to rest the rubric that "they all speak English." We finally point to the menu of the day written in longhand on an appended card and are pleasantly surprised by a quite palatable sauerbraten-type dish, together with salad.

The road now descends rapidly into Baden-Baden where it plunges with zero warning to the non-German reader into a tunnel perhaps three or four kilometers in length which takes much of the traffic (but not enough as we later discover) under the city streets. It emerges at the north end of town where we finagle our way back to the "Romantik Hotel Kleine Prinz." It is "romantic" only in a sense that it is part of a chain of German hotels which call themselves that. Our room, on the second floor, directly overlooks Lichtentaler Strasse, the city's main aboveground drag and its like trying to sleep in the oval at Indianapolis. We can't close the windows, which are of the ubiquitous German variety which tilt inwards from the top, because it's oppressively humid and hot and we'd suffocate if we did.

We perambulate around town during the afternoon, listen to a part of an open air concert in the park, noting the large numbers of silk-frocked ladies, including one being escorted by an impeccably dressed but etiolated middle aged man whose role could not have been plainer if he had a sign of his back saying "I am a kept man." We have a coffee at a sidewalk cafe and observe the innumerable hausfraus with young children in prams, pausing to converse with each other and admire each other's kids while secretly thinking, as Kate observes, that "my kid is twice as cute as hers."

It starts to rain as we return to the hotel—en route we spot "La Terrazza," an Italian restaurant in a court along Lichtentaler Strasse where we make reservations, having by now a distinct antipathy to our hotel and everything about it, including its restaurant, even though we haven't tried it. So we eat at La Terrazza and enjoy a pleasant Italian meal served by a highly talkative waiter of many languages and indeterminate nationality who speaks enthusiastically about the baths, urging us to visit the Friedrichsbad, which requires two hours to visit.

Friday, August 31—So after very little sleep in our overheated racetrack infield, we struggle out to the accompaniment of unmuted bitching and whining, determined to try the baths. We approach the Friedrichsbad through an underground parking garage and find to our surprise that the two hour time requirement is totally non-negotiable. The lady recommends instead that if we have brought "costumes de bain" we go to the Caracallabad, which is adjacent.

What a revelation! It is organized with thorough Teutonic efficiency: (1) One enters a white marble dressing cubicle (one of hundreds), changes, emerges from a door opposite, inserts one's coded entry ticket inside the lock of the facing numbered lock, which releases a key which one straps to one's wrist; (2) one now advances into the bathing chamber, theoretically carrying a towel which we did not bring (and did not know we could rent at the downstairs ticket counter), and also one's wallet for which is now found a matching numbered lockbox into which the wrist key fits; and (3) one now is ready to enjoy the baths—"enjoy" is indeed the operative word.

The scene is astonishing. We are in a huge domed circular room, perhaps seventy-five yards in diameter and forty feet high, with a terraced floor of three or four levels, each with swimming pools which flow into each other from top to bottom. At the high end is a small pool twenty feet in diameter which extends into an apse at the back wall in which there is a hot water fall twenty feet high cascading from a rocky ledge. In the center is an upgushing fountain which surges on and off. The water temperature is about 110 degrees.

The next level down is an enormous pool almost as wide as the room itself with various overhead and underwater jets. The temperature here is about five degrees cooler than the first one. There are bodies of all sizes, shapes and ages, all with large smiles on their faces, frolicking about, including a fair number of young maidens of Junoesque proportions, very little of which is concealed from the interested observer. Also young men and women seeming to feed on each other's faces while bathing. At the back of a lower pool is a glass wall into which are set several plastic-flapped apertures leading to a continuation of the pool into the outdoors, which on this day is cool and rainy.

We slip out these doors and find in the large outdoor pool a sort of watery merry-go-round. The circular pool has underwater jets in its circumference, all pointed in a counterclockwise direction. There is also a concentric wall about six feet inside the exterior wall which serves to speed up the flow of water and propel the laughing bathers between the two. All in all it's a riot and we spend an hour and a half of sheer pleasure. The pouts of the morning have vanished long ago and even the lack of towels to dry off with does not alter the mood. I find an overhead tanning light location where one can stretch out on a chaise lounge and let the rays evaporate the drops.

A uniquely memorable experience, all agree, fully justifying the maternal response to the peevish remark when turning away from the Friedrichsbad, "Who's idea was this anyway?", the response being "I'm sure this will be something we will never forget!"

We drive no more than five minutes from the Caracallabad when Kate espies a Japanese restaurant to which we instantly repair for a delicious Nipponese lunch, during which I learn that as I was dressing the girls had gone up a spiral staircase in the main room of the bath where they had discovered a room full of naked men. Susan apparently reacted with such surprise that one fully-exposed gentleman felt impelled to compulsively cover himself.

En route now to Cologne through rain and fog. As dusk is falling we journey northwards down the Rhine on its west bank not really seeing very much in the way of castles or vineyards and nothing of any Lorelei. Only a few barges appear through the gloom.

We pass through Bonn, and having heard that it was originally a sleepy little university town are surprised to discover how big it is.

On entering Cologne I am suddenly completely disoriented because the autobahn whose "Koln" arrows I have been following has somehow managed to cross the Rhine from the east to arrive in the downtown. I have to stop at the railroad station to look at a map and reorient myself exactly 180 degrees. It takes a few minutes to do this, during which we are startled to discover our vehicle in the middle of a pedestrians-only shopping district, but we finally arrive at the Hotel Eden, directly across the square from the red sandstone Cathedral. We install ourselves in our room, go for a drive to the Intercontinental Hotel to find grass for the dogs, and then go to the restaurant right next to our hotel where we have something Germanic. And so to bed.

Saturday, September 1—After our usual protracted organizational period, we finally get everyone going and visit our very last cathedral on a very dark day which doesn't set it off too well. We notice some smeary blue stained glass of obviously modern origin in the chancel area and another modern effort, seemingly much better, which is obscured in large part by the organ pipes just inside the main door.

Much more interesting is the German-Roman museum in a stunningly modern two story building just north of the cathedral. There are mosaic floors discovered in this location in 1941 which are fascinating if somewhat faded, and displays of glass, pottery and jewelry which are stunning. Particularly impressive to me are two gold tiaras of free-flowing design which have sustained no tarnish whatever through the ages.

We now embark on the long haul to Berlin, distant by 575 kilometers, in the course of which we learn that the autobahn system is a very mixed blessing. Items: (1) Traffic is dense and includes everything from Citroen 2 cvs., house trailers and semi-trailers to Porsches, BMW's and Mercedes straining to go 170 kilometers per hour. This results in many slow downs as when a truck, for example, wants to pass a slower one and breaks into the passing lane, where it takes two or three minutes to pass the other vehicle(s) during which no one goes faster than 90 kilometers per hour; (2) another phenomenon is when one is going along at 135 kilometers per hour and a fat-assed Mercedes, typically, barrels up behind with its turn signal and headlights flashing to tailgate tightly until the way is given; the driver is invariably a plump and solitary German of intense seriousness and importance; (3) the legal speed limit on the autobahns in Germany is 130 but no one pays it any heed; speeds of up to 160 are not unusual and higher are occasionally seen; (4) the traffic is now much too dense for the two lane portions; three lane roadways are not general and except in the Ruhr exist largely on the hills where they help greatly, but most of the topography is flat.

I don't really know what speed we were able to average—maybe 110 kilometers not counting pit stops. These fortunately are few because the Opel Vectra 1.6 liter can go a whole day on one tank of gas, yet it really rolls at 160 kilometers. We stop much more often to refuel the persons than the auto. We make one such stop for lunch at an autobahn "gasthof" where a sit-down meal is enjoyed at linen-napped tables. Our struggle to translate the German menus has not greatly advanced.

Our first glimpse of Helmstedt, the town which from 1945 until the reunification in 1989 marked the frontier of East Germany, is a revelation. As we approach we begin to see more and more eastern-Europe-looking vehicles. Before long we are able to identify the curious eave-roofed Trabants and the dinky Ladas most of which look as though they were made from tinfoil. Some of them are towing—with loose ropes—other vehicles and trailers. A pattern seems to emerge: old and partially-wrecked western vehicles are being towed to the east where they can presumably be repaired much more cheaply than in the west.

But in Helmstedt we finally see how it "used to be." The autobahn fans out into something like twenty elaborate check points where before the wall came down all incoming vehicles and passengers were checked by DDR soldiers. Now they sit idle and deteriorating as traffic whisks past in a wide arc.

The way things "used to be" is likewise readily apparent from the farmland alongside the autobahn. Zero habitations, and, with the exception of Magdeburg seen in the smoky distance to the south, zero towns. Advertising has appeared on the overpasses, however, but we can't say how recently.

It darkens as we approach Berlin and the driver, me, is confused as we see signs to "Westberlin" when we are still 80 kilometers away. I elect to drive straight ahead (rather than turn north) following the signs to "Berlin." These as it develops, take us south of the city rather than to its center. False hope is raised by the appearance of the small jet airplane sign which we assume means Tegel Airport. Not at all; it means Schoenefeld, the East German airport. Oops! So we now head towards Berlin "Zentrum," to the west which it turns out takes us right across the city, past Unter den Linden and Alexander Platz, which are duskily impressive, but not clearly visible. Finally about 9:30 p.m. we get to Tegel

Airport and find our "Novotel Berlin Airport" which is located next to a small woods off the airport entrance. Given what it is—an airport hotel—it's not too bad (though Kate may disagree—she got short shrift on beds the whole trip) and the restaurant which has a limited but quite well prepared menu is not half bad, as witness the fact that we eat here all three nights of our stay in the city.

Sunday, September 2—We struggle out into a fairly nice day and find our way without great difficulty to the Tiergarten, denuded of all trees and vegetation in 1945 but now all beautifully wooded and manicured. At its eastern end we find the Brandenburg gate.

What a curious scene! It is more than a little reminiscent of counterpart scenes forty-five years ago, when the objects in demand were American cigarettes, food, gum, etc., and the currency was occupation marks. Now the objects sold are (1) pieces of the Berlin wall, large stretches of which remain quite intact both north and south of the Brandenburg gate, and (2) all manner of Soviet uniform items, including caps, fur hats, medals, and insignia of all kinds.

In approaching the gate, we pass the Soviet War Memorial, the sight of which instantly resuscitates in me a dormant memory of having attended its dedication in 1945 as an official American representative. We observe two Russian sentinels standing on its top steps with rifles under their raincoats. Kate says they are statues—not real—only conceding that they are flesh and blood when the guard changes and they goose-step down and away.

As we leave the War Memorial we espy an emaciated Russian soldier behind a concrete pillar at the corner of an iron picket fence and hidden from behind by an adjacent yew tree. He offers his garrison cap for sale through the fence, furtively hoping not to be detected by his superiors.

At the Gate we observe pieces of the wall for sale by various vendors and also hammers and chisels for those interested in chipping off their own pieces. We decide to try the latter and for three marks ($2.00) rent a set for half an hour and chip away, only to discover that to get sizable chunks out, of the size, say, of a pack of cigarettes, an effort both long and hard would be necessary. We garner a few chips of our own, none larger than a dime, but carefully squirrel them away in a plastic sandwich bag gratuitously provided by the tool renter and finally return the tools and proceed to buy a substantial hunk (about two pounds) for four marks.

We then move over to the Kurfurstendamm to find lunch, first spending an hour or so in the aquarium which I had read had more kinds of fish (6,000) than any other in the world. It is indeed impressive as is my daughter's knowledge of its contents. She is able to identify many species (the nameplates being only in German), state whether salt or fresh water, and in other ways display various insights.

We find a Viennese style cafe on the Kurfurstendamm and elect to eat on a terrace where the wind is somewhat chilly and the service also quite cool. We eventually get served after a couple of forays within to scare up the waitress.

Susan has obtained directions from the official West Berlin tourist information office to the "Museum fur Nature Kunde" thought to contain mineral and fossil specimens, in East Berlin. A map furnished as a means of identifying its location takes us deep into the southeastern part of Berlin but just inside the East Berlin border, thus enabling us to see and be stunned by the *enormous* size of the Russian military cemetery just to the north.

We finally come upon an address bearing the correct name, only to discover (at 5 p.m. closing time) that this location houses, very delapidatedly, a biological museum and that the one we really wanted was on Invalidenstrasse back in the middle of downtown East Berlin. (It is evident that the West Berlin tourist office's sources regarding East Berlin are haphazard at best.) Meantime, it is fascinating to drive along the wall, which remains firmly and solidly in place except where breached only at road crossings and to observe the contrast between the drabness of East Berlin and the well painted and maintained structures of the western city. The difference is also readily apparent in the dress and demeanor of the citizens of the two areas.

We hasten back into town, marveling at the grandeur of the reconstruction of downtown East Berlin (broad avenues, high-rise hotels, and a huge broadcast tower together with the repaired or rebuilt buildings of Humboldt University), and comparing this scene to the uglier but infinitely more varied and human scale of the KuDamm. Eventually we find the Natural History Museum about one half a kilometer east of the border in a dingy institutional building which had been damaged in the war and only partially patched up. It will not open up until Tuesday at 9:30 a.m.

So now back to the airport where we dine and go to bed.

Labor Day, Monday September 3, 1990—With the aid of a street map showing Im Schonower Park we drive from Tegel through the Grunewald south to Zehlendorf. I find myself surprised by the shortness of the distances. And after a little backing and filling, there it is: No. 7 Im Schonower Park which was my home with three other junior American staff officers from September 1945 until June 1946. It looks a trifle larger than I remember it and has acquired a coat of light colored paint on its stucco exterior. A glassed-in porch appears to have been added at the right rear, where I remember the living room to have been. But the layout and park-like cul-de-sac neighborhood remain totally unchanged over the forty-five years.

No one appears to be home, and after a few pictures we drive away to try without success to find the Telefunken building, where I had my office as the Assistant Provost Marshal of the U.S. Berlin District.

So now we head west towards Babelsberg to see what can be identified as the homes occupied by Truman, Stalin and Churchill at the 1945 Potsdam conference. En route we drive along the shores of the Wannsee to the approximate location of the yacht club where I sailed and reveled with American and British friends in the summer of 1945. All now grown up with tall trees in full leaf, making identification impossible. A large and growing hospital seems to have usurped much of the area.

There is an extension of the Wannsee called the Griebnitzsee—more on the order of a canal than a lake—which leads to the Babelsberg compound where the Potsdam Conference dignitaries lived during the July 1945 sessions. I am surprised to discover that when the Berlin Wall was built in 1961 the Griebnitzsee became the boundary between West Berlin (here to the east) and East Germany, which included Babelsberg. The grand turn-of-the-century lakefront mansions on Babelsberg's main street, renamed and still known as Karl Marx Allee, were cordoned off from the shore of the lake by a paved roadway perhaps seven yards wide. Along its west edge was placed a barbed wire fence staggered at intervals with watch towers with search lights and machine guns. On the side of the road next to the lake ran the infamous wall, here not quite so tall or thick as in downtown Berlin.

On first driving up the street my eye falls on a large stucco residence in whose northern side yard are several flag poles with flags showing the logo of a computer firm. I do not clearly identify this as Truman's house, so we proceed along for perhaps another kilometer until we come to another large house on the lake shore which is likewise unrecognizable to me but which on close inspection is found to bear a plaque in German indicating that it had been the house occupied by Stalin during the conference. (This is the building to which I apprehensively delivered Truman's gift of luggage to Stalin after a state dinner at Truman's house while several NKVD machine pistols were aimed at my head.) I go in and find a bearded German who speaks a little English and to whom I make known my desire to identify Truman's "Little White House." He does not know but knows someone who does. He phones this latter who arrives shortly. He turns out to be Herr Rudolph Franke, who is a teacher at a television school which now occupies the Stalin residence. I take some pictures of the house and with Franke in tow, we drive back south along Karl Marx Allee, as Franke tells me that the house at Number 2 Karl Marx Allee, being the place with the computer banners, is indeed the location of the Truman Little White House.

We go in, and while the place is in an advancing state of deterioration (walls unpainted and crumbling, floors and woodwork badly scarred, etc.) there is no doubt that it is the right place. Computer installations occupy the main salon but all else is empty. The back terrace, where the Truman-Churchill-Stalin state dinner took place, is intact, if decaying. Somewhat at odds with my recollection, there is no access to this back porch from the side drive on the north, which is the way I remembered that Stalin had arrived in his limousine. Thus it becomes clear that his arrival could only have been at the flight of stone steps leading to the front door.

I go upstairs to the third floor and am able without question to identify the maid's room up there where in June 1945 I had been found sound asleep at 10:30 a.m. and therefore relieved of my job as officer-in-charge of the house which Truman would shortly occupy. (The bird-colonel advance party man from Washington could hardly have known that I would then be reassigned with duties including supervision of the military police detachment around the President's house.)

Herr Franke turns out to be marvelously informative about Babelsberg in other respects. He takes us to Churchill's house, which he says had previously been occupied by Joseph Goebbels and family through a connection between a relative of his wife's and a former owner. (It sounds to me like Goebbels simply requisitioned the house.) He also shows us in the second street back from the lake the home of Admiral Dönitz, Commander of the German Navy during World War II, and another house which was used as a communication center by the Americans during the conference. He says that John F. Kennedy served as a naval communications officer in the house during the conference. (Through later correspondence with the Kennedy Library in Boston I learn that this is apocryphal.) He also tells us that it was through this facility that the order to drop the atom bomb on Hiroshima was issued from the Babelsberg White House in the course of the conference. (There is no question that this order indeed did come from Babelsberg.)

Before leaving Babelsberg we return once again to Number 2 Karl Marx Allee to photograph the chilling evidence of how the front lawn of this house—where the President lived while (vainly as it turned out) attempting to forge a durable and democratic peace—became a front line trench of the Cold War.

On the way back to Berlin we have a pleasant lunch in the sun at a cafe which finally satisfies Susan's urge for a "typical German meal," including red cabbage, schnitzel, etc. St. Hubertus is the name of this place, where we feed the ducks and watch rowers and boaters glide slowly by.

Then it's back into town along the Potsdamer Strasse through Steglitz and to the museum at Checkpoint Charlie on Friedrichstrasse. This provides unique insights into the tunnelers, the balloon and ultra light aircraft builders and the automobile alterers who devised sometimes incredible methods of escaping to the West.

One of the more impressive among many and among the simplest and least expensive, was the alteration of the suspension arrangements of a small East German Trabant equipped with helical rear springs. Rubber balls were placed inside these springs with the result that even though heavily loaded, the car would still ride high and thus appear to be carrying little cargo. The escapers hid under a false rear seat, while the contraband car was preceded and followed by others which actually were, and appeared to be, heavily laden. The Vopos did the natural thing—they inspected the low slung cars with a fine tooth comb and did not bother the guilty one.

The museum also displays considerable "art" of a highly propagandistic and ugly nature, but on the whole it was well-worth visiting.

Susan goes to do shopping on KuDamm while Kate and I visit the zoo. A pleasant stroll for an hour reveals among other things the most enormous red orangutan—he had to be 200 pounds—cruising from one handhold to the next up and along the side of his cage; a fur seal slithering languidly off the edge of his pool back into the cool water of his tank; a baby red monkey who according to Kate has 1,000 things on his list to do every day: pick up the string, jump on the log, put the string down, etc., etc.; and an enormous giraffe who must be his veterinary orthopedist's dream or nightmare.

We go back to eat and bed. It may be fairly stated—if not already inferred by the reader—that we all feel a little out of gas by this time. Lots of driving and new and varied stimuli on all sides. We thus don't feel particularly exploratory in the evening.

Tuesday September 4, 1990—Prior to leaving the U.S., my old friend Tom Korologos, a well-connected Washingtonian, had been kind enough to arrange contacts with the Army's public affairs office in Berlin, to whom I had explained that I had been in on the "ground floor" in establishing the American military police presence in Berlin in 1945, and that I would be greatly interested in meeting my 1990 successors and finding out about contemporary U.S. military problems in Berlin.

As a result of these discussions, the following unexpected events now ensue:

As Susan goes off in pursuit of her consuming interest in minerals to visit the Museum of Natural History in East Berlin, Kate and I are met at our hotel (over her protests at the earliness of the hour) at 8:15 by M/Sgt. Lein of the 287th MP Company and a driver, who take us around to show us Berlin's U.S. military installations. We are greatly impressed. There are three separate "barracks" that we see.

The first is "Andrews" which is located adjacent to the U.S. Army's Berlin Headquarters building in Zehlendorf. It consists of (1) a large compound with half a dozen large apartment buildings (separate ones for married enlisted personnel, unmarried enlisted personnel and similar for officers); I am astonished to learn that only twenty percent of the soldiers on duty here are not married and living with their families; (2) a shopping area which includes a couple of fast food outlets—one a Burger King—a huge PX, new and used car dealerships, all of these things being available to the troops at only a slight markup over cost; (3) day care, elementary and high schools, etc., etc., indoor tennis courts and swimming pool and on and on. It becomes apparent in talking with our guides that they love what they are doing and are making a good living doing so. The other barracks are "Clay" and "McNair," to which we go somewhat later.

In the meanwhile, we return to the Headquarters building and are ushered into a theater which has seats for 100 people. Kate and I and our military police escorts are the only ones in attendance. We view a multimedia presentation called "Perspective Berlin," which is a quite comprehensive review of what the Berlin U.S. presence (5,000 soldiers) is all about and the historical reasons for its existence. At the end of it, having described the knocking down of the wall in October of 1989, there is a distinctly self-justifying segment suggesting that U.S. forces will in all probability be necessary indefinitely in Germany and Berlin.

Kate and I are then escorted into the presence of Major General Haddock, the commanding general of the U.S. Berlin garrison. We spend a good half-hour with him in his sumptuous white marble office which it turns out had been that of both General Lucius Clay during his years in Berlin and, prior to that of the German Luftwaffe's eastern command.

I open our conversation by describing my reaction to the closing moments of the multimedia presentation: that it seemed quite aggressive in its suggestion that the continuing presence of the U.S. Army in Berlin would be necessary indefinitely. (Kate observes later that in her opinion I came on a little strong in this opening remark, but I still think both the slide presentation and the General's defense of it somewhat self-serving.) But he says that opinion polls of the Berlin populace and innumerable other indications satisfy him and most other Americans in Berlin that they are not only supported by the Germans but that the latter are deeply grateful for the results of the U.S. presence. He and his command are making a concerted effort at every level (schools, clubs, speeches, personal appearances, etc., etc.) to get the message across.

Q. Will the need not disappear when Germany is unified in October, 1990?

A. No. It will certainly go on until the Russians leave East Germany, which will not be earlier than 1995. It may well seem desirable to continue it thereafter.

Q. How does the General explain the political turnaround in the USSR and the sudden collapse of the East German regime?

A. A combination of factors which go back to the middle Seventies when the Soviets determined to beef up their missile and military commitment and to increase the allocation of their gross national product to that purpose from about fifteen percent to as much as twenty-three to twenty-four percent. This subtracted heavily from their ability to support their civilian economy, but they did it out of the conviction that the West did not possess the political will to counter it. They were wrong in this assumption because in the early Eighties, the U.S. decided to build and deploy the Pershing II missile ("a magnificent weapons system with a range of 1,100-1,300 miles and pinpoint accuracy; I was personally responsible for its deployment in Germany"), and the Soviets "blinked." Gorbachev has recently admitted to Prime Minister Kohl that the Pershing II is what brought the Soviets to the bargaining table, that plus the looming collapse of their civilian economy.

Q. Is it foreseeable that an entente of some sort will now emerge in U.S. relations with the USSR?

A. It's clear that our relations are now being conducted on a basis of mutual respect and understanding, but the General doubts that it is the correct long term relationship of the "two super powers" to be in each other's "close embrace."

We are much impressed with Gen. Haddock's persuasiveness, and somewhat awed by the extensive audience accorded us, and thank him profusely at the conclusion of our meeting.

(An interesting sidelight to the General's comments about the Army's future in Berlin is provided by our principal host, Lt. Colonel Pittman, the Provost Marshal, and others of his unit with whom we later take lunch. They put a slightly different perspective on the situation when they make clear that they are extremely nervous about their futures in Berlin, if not in the Army. With a handful of exceptions, largely for soldiers with language specialties who have been shipped to the Middle East, the Berlin garrison remains substantially intact at its traditional 5,000 men, but these guys are quite apprehensive that the days of their privileged life in Berlin may be numbered. Well, there always has been a large gap between rumor and reality in the Army and it is obviously no different now.)

The General gifts us with a Berlin paperweight as we leave and I am ushered into an adjoining conference room where a photographer and reporter for the Berlin *Morgenposte* and a female soldier, correspondent for the local army post newspaper, interview me for fifteen minutes. The questions are what might be expected—what impresses you most as you come back forty-five years after you left, etc., etc. A PR Captain says he'll send copies of this stuff back to us at home. He forgets to do so.

— Not Me! —

Our lunch is with the officers and NCO's of the 287th Military Police Company, who to a man—and woman—are most impressive. Some of them—a Staff Sergeant Yount who has escorted Susan this morning speaks both German and Russian, and Major Godeck—have direct responsibility for U.S.-Russian relationships regarding military police affairs. The captain of the 287th, a light skinned black man is as handsome and personable as can be imagined.

To my surprise after our lunch I am presented with two plaques, one by the Captain and the other by Major Godeck, both of whom say nice things about "handing the baton along," etc., to which I respond thanking those present for the sensational job they are doing, which is a sentiment I find I strongly hold. It's clear they find their Berlin billet sensational duty and will be sorry to leave it if and when that happens.

Now Sergeant Yount and Major Godeck lead us off to see the McNair barracks which does indeed turn out to be the old Telefunken building and which is now occupied by the U.S. Tank Force in Berlin. Some of the tanks are out in the large paved parade ground when we come by. Unfortunately we cannot gain access to the building to find my old office which I think I can pinpoint as I look through the fence.

Yount and Godeck now take us through choking traffic to Karlshorst, a southeastern suburb, where a Russian military museum is located and where we are expected. We spend the next hour being led through the museum by a blonde Russian lady who speaks fairly good, if heavily accented, English and who explains the displays, almost all of which relate to the final battle of Berlin, waged by the Russian Army in April 1945. Heavy stress, naturally, on the heroic nature of this conflict—"no one feared death"—and much reverence displayed before the busts, uniforms and other relics of the generals in charge, including especially Marshal Zhukov. There is no slightest hint either of a contribution to the victory by the other Allies or that any significant change in Communist ideology has occurred within the last year: Lenin's giant statue still dominates the lobby.

The tour does explain a lot more than I knew about those last two weeks or so when the Russian command, seemingly bent on vengeance for the havoc wrought in their own country, pursued and slaughtered thousands of Germans who could not have failed to know that their cause was totally lost. This effort also cost thousands of Soviet lives—I did not note the precise number but perhaps 15,000 would be in the right range;

the size of the Soviet cemetery which we happened upon yesterday is altogether consistent—when you would have thought that the drawing of a ring around the city and the issuance of a "surrender or starve" ultimatum would have done the trick.

We are shown a fifteen minute movie of actual combat footage which shows graphically how terribly Berlin and the now-rebuilt Reichstag were destroyed in April, 1945.

They keep the best until last—a visit to the impressive room where the German surrender was finally signed. Much of the same furniture is still in place. A film account depicts Field Marshal Keitel, later executed following the Nuremberg trials, signing the Act of Surrender, and our lady guide characterizes his manner as so arrogant that Zhukov required the actual signing to be at an insignificant side table. No mention is made of the simultaneous ceremony conducted by the Western Allies and Germans at Reims, France.

We take pictures of our hosts who include a sunken-chested Russian major who is the curator of this museum, and who somewhat plaintively tells us how a U.S. Senator who visited (there are no guests in the building but us and it appears that the place is not now much frequented) promised to take under advisement the major's suggestion that a "room" could be made available in the museum for installation of U.S. exhibits—he has made the same offer to British and French visitors—but so far he has received no response or encouragement. We are apparently being solicited to assist in this endeavor but we don't bite.

So at about 4 p.m. we are off in the rain—led by our hosts along the south autobahn route by which we had entered—back west while they swing off at the Potsdamer interchange to go back home.

They have really been most accommodating and warm throughout our visit, well beyond the call of duty. Tom Korologos' hand is in the wings and he has surely pushed the right buttons!

After 8 p.m. we arrived in the little town of Bilm, an eastern suburb of Hanover, where using the "Relais du Silence" pamphlet we took away from Le Moulin in La Wantzenau, Kate has identified the Park Hotel Bilm, which, like Le Moulin, turns out to be one of the nicest we have stayed at. Dinner is good but greatly delayed. Our room is impeccable and Kate even has a separate one of her own!

Wednesday, September 5, 1990—Our last in Europe. We leap across the kilometers on autobahns much less crowded once we get past the

Rhine. Then we are suddenly in Holland, where we lunch at a pleasant autobahn restaurant, where the great sensation is the coffee, served in a copper pot on a candled heater, with chocolate and other appurtenant fixings. It appears that this is a regular Dutch treat. Then in to Belgium, past "Antwerppen" where we miss a turn and go under the Scheldt River through the John F. Kennedy tunnel, only to come back and get on the right road to Brussels.

We have further trouble finding the right road to the Mercure Hotel, about three kilometers from the Brussels airport, where we finally collapse after watching Pete Sampras take the first two sets from Ivan Lendl in the quarter final of the U.S. Open in New York.

Thursday, September 6, 1990—Plane scheduled to leave at 11:40 finally loads up at 12:15, leaves the gate promptly thereafter only to come back from the runway with a mechanical problem. We don't actually get into the air until 2:15 p.m. and don't land in Boston until 3:15 EDT.

We are happily met at the airport by Margaret Sheldon with our car and her two children who find it a lark. Also by Kate's boyfriend. Much smooching. We ferry the Sheldon's back to Jamaica Plain where dogs enthusiastically relieve themselves and bleary eyed humans try to regroup.

Finally on the road home at which we arrive at 7:30 p.m. Stay-at-home animals (two each of dogs and cats) gleeful if a trifle suspicious. Six pound Poodle Attilla has been in a crisis of nerves for the last two hours of the trip—he can sense we are almost home and can't wait.

We are exhausted, body clocks awry, but very glad to be home.

View of approximate location at Lutzkampen, Germany, of author's foxhole on morning of December 16, 1944 when German offensive was launched from the east (right).

— Not Me! —

Sigolsheim, France, August 1990. View from the north of the town (top photo) with vineyards (left) in which outpost was located, and (bottom photo) rebuilt town.

Suzanne and René Bucaille, Kate and Susan Hadden, Carentan, France, August 1990.

Trois Epis, France. Exterior of Chapel of Notre Dame, where service of liberation was held, February 1945.

Trois Epis, France. Interior of the Chapel of Notre Dame where liberation service was held, February 3, 1945.

— Not Me! —

Susan Hadden at Lutzkampen, Germany, August 23, 1990. Only remains of a "Dragon's Tooth" of the Siegfried Line.

— Not Me! —

Kate Hadden wearing Bernard Dietrich's World War II helmet. Sigolsheim, France, August 27, 1990.

Sigolsheim, France, August 27, 1990. Author, daughter Kate, and poodles Attila (left) and Geronimo (right) with Bernard and Martha Dietrich, owners of the Restaurant De La Viniculture.

Lakeside façade of the "Little White House", Babelsberg, Germany, on the porch of which Truman hosted state dinner for Churchill and Stalin, July 1946. Photo taken September 1990.

— Not Me! —

Front steps of "Little White House", Babelsberg, Germany, where Truman greeted Churchill and Stalin, July 1946. Photo taken September 1990.

— Not Me! —

Machine gun tower built in 1961 on the front lawn of the "Little White House", Babelsberg, Germany. Photo taken September 1990.

"Unconditional Surrender" The Wrong Policy

THE policy that unconditional surrender would be the only terms on which the war with Germany would be terminated by the Allies was announced by President Roosevelt at a press conference held on January 23, 1943, at the conclusion of the Casablanca Conference with Churchill. The Russians did not attend. The idea was clearly Roosevelt's, and it stemmed at least in part from the intense press and public criticism of the unfortunate political situation in which the Allies found themselves immediately following the American invasion of North Africa in November 1942. As a means of eliminating the unexpectedly fierce opposition to the landings by the Vichy French military forces there which had proved costly in terms of U.S. casualties, it had been deemed expedient to negotiate with a French command structure to whom the French troops would be loyal and by whom they could be controlled. An effort to cut such a deal with French General Henri Giraud collapsed when he refused to take orders from the Allies. The next in line was Vichy's Admiral Darlan, with whom the Allies felt they had to deal notwithstanding a record of close cooperation with the Nazis. Because it was then far from clear to many of the Vichy French that the Germans would ultimately be defeated, this cooperation had anomolously resulted in the perpetuation of many Vichy policies such as persecution of the local Jewish population, imprisonment of supporters of the Free French, etc., to all of which the responsible Americans, who included Dwight Eisenhower and Robert Murphy, had felt compelled to turn a blind eye. This experience appears to have influenced Roosevelt away from any future course which might reopen a similar quagmire.

Roosevelt also drew on an inaccurate analogy between World War II and Robert E. Lee's surrender to Gen. U. S. Grant at Appomattox at the end of the Civil War. FDR recalled that Grant had earned the popular nickname "Unconditional Surrender," but that was because early in the war he had successfully imposed those terms on a surrounded southern garrison. No such policy was ever adopted by the Federal Government with respect to the Confederacy as a whole. Indeed, about the only documented precedent in which such terms were applied to end a war was in the time of Ancient Rome when the Punic Wars were ended by the complete destruction of Carthage and the total extermination of its inhabitants.

The announcement of the policy was regarded as a godsend by Nazi propaganda minister Josef Goebbels, as well as by Hitler. Thereafter and until the bitter end of the war, they lost no opportunity to remind the German populace that the Allies would show no mercy either in their conduct of the war or in the peace terms that would end it, and thus repeated, the message had a profound effect on future events.

If the result was so predictable, why did Roosevelt make the announcement? The answer is found in the emotional and quite moralistic view which he took of the war. It was his belief, one which was shared at the time by large numbers of Americans, that Hitler, the German General Staff, and to a considerable extent the German people were remorseless in their appetite for world power and domination, that they could not be trusted and that they needed to be "taught a lesson." Lest its meaning escape them, it would be made concrete by depriving them of their industrial and economic base so that their capacity to wage war would be destroyed into the indefinite future. So firmly was the President convinced of the correctness of these views that no amount of persuasion ever succeeded in modifying his position on surrender, although many able persuaders, among them Winston Churchill, tried hard.

The trouble was that Roosevelt's hypotheses were seriously flawed. There are few if any historical examples of tyrants more bestial than Hitler, but FDR seriously miscalculated with regard to the German General Staff and the nation at large. His view was that the Prussian elite had established a tradition of military conquest culminating in two of the bloodiest wars in history. The truth was quite different. The Prussian tradition had been to stand apart from politics and to serve instead as the servants of the civil authorities, which had been Bismarck in the late nineteenth Century and Wilhelm II during the First World War. More importantly, however, the General Staff had been among Hitler's most vocal opponents prior to the start of World War II. Indeed, Ludwig Beck, who had been the Chief of Staff of the Army, resigned to voice his opposition to Hitler's violation of the terms of the Munich Accord in occupying Czechoslovakia. Beck thereafter became the leader of underground resistance to the Nazis and succeeded in organizing—in the face of the unconditional surrender policy—a large group of co-conspirators with elements in all segments of German society, including the churches, trade unions and the aristocracy as well as at all levels of the military. The group may not have represented a significant percentage of the population, but in terms of both status and numbers it was substantial: no fewer than 20,000 were brutally executed by Hitler after the unsuccessful attempt on his life on July 20, 1944.

That episode was the sixth time that Hitler's death had been plotted. Literally dozens of efforts had been made through the Pope, the Swedish and especially Allen Dulles, the OSS agent in Switzerland, to acquaint the Allies with the existence and plans of the conspirators. The latter included the establishment of a democratic regime, the naming of particular anti-Nazis to a replacement or shadow cabinet, trials for war criminals and the payment of reparations to the Allies. Because of Roosevelt's intransigence, no one would listen. A former Berlin bureau chief for the Associated Press, Louis Lochner, twice attempted to pass along information about the German resistance only to be told that the matter was "embarrassing" and that a "personal regulation" from the Commander in Chief forbade mention of the subject in the press.

While the policy thus sprang from Roosevelt's personal emotional orientation, as time went by additional complications arose from his dealings with the Soviet Union. At the "Big Three" conferences in November 1943 in Teheran and later in February 1945 at Yalta in the Crimea, extended discussions took place both with regard to plans for the invasion of France and with regard to dealing with the Germans once the war was over. Stalin pressed relentlessly for a firm commitment from Churchill and Roosevelt with respect to the timing of the invasion, then set for May 1944, and also made plain that he shared fully in Roosevelt's view that emasculation of German war potential was absolutely essential. It was agreed that German industrial plants would be dismantled, that huge reparations were to be paid and that large drafts of German manpower would be turned over to the Soviets to help rebuild their country. With these subjects on the table, it became clear if it had not been before, that unconditional surrender meant not only no negotiations with any surviving government, but also that total ruination of the country's society and economy would be exacted. It is no wonder that some of these conclusions were relegated to "secret protocols" which never saw the light of day until years later. Against this background, it is not surprising that FDR refused to negotiate with the dissidents or that he characterized their mere existence as an "embarrassment." They were an embarrassment because he did not believe in them, or at least in their sincerity, and there was thus absolutely nothing to discuss with them.

This review also lays bare another incredible strategic error by the President. Notwithstanding counsel from many sides including Churchill, his own State Department and, to a lesser extent, the Congress, that planning for the post war should include some provision for a viable economic entity in the center of Europe which would relieve the West of the need to sustain its population, he had become convinced that those problems could be dealt with by establishing a relationship of trust and confidence with the Russians and by obtaining their support for the creation of the new United Nations, in which, for God's sake, they would possess a right of veto! In the light of the developments which took place over just the next two years, such naiveté is astonishing. There was already plentiful evidence that Stalin was talking out of both sides of his mouth, that he was as much a brigand as Hitler, and that the only sane approach to the post war was to require of Eisenhower that he press forward to conquer as much of Germany as he could before the Russians did so, and that the means to create and support a self-sufficient Germany should be found posthaste. This is exactly the program advanced by Churchill and the British and ultimately adopted by the U.S. two years later, but in 1945 it caused many heated debates between the two countries. In the end, blinded by what appeared to be the military need of pursuing and destroying the German Army, Eisenhower, supported by the President, chose to turn the offensive away from Berlin to the south where it was thought, erroneously as it turned out, that the hard core Nazis might be holing up in a "National Redoubt." It is reported that Churchill wept when he learned of this decision.

But what if it had been different? What if the Churchill strategy had been adopted and the desirability of recognizing and supporting a viable ongoing Germany had been pursued? What would have happened? It seems likely that such a course would have profoundly altered postwar events.

— Not Me! —

As has been amply documented, there were a number of junctures during the war at which substantial elements of the German High Command were prepared to concede that the war could not be won, and that an accommodation should be sought with the West. The first of these may have been as early as the fall of Stalingrad in January 1943. In the first serious reverse of the war, Hitler had insisted that the Sixth German Army, which had been surrounded by the Russians in that city, should stand its ground rather than retreat as the high command had urged, with the result that several hundred thousand crack troops had been killed or taken prisoner. A book published in 1961 entitled *Unconditional Surrender* by Anne Armstrong (Rutgers University Press) has carefully researched the views of the controlling generals and has concluded that had it not been for the Casablanca declaration, issued a scant six days before the fall of Stalingrad, a substantial initiative would have begun which, then or later, could well have opened the doors to an armistice.

There were a number of later moments when, as their battlefield defeats accumulated, it became ever more apparent in Germany not only that the war could not be won but that a disaster of major proportions was near at hand. Two in particular stand out as representing occasions when it fairly could have been said that the Allies had been "victorious" and yet that many hundreds of thousands of lives could have been saved. The first was after the Allied breakthrough in Normandy in late July 1944 which led to the frantic retreat of the Germans and the capture of 200,000 of their troops. But even if the inevitability of defeat had not by that time become apparent, then surely after the Ardennes campaign had resulted so disastrously, the lesson had clearly been brought home to the German nation as a whole, as it so clearly had to the hundreds of troops whom I myself had a hand in capturing.

As an indication of what might have happened on these two occasions if the door to negotiations had been ajar, it is instructive to look again at the July 20, 1944 assassination attempt and to realize that even though Hitler escaped death from the bomb that exploded under his conference table that day, the coup came within an ace of overturning the regime. Troops loyal to the conspirators had already been deployed in the streets of Berlin and General von Kluge, commander of the forces in France, teetered on the verge of throwing his support to them. He finally decided not to do so because he doubted that there was anything to be gained in light of the unconditional surrender policy. As Eisenhower aptly said in a press conference, "If you have a choice of going to the scaffold or charging twenty bayonets, you might just as well charge the bayonets."

As noted at the outset of this review, though the logic favoring an earlier negotiated peace today seems compelling, it was just not in the cards at the time. Among the decision makers—whose judgment was not clouded by concerns of personal safety—there was still a strong component of the outrage created by Pearl Harbor and Nazi excesses, and even as late as April 1945 when Truman came to review the question, there was virtual unanimity that unconditional surrender remained the right name for the country's German policy. By the time of the Potsdam Conference in July, however, there was a noticeable slippage: in the official document embodying the Potsdam Declaration, the phrase was relegated to the last (13th) paragraph, preceded by a variety of other terms which clearly limited its sweep, such as pledges that Japanese military forces when disarmed would be permitted to return to their homes, that national sovereignty and the right of self-determination would be respected and that the country would be entitled to maintain industries to sustain its economy and to have access to world markets. In other words, Japan no longer confronted the possibility of national extinction and it had become apparent that there was considerable room for negotiation.

That the policy was badly flawed came to be recognized later by many including Truman. In 1964 Eisenhower opined that it had lengthened the war in Europe by as much as ninety days, while Charles Bohlen called it Roosevelt's "greatest single mistake." See Robert J. Moskin, *Mr. Truman's War*, Random House, 1966, p. 102.

If that belated wisdom had only become apparent at the start of 1945, and it had been decided to hew a little harder line with the Soviets and a little softer one with the Germans, it seems entirely possible that many of the 222,360 American casualties incurred in 1945 might have been prevented, and who knows what benefits might have resulted as regards the Cold War..

Baker Company's Reunions

June 1992 and August 1994

IN the spring of 1992, three veterans of Company B of the 112th Infantry Regiment of the 28th Division combined to organize a reunion of the fourteen men whom they had succeeded in identifying as survivors of the company. The three in question were George Knaphus of McCallsburg, Iowa, a professor of botany at Iowa State University, who had been the company's communications sergeant; Charlie Haug, the retired president of a bank at Sleepy Eye, Minnesota (a town of 3,200 souls named after an Indian chief whose eyelids tended to droop), a runner; and Cliff Hackett of Greenville, South Carolina, of whom I already have written much. Like me, all three were ASTP cast-offs and joined Baker in the Hürtgen Forest on November 11, 1944.

The plan they put together was for fourteen of us whom they had been able to identify as Baker veterans to convene with wives at Charlie's vacation home on the shores of Lake Koronis, Minnesota. Lake Koronis is located about 65 miles west of Minneapolis, is about five miles long by two wide, and is deep in Garrison Keeler country and may possibly even be a model for Lake Wobegone. We all gathered there on Sunday, June 14, 1992, and spent three days getting reacquainted and sharing memories. Elaborate housing arrangements were developed utilizing not only the facilities of Charlie's cabin but of nearby summer homes generously made available by Charlie's neighbors. A schedule of meals, both at the cabin and in local clubs and restaurants, was arranged by Charlie and his warm and unflappable wife June, both of whom could not possibly have been more hospitable. None of us left Lake Koronis weighing less than we did on arrival.

The instantaneous and warm rapport developed in 1992 was so memorable that a second reunion was organized and held in August 1994 with largely the same cast of characters. What follows describes those who attended and adds a few words about the roles of each of the men in Baker's activities in 1944-5.

Bill and Joann Edwards, of Buffalo, New York. Bill was Baker's supply sergeant, and the only member of the company, so far as anyone can now document, who managed to serve throughout the entire war from its commitment at St. Lô in Normandy on July 22, 1944 until the armistice in May 1945. His job required him to shuttle fairly continuously between the front line and sources of supply to the rear, and as a consequence he was at risk somewhat less than many of us, but that did not mean that he was not plentifully exposed to danger. He managed to develop a case of trenchfoot in the Hürtgen Forest and spent a period of weeks recuperating in the hospital as a result. It is perhaps the best possible measure of what a devastating meat grinder Baker went through that he was the only soldier of the five hundred or so who saw combat service with it who even came close to enduring and surviving the entire experience.

Tom and Mary O'Malley, Chicago, Illinois. Tom was also a member of the company from the beginning, serving as Platoon Sergeant of the third platoon, and helping to lead the company in its bayonet attack on Spineux, Belgium. His service ended, however, when he was wounded a short time later, and my first acquaintance with him did not occur until our reunion. Tom was unfortunately one of the few who passed away shortly after our first reunion, and I was thus unable to renew the acquaintance in 1994.

Bill Kleeman, of Patoka in southern Illinois, east of St. Louis. Bill made a number of comments in the camcorder session we all participated in. One was that in his first exposure to fire in Normandy, "It was pretty rough on this ol' farm boy" to get up the courage to move out on command to attack the hedgerow across the facing field, but that he had somehow found the will to do so. He also said that the 11th of November 1944, when all of us ASTP-ers joined the company, was a good day for the company, giving it "a whole new character."

Bill was wounded by shrapnel in the lower leg in an engagement in Germany just prior to the Hürtgen Forest and thus had the great good fortune of avoiding both that awful time and most of the Ardennes battle as well. He rejoined the company in January in time for the attack on Spineux and the trip to Alsace and then served through as third platoon sergeant, replacing Tom O'Malley, until the end of the war.

— Not Me! —

As I talked with Bill, a rangy 6' 3" or 6' 4" with a wonderful farmer's drawl, I found that clear recollections of him and his stalwartness came back to me. We discovered that we shared our admiration for Slick, whom Bill was able to identify as Marvin Lefler. He believed Lefler had survived the war but had lost touch with him. About Slick, Bill said modestly that if there had been an award for the single outstanding enlisted soldier of the company, it would almost certainly have gone to him. He, too, recalled Slick's refusal to accept the battlefield commission offered to him, and believed it was due at least in part to the fact that Slick couldn't read or write, notwithstanding which Slick was able to deliver as good a lecture to the men on training subjects as any other non-com during pre-invasion training in England, according to Bill.

It came as a surprise to me to discover that the friendship which I quickly developed with Bill was among the warmest of those I formed at the reunion. No small part of that was due, I am sure, to the genuineness of his personality. He was deeply moved by the experience of the reunion and did not hesitate to say how glad he was (as he blew his nose and wiped his eyes) he had let himself be talked into coming.

At our 1994 session, I was able to let him read one chapter of my book which sums up my combat experiences and voices my strongly-felt views on the inadequacies of our division leadership. I was anxious to have his views because I knew that at least as regards our regimental and battalion leadership they were similar to mine. He returned the pages to me with the single comment: "Right on!"

Carlton and Kay Coats, New York, New York. Carlton was also one of the original members of the company, with service from Normandy to the Hürtgen Forest, in which he was taken prisoner. He had been the third platoon sergeant before Tom O'Malley and Bill Kleeman, and for about a four-day period during the Hürtgen horror, had actually been in command of B Company, after all of the company's officers had been killed. He remained in a German prison camp, which he describes as "not too bad," until the end of the war. He relates how he arranged food distribution for his group of twelve prisoners: each day responsibility for food sharing would rotate to a new man, and that man was required to take the last portion as his share. He says this system worked so well that a jeweler's scale could not have improved it. Since I did not join Baker until four days after he was taken prisoner, I did not know Carlton in Europe, but found him to be a warm and engaging man who with his wife had brought up a houseful of adopted kids who have in turn provided them with an abundance of adored grandchildren.

Carlton's most revealing comment related to the great kindness shown him by the German soldiers who had captured him. He found it difficult to speak of this, but managed while wiping his eyes to get it out, saying that they had very little food but willingly shared it with their prisoners, and that one German who spoke English had said to him, "Isn't it a miracle? Here we are sharing the same food when a half an hour ago we were trying to kill each other."

The remainder of the group, Bill Gibler, Emerson Hazlett, Ken Janne, Charlie Haug, Ray Schlosser, George Knaphus, Walter Gustafson and I (Cliff Hackett was unfortunately unable to attend in 1992 but did in 1994) were all among the 150 replacements who joined the company on Armistice Day, November 11, 1944, and all of us were also refugees from the college-oriented Army Specialized Training Program. The extent to which the character of the company had changed as a result of this infusion of intellect can be gauged by Bill Kleeman's reaction on returning to the company from the hospital in January 1945, "Ah never thought Ah'd see the day Ah'd find GI's a-playin' *bridge* in a foxhole!"

Bill and Pat Gibler, Green Valley, Arizona. Bill's cheerful and happy-go-lucky personality fixed him among the small handful of whom I preserve a clear memory from 1944-45. He was in my second platoon and a close friend of Emerson Hazlett before the latter was taken prisoner in Sigolsheim in February. Bill had what he characterized as a "million dollar wound," although I'm not sure I'd agree with that description. He was hit by shrapnel in the lower back and spine while we were in Alsace. The shrapnel tore through his webbed cartridge belt and caused instant paraplegia. Bill was of course evacuated to the hospital where he languished for several weeks with no apparent improvement in his lower limbs, which remained completely paralyzed and devoid of feeling. He had begun to reconcile himself to life as a paraplegic when he somehow rolled or fell out of bed while asleep, and the resulting jolt brought about a complete, instantaneous and miraculous cure. Just as Bill Kleeman in England and I at the hospital at St. Dié, he did absolutely nothing to hasten his discharge, moaning and complaining at the slowness of his improvement. He even enjoyed the cooperation of the head nurse at his hospital, with whom his relationship was on anything but a professional level. Eventually, however, the doctors in all three of our cases wised up and sent all of us back to duty, but I think Bill didn't make it back to the company until after the end of hostilities. Bill and Emerson Hazlett are among the very few from Baker who found the means to carry their service friendship into civilian life.

Charlie and June Haug, Sleepy Eye and Lake Koronis, Minnesota. Charlie was one of the company runners, assigned to its headquarters. In 1949, he wrote an account of his experiences in Europe, folding into it a meticulously kept record of salient dates and the various units to which we were all assigned as we made our way through the Repple Depples. His account of the events in the Ardennes immediately following the start of the German offensive is both graphic and harrowing, telling as it does of his escape on the first day of the breakthrough by having buried himself so deeply in snow that the Germans didn't know he was there, and of the constant flight of Baker's survivors before the relentless pursuit of the German panzers, with new casualties being suffered every day. This account filled a wide gap in my knowledge of the company's activities during the five days I was driving around Belgium in the jeep trailer.

George and Marie Knaphus, McCallsburg, Iowa. George, the botany professor, specializes in mushrooms, and as any other proud author, he brought to Koronis a supply of a handsome book he has recently published on this subject. Another talent which he is not slow to demonstrate is the ability to throw pennies or other coins four or five feet into the air and hit them unerringly with a .22 rifle. George says one has to hit them on the rim, because if they are hit in the center, "I never can find them." George was communications sergeant for the company, and according to all accounts was indefatigable, especially in the vineyards of Sigolsheim, in keeping the telephone wires to the outlying observation posts in some semblance of repair. I obviously encountered him in this context, but it required our reunion meeting to revive my recollection of him. This was odd because he is not a man who is easy to forget once you have known him. He served as informal master of ceremonies at both our reunions and did a wonderful job of it. In one session attended by a group of outsiders, he spent a half-hour describing what had happened to the company and the roles each one of us had played. He gave strong emphasis in this presentation to the absolutely pivotal role played by Baker Company on December 16, 1944 in deflecting the initial thrust of the Fifth Panzer Army, observing that to rupture the American line between the

28th Division on the south and the 106th on the north, and thus to capture the two bridges at Ouren, was the key German objective for that day. They were prevented from achieving this goal for almost two days by our defense, which gave equivalent breathing space to the Allied efforts to bring reinforcements up to contain the German thrust. It is George's feeling, shared I'm sure by every one of us at the reunion, that this delaying action was fully as important to the ultimate defeat of the Germans as was the stand at Bastogne, but "We'll never get the credit our effort deserved," says George, adding that, "If there hadn't been a Lutzkampen, there never would have been a Bastogne."

No account about the Knaphuses would be complete without a word about George's petite and gutsy wife, Marie. Like her husband's, her view of the world is a happy one, which is truly remarkable in light of the fact that she has undergone more than a dozen surgeries to replace hip, knee and other joints over the years. She smiles and says, "I just don't pay any attention to it and go on about my business."

Ken and Doris Janne, Wichita, Kansas. My recollection of Ken was dim at best, but evidence of our close association in Baker was miraculously provided by Ken in the form of a photograph of the two of us with happy smiles and arm in arm, standing in front of a picket fence, somewhere, I'm sure, in Germany in 1945. The photo shows me with an M1 rifle slung over my shoulder. I've puzzled over when and where this might have been taken. We are in shirtsleeves, so it must have been fairly warm. I'm wearing the Combat Infantry Badge, so it must have been 1945. I do not have sergeant's chevrons on my sleeves, but that doesn't mean much because there was never any reason to wear them on anything but my field jacket. I believe the photo comes from the time we spent on the Rhine at Andernach, after I had lost my Tommy gun (after that I had a rifle and no longer let it out of my possession), and just before I went to OCS. I cannot conceive that we could have been frolicking in the sunshine in such a carefree way, or that anyone would have resorted to the frivolity of a camera, any earlier than that.

Ken was one of three of the men attending the reunion who, like me, had been reported MIA in the first several days of the Ardennes breakthrough. None of us was told at the time that we had been so reported nor did the Army ever correct the record by follow-up messages to our families. George Knaphus ascribes this snafu to the company clerk's mandatory duty to account for each man in the company in some fashion in the

Morning Report which had to be submitted daily to higher headquarters. Perhaps, but an immediate follow-up with correcting wires home should also have been mandatory.

Ken spent his working career in the aircraft construction business in Wichita. He was "on the flightline" for Cessna, meaning that he was responsible for final inspection of completed aircraft just before their first test flight, a job of high responsibility, obviously. He suffered a heart attack not long ago and has since become very accomplished as a woodcarver, making small animal carvings and other more complex objects of real beauty and purity of line.

Ken related an anecdote about what happened to him and Charlie Haug, both runners, late in the day on December 16, 1944. He and Charlie had been detailed by the first sergeant to go to the position of an artillery forward observer about a half kilometer to the rear to request artillery fire on the approaching tanks. When they got there, they found that the forward observer position had been abandoned. Just then one of the German tanks let go at them with an 88mm cannon, narrowly missing. They decided to retire to the rear, at which time he noted that Charlie's legs weren't moving back and forth as in a normal run, but were actually "going around in circles" like a wheel.

Emerson and Betty Hazlett, Lawrence, Kansas. I have already spoken much about Emerson. In spite of his months in a Stalag, time has dealt with Emerson more gently than it has with most of us. His weight can have changed little over the decades. Betty produced a couple of portraits of him taken right after his discharge which brought the 21-year-old Hazlett vividly to life for me, wearing the insouciant, Tom Cruise-like smile I remember so well. He still wears it today, now surmounted, however, by a full head of white hair. For whatever reason—I would surmise it might simply be a desire to forget—Emerson recalls very little of the places, events and people of Baker. He made the observation as a part of the camcord record we all made at Koronis, that he had never really felt a part of any particular Army unit and that his trip to the reunion established for the first time for him a sense of identity with our Baker group. His sole recollections were of Bill Gibler, with whom he had been very close, of me and perhaps of one or two others. One thing he did recall, however, was the circumstances of his capture at Sigolsheim. It seems that he as squad leader and two of his men had manned the outpost the previous night and that another trio had been scheduled to cover it the next night. Some mix-up ensued; those who were supposed to man the hole couldn't and thus Emerson and his guys had to do it two nights in a row. The routine was for two men to keep watch while one slept in the bottom of the hole. Emerson was the one asleep when the Krauts snuck up through the vineyards and got the drop on his two men. He says, "It was all over before I knew it was happening." Thus, forty-seven years after the event, I finally learned the answer to the question which perplexed me for so long.

Emerson is now retired from a distinguished career as a professor of economics at the University of Kansas at Lawrence, and he and Betty spend their summers in Estes Park, Colorado, where he enjoys helping run a summer hotel. His family had scheduled a reunion of its own in August of 1944 and they were hence unable to come to Minnesota.

A new entrant at our 1994 reunion was Mayer Goldstein of Memphis who attended with his wife Hannah. Although our paths must have crossed when we were at Lutzkampen, I did not recall him, since he was a lieutenant and was Baker's second in command. He had also participated in a portion of the Hürtgen debacle, and I was anxious to try to elicit from him his views as to how and why it had happened. I was unsuccessful in attempting to draw him out on this subject. I handed him my copy of Gen. Gavin's book, *On To Berlin*, having marked the passage which is so bitterly critical of Cota and the 28th Division's leadership in Hürtgen. The only comment on the subject came from Hannah, who said as she returned the book, "Awful!"

But Mayer did confirm in spades that the German column that attacked us at Rogery, Belgium, on December 23, 1944 was driving American vehicles. He had the best of reasons for remembering that afternoon: one of those vehicles was the source of the shell which destroyed supply sergeant Bill Edwards' jeep which Mayer had commandeered when his own vehicle was lost, wounding Mayer and ending his combat service for good and all.

Mayer also recounted an interesting experience he had in Normandy when he came to the attention of our Division's Assistant Commanding General, Benjamin Davis. As I had learned from collateral reading, Davis was a stormy petrel and a lone wolf, much detested by staffers at division headquarters. In any case he tried to form a relationship with Mayer, apparently with a view to attracting him to serve as his aide de camp. Mayer resisted and hence was assigned to the front line duty with

Baker. There is obviously more to the story than I here record, but Mayer did not offer any additional detail.

Finally, there was Walter Gustafson, of Venice, Florida. I remember Gus with great vividness, and have written much of him. In 1992 he had changed not at all in bearing or way of speaking. When Susan and I drove into Charlie Haug's cabin at Lake Koronis, Gus was standing out on the driveway smiling and asking somewhat anxiously, "Do you remember me?", and immediately supplying his name in case I didn't, which was not the case. We embraced warmly and immediately embarked on a series of conversations all starting with the words, "Do you remember the time that... ?" For the most part, we both did remember the same events, including our traipse through the winter woods in Belgium to the farmhouse and the assault on the German bunker in Sigolsheim. One minor change I did notice in Gus—probably a good one— was that the steely look I used to see in his eyes in Europe, one of absolute implacable purpose, seemed to have relaxed and to have been replaced by an easy going outlook which says little but sees much. In our taping session he made the remark, echoed in different words by a number of others, that the bond and kinship formed by soldiers in the stress of combat is like no other and lasts forever. Amen.

Over the 1993-94 winter Gus and I tried valiantly to get together one-on-one in Florida, he being at his home in Venice on the west coast just south of Sarasota and I in the Florida Keys. I was anxious to really renew our friendship and to get his detailed recollections concerning the events of December 23, 1944 when we were ambushed by the German armored column masquerading as Americans. Since we were together throughout that experience and most others I was hopeful that Gus would provide insights that would enable me to clarify my recollections as to our exact location on that day, and perhaps better yet, to help me clarify where we were when I saw all of the landmarks which I so vividly but erroneously remember as connected with December 23, 1944.

Unfortunately it was not to be. He was north attending a family reunion when Susan and I went up to attend a meeting in Sarasota, and he later had to cancel a planned trip to visit us in the Keys when his wife became ill and could not travel. And then some months before our 1994 gathering in Minnesota and with stunning suddenness, he contracted a rare and invariably fatal disease which robbed him first of his reason and memory and then of his life.

— Not Me! —

Gus, you may be gone but you will never be forgotten.

— Not Me! —

Baker Company "50 Year Reunion", August 1994.

Front Row: (left to right) Bill Edwards, Cliff Hackett, Bob Smith, Mayer Goldstein, and Charlie Haug.

Back row: Ken Janne, George Knaphus, Bill Kleeman, Sandy Hadden, and Bill Gibler.

— Not Me! —

Bill Kleeman, Lake Koronis, Minnesota, June 1992.

— Not Me! —

Our reunion hosts, June and Charlie Haug, Lake Koronis, Minnesota, June 1992.